# Nobody Told Me

## Cassie Harte

For everyone who has become dependent on GP prescribed medication.
Never give up the struggle to break free.

# Foreword

Life had not been easy for me as a child, as I have written in my first book I DID TELL I DID. My childhood had been fraught with fear from sexual abuse that I suffered and the cruelty from my mother. At the age of fifteen, I sought the help of my family doctor, on the advice of a teacher at my school. The abuse had been going on since I was too young to remember, since forever and it had taken its toll on me as a person.

Many readers of my autobiography, have asked about the medication I took for many years. Some have asked why the abuse continued into adult hood, why I didn't fight back. I am hoping this part of my life story will explain the 'why's' to those who asked and will show others, the dangers of some GP prescribed medication.

Back when this story took place, the medical profession were beginning to use anti-anxiety and anti-depressant medication freely. At first they didn't know the dangers, the long term effects. They were not aware of side effects and withdrawal. They saw this medication as a wonder drug. Something that will make patients better. The prescribing of Benzodiazopine drugs increased and were used world-wide without fear. Today, many GP's still offer these drugs as a first solution, to patients needing help with depression or anxiety. Not as many as a few years ago but sadly the numbers are increasing every day.

I have written my story, not to scare patients or to blame doctors but to explain the effects this medication had on me, from the age of fifteen. I wasn't aware of what I was taking, I just needed to be able to cope with my life. They never made me feel 'high', they never gave me any kind of 'kick', they only made living, without the pain in my head, bearable and dulled my senses to enable me to survive. The hold they had on me, left a mark on my well-being and made me acutely aware of the dangers of these so called wonder drugs.

There is a place in society for Benzodiazopine medication and similar drugs, in my work as a psychotherapist, I know this but they should come with a warning. Patients should be told that coming off is hard, that withdrawal in some people can be horrendous and dependency can happen without you realising.

I hope this book enlightens people who have no knowledge of this kind of drug therapy. I hope it comforts others who have suffered the way I did, comforted by understanding that they are not alone

I don't today, look on myself as a victim, either of the abuse or the medication, I have a wonderful life and gained a Masters in Cognitive Behavioural Psychotherapy and now have my own Practice. There is life after dependency, I know, I live it!

# Acknowledgments

Special thanks to my husband and youngest daughter for their amazing and unfaltering support, not only during the writing of this book but for the past years. Although Daniel didn't know me during the awful time I have written about, he has always encouraged and loved me in every way since we have been together. During the withdrawal, Lucy and Melissa were always there, Lucy telling me straight how it was and she was always able to make me laugh. In later years, my husband and daughter have taught me to be myself and to like the person I am.

I would also like to thank Peter for his encouragement, love, support and friendship in everything I do. He always believed in 'me' I especially want to thank him for his creation of 'little coloured badges'!

My thanks also go to the Spiffing Covers team, for their help, patience and support throughout the publishing of this book. My ignorance of the technical aspect of this venture, must at times, been frustrating for them all. We got there in the end guys! So thank you.

# Chapter One

The ceilings of the waiting room were very high with ornate cornices, giving an air of grandeur. It was a large room with chairs around the edge and a coffee table in the centre holding books and newspapers. The walls were a creamy colour and the windows had long, floor length brown drapes. I briefly wondered how the people who had lived in it before it had become a doctor's surgery, would feel about its use today.

I was quite nervous about this appointment. I was only fifteen and had agreed with my form teacher, to go to the doctor. Miss Harris had noticed that my concentration was sometimes almost non-existent; I was worried all the time, scared and not feeling well. I had told her about the headaches. She was a kind person, not very tall and looked a bit like Margot Fonteyn, the famous ballet dancer, having her hair tied back in the same style. She wore long skirts that rustled as she walked around the classroom. She suggested that I went and talked to the doctor and had assured me, that he would help with my constant headaches and would make me feel much better. I thought, if I thought anything at all, that I had nothing to lose and hoped, that she was right and he would make them better.

So now I was there, waiting to see him.

*What will he ask me?*

*How will I explain how I feel?*

*Should I tell him how scared I am, all the time, how my life is full of pain and fear?*

This could be my chance to get help, my chance to escape from the horrors in my life. I looked around at the other patients, waiting to see their doctor and wondered if they were here looking for the same help as me. They looked okay so I didn't think they had someone in their lives who was hurting and terrifying them. But I did and I wanted it to stop. But where would I start? Could I tell him how I have been scared all my life, since forever?

*Will he ask me the right questions?*

*And if I tell, will he believe me?*

I probably didn't look out of place among the other patients; I was very small for my age and quite frail looking. My long dark hair did nothing to enhance my pale appearance. I looked tired because I didn't sleep very well.

I suppose there were about twenty other people sitting round the large room, some coughing, some reading and a couple talking. There was one woman, dressed all in black and who looked very unwell. She stared across the waiting room and I wasn't sure if I should smile but I didn't feel much like smiling so I looked away.

So many things went through my head. Dr Oxley was our family doctor; he knew my Mum very well so how could I tell him of her cruelty and lack of love for me? How could I tell him, that *she* was part of my problem? I looked again at the people sitting in that cold waiting room. I wondered if they could see how I felt. If they knew what had happened to me.

*Does it show?*

Suddenly, my nerves started to get the better of me; I began to feel very shivery. I thought of leaving, running out of the waiting room, afraid that I might say too much, but more afraid that I might say nothing at all. But it was too late.

"Cassie Black," came a voice from the door "Doctor is ready for you now." The receptionist stood, holding the door open. Miss Pringle she was called, a large lady who wore twin-sets and pearl necklaces. A bit scary and you wouldn't argue with her!

*He may be ready for me, but am I ready to see him?*

I stood up nervously and walked through the open door. The consulting room was formal and sparse, just a couch, a filing cabinet and a large wooden desk at which sat our family doctor. He was a big man, smartly dressed in a brown suit. He was a bit overweight and I suppose middle-aged. He had grey silvery hair and kind eyes. That's what I remember most about him from when he had come to see Mum, the kindness in his eyes. But I couldn't see his eyes that day. He was looking down at something on his desk.

"Sit down Cassie," he said, gesturing to a chair on the other side of his desk. He didn't look up at first. "How can I help you?"

*He wants to help me; at last, someone wants to help me.*

I was fidgeting nervously. It was a good job Mum wasn't there since my fidgeting really annoyed her. I was afraid of Mum. She was a large formidable woman who never said a kind word to me. I was a timid child and fidgeted a lot in front of her. "Keep still girl, for goodness sake, your wriggling around in the chair really makes me mad, you are so irritating," she would say, often followed by a slap or a push. I recoiled at the thought of her anger and continued to look at Dr Oxley. There was a silence in the room, so I felt it was my turn to speak.

"I'm having really bad headaches," I said, feeling quite strong now. He looked up at me and I gained strength in his kind eyes. "When they come, which is most of the time, I feel as though my head is going to explode and sometimes I feel a bit sick. When the pain comes, I can't seem to get rid of it."

My doctor, leaned forward and spoke quite softly, "Your Mum told me you've been chosen to take O Levels, does this entail more work?"

The memory of the day I took the letter home; the letter that said I had been chosen to take these exams came into my head. I was in a Secondary Modern school at that time and O Levels were taken only in a Grammar School. The letter had announced that six pupils had been chosen as part of a new Government scheme to sit these examinations, and I was one of them. At first I thought I saw pride in her eyes but it didn't last. She threw back the fact that I had failed the 11-plus exam and she had never forgiven me for that; even though she knew I had been ill at the time. No discussion, no congratulations, just telling me I would take them whether I wanted to or not!

"Well, yes, it does and the headaches make it hard for me to concentrate," I answered hopefully, wanting the doctor to ask more. I could feel my heart beating fast.

*Now's my chance.*

*Stay strong he wants to help.*

I looked straight at him, pleading with him with my stare, to help me. Silently begging him to see my distress, to ask me if there was anything else worrying me. I was hoping so much that I would be able to talk to him, tell him everything.

But then, suddenly, without warning, I started to cry; the sheer memory of Mum and her expectations of me, made me cry. I was so miserable all the time, what with her treatment of me, the pressure of my schoolwork and the *'nasty's'* in my life. I was really down and felt so alone. He looked at me again.

*If he asks, should I tell him?*
*Should I tell him of my scary life?*
*He will ask, surely he will ask.*

But he didn't ask, he reached for his prescription pad and began to write. "These will stop the headaches and you'll feel much better. If things don't improve, come back and see me. I'm sure if you take the medication properly, you will feel much more able to concentrate because the pain will have gone." At this, he stood up, handed me the prescription and said goodbye.

There was no arguing, no 'Yes buts….' from me. I was dismissed.

*Was that it then?*
*Was that helping me?*

I had only been in the surgery a few minutes. My doctor wasn't concerned about the headaches, and he didn't want to see me again. The pills would sort it all out! The fact that I had been suffering this pain for the months, even years, seemed irrelevant. I had realised, that as my life became scarier, so the headaches became more severe. I didn't get the chance I had hoped for to tell Dr Oxley this. He only seemed to be treating the headaches. But the pills would put all of this 'right', or so my GP said.

At first I felt cheated, cheated out of the opportunity to tell someone what my life was like. How my days were filled with fear, a darkness that I kept secret. I so wanted to tell of the emotional cruelty at the hands of Mum. I felt angry that I hadn't been able to tell how life was, not able to ask for the help I really needed. I had summoned the courage to see the doctor and had truly hoped that he would question why I was having the headaches and more importantly, try and find out what was worrying me.

But…

*He never asked me.*

*Why didn't he ask me?*

*Couldn't he see my pain and fear?*

*Didn't it show in my whole being?*

I suppose, to be fair to our family doctor, why should he have done anything else or even suspect anything. My school work had become much more intense and he felt that was the reason for the pains in my head. I was from, what the outside world saw, a 'good' family. We lived in a council house in the 'better' part of the estate and to all who thought they knew her; Mum was a pillar of the society. I attended the local church where I was a member of the choir. My brother Tom was a popular lad and my two older sisters, Ellen and Rosie, were both working at the local hospital. Anne the baby of the family was a happy child but would always side with mum when our mother was cross with me. No, he had no reason to suspect anything was wrong in my life. So he treated 'just' the headaches.

He had said he wanted to help me, this doctor with kind eyes, but he didn't. Because I never told him. He never asked me, so I never told.

On arriving home, nothing was said. As usual Mum wasn't interested. I'd told her about the pains in my head, as I had told her about my fear, right at the start, but she wasn't interested. "Headaches?" she had said, "What earthly reason should you have headaches? You've nothing at all to worry about, you have it easy, you should have the stress that I have, and then you'd have reason to have headaches."

With that she had sent me off to carry out the

numerous household chores that were part of my day. How could she say my life was easy? She knew, didn't she?

*"He kissed me, Mum" She sat looking at me with raised eyebrows. "He kissed me and it hurt. I don't like him kissing me like that it's horrible. And he touched me there." I pointed between my legs. "In my panties and it hurt" I was looking at Mum, waiting for a response. Surely she would hold me now. Surely this would make her care. She remained calm and left the room. After a while I heard raised voices from downstairs. I thought she must be shouting at Uncle Bill. Forbidding him to ever come near me again. That's what Mums do. But no. After peaking out from the top of the landing and seeing him about to leave; I was shocked to see her kiss this man who had hurt me and tell him she didn't believe me. He left. She called me downstairs. "How could you be so wicked? Telling such lies about Bill. He loves you." With that, she slapped me hard across the face. "Get up to your bedroom; I don't want this mentioned ever again. You're an ungrateful liar." I ran up to the safety of my room.*
*I was six years old.*

So she didn't believe me then, why should she believe anything I say now. She just didn't care about what happened to me, I knew that. Just didn't love me or even care about me enough to ask what the doctor had said. For nine years after I had told her about Bill, my horror continued.

So on the day of the doctor's appointment, I was now 15 years of age and nothing had changed. My Mum still had no interest in my welfare and I said nothing. I didn't tell her about the tablets or what had happened at the surgery. I didn't need to. She didn't ask.

I'd never taken medication regularly before but wasn't afraid. I just wanted to feel better, to be pain free so that I could cope. I took the prescription to the chemist without reading it, I trusted that they were what I needed, so I didn't even consider looking to see what they were called. I don't think my GP mentioned the name of the tablets. It wouldn't have made any difference if he had. I had never heard of Benzodiazepine drugs or Valium, and I don't suppose many people had. It was the 1960s and we were in awe of doctors; if they gave us tablets, we took them. No questions, no thinking about it. I took them. I remember hoping, that if one little pill could make me feel better and take the pain away, then things would at least be bearable.

As the headaches lessened, my condition improved, so I continued to take them. I was feeling better and I hadn't had to tell. So he had helped me, *hadn't he?*

The medication was available to have on repeat prescription, Dr Oxley had told me "If these make you feel better and take the headaches away, just ask for more and I will write you a prescription" he had said at the first appointment, so repeat them I did. My life became slightly more bearable. The headaches stopped and I was able to function as though there was nothing wrong. *Pretend* became easier, blocking the *evil* became something that I could do, had to do to survive. For years, I had always done this, but now it was easier. As the headaches lessened, I seemingly was able to cope. Life was hard and the horrors continued, but nothing seemed quite as bad as it had before. Maybe being resigned to it, made it more bearable. I didn't realise that my judgement was already becoming impaired. I felt different but I wasn't aware that my character was changing.

After a few weeks, my concentration improved. My school work became easier and reading had begun to be enjoyable again. I was sleeping at night, something that had not been happening up until then. Did I wonder at the power of these tablets? At this stage I don't think I did, I was just relieved that I was pain free and coping better. Without the pain and with the benefit of sleep, life was easier. Seeing my GP had been useful, even if he didn't give me much of his time.

I was still seeing my childhood best friend Claire. She was a *happy*, an *in-between*. We had been friends for years, since starting school. She was a cheery girl who could see no bad in anyone. People said we complimented each other, she was blonde and blue-eyed and always smiling. I was dark haired with blue grey eyes and only smiled, I think, when I was with her. A good match as friends. My times with her and her lovely family helped keep me sane.

Throughout my childhood, her Mum and Dad, treated me as though I was theirs. *If only*. We used to spend a lot of time together but these times became fewer as we grew older. At this time, her family had moved, and she now lived a bus ride away from me. With schoolwork, the church choir, chores at home and my 'outings' with the man they called my 'Uncle', I didn't have time for anything else; so I didn't see much of her at all.

Life was still hard and although I was finding things a little less stressful, Mum was still the same with me. Nothing had changed but somehow I didn't seem quite as scared of her as I had always been.

During one of my mother's outbursts, shortly after seeing Dr Oxley and a few weeks on the medication, I realised that something was different. Her words were the same, belittling and berating but I didn't feel so upset by what was said.

Mum was a larger than life woman, physically big with dark hair that she kept permed and neat. She had blue eyes but not the same blue/grey as mine. Always dressed very well with matching outfits and jewellery. She was a very powerful character who dominated the whole family. Although she wasn't unkind to my siblings, she was no match for my Dad, William. Tall, thin and placid, with brownish hair kept short, as most ex -servicemen did and soft brownish green eyes; he was a kind gentle man who was regularly the target for her venomous tongue and nasty ways. He would do anything to please her. He did try and stand up to her for me, on occasion but she would all too soon shout him down. When Mum got angry, it scared me.

But I remember one occasion, about two weeks after starting on the medication; she began shouting at me because we had run out of milk.

"Why didn't you notice?" she screamed. "You know I needed some extra for a rice pudding. You can't do anything right. You're useless; I don't know why I kept you. No good for anything you're not!"

I didn't try and stand up to her, or even apologise as I would have once done even though it wasn't my fault. I didn't question the 'kept you' part of her shouting as I had before. I just went upstairs out of her way. I noticed that instead of feeling really sad and hurt that she was picking on me once again, I felt nothing. It didn't seem to bother me.

I put this down to my feeling better in myself, getting some sleep and so perhaps I was less sensitive. On the occasions that she hit, slapped or pushed me, it didn't seem to hurt as much. If I was in her path, or close to something she wanted, she never asked me to move, or said excuse me. Oh no. She would push or slap me so that I moved away.

"Get out of my way!" she shouted, on one occasion, pushing me so hard that I fell against the banister. I saw her look at me. "Story of my life that, you, always in my way, get out!"

I think she was waiting for me to complain or something, so that she could continue her onslaught. But now, her words now just seemed to float over me without effect. I didn't react in the usual way. Instead, I calmly walked away and went into the garden. Her aggression didn't seem to touch me as it had before. I still felt hurt, still felt that I wasn't wanted, but I felt calmer and a little removed from what was happening. Perhaps I thought I was becoming resolved to the fact that I wasn't wanted by her; I had found that out just before I had told her about Uncle Bill.

*"She was a mistake. A very unfortunate mistake. Having her ruined my life."*

*I was six. Mum had told me to lay up a tray for her and my Auntie Prue, when I heard her say these words. I think I may have taken an intake of breath and she had heard me outside the door. She came out of the room and screamed at me. "You're the reason for all the unhappiness in our family, you know that don't you." As she screamed she dragged me by my hair to the back door and threw me into the garden.*

*I was a bit confused, how was I a mistake? Did people have babies that were a mistake? I was upset and scared, after a while I crept back indoors and ran into the bathroom.*

This was my place of safety when I was scared of Mum or after being out with Bill; I would go to the bathroom and lock myself in. Often he would arrive at such times and coax me out of the tiny room, saying he would put things right, telling me he loved me.

He wasn't my real 'Uncle', but my Godfather. Bill was a friend of Mum's and had been there forever. He had always cuddled me and tickled me; sometimes it didn't feel right but I was a tiny child, so it didn't feel wrong either. Anyway, he loved me; he told me that he did. I don't remember when the abuse began, I suppose it had always been there. At first I wasn't scared. But things changed and one time I realised that Uncle Bill

19

wasn't loving me, as he said he was, but hurting me. Life at the hands of Mum, who had never shown me love, was unhappy and at times scary. But not as scary as what happened in the back of the car after a lovely afternoon out. Nothing at home was that scary.

I had never taken pills in my life before but the effects were life-changing and I hoped I would be able to continue taking them. After a month I had run out, Dr Oxley had said I could ask for more. I rang the surgery and was told a new prescription for a three months' supply, would be ready for me to collect the following day. I felt so much better taking this medication, these pills I was told were for my headaches, that I saw no harm in taking them. I remembered that one of my Nans, not sure which one, said she took aspirin every day to stay well. So taking tablets everyday didn't seem a problem.

At that first consultation, when I was 15 years old, my doctor hadn't encouraged me to talk; he hadn't given me much time. Doctors didn't back then. The practice was a large one and he always had lots of people waiting to see him. He hadn't told me what the pills were, just that they would help me. He didn't ask the right questions, any questions. But if he had, would I have felt strong enough to tell him?

I continued to take the tablets as instructed, not knowing that this was the beginning of the slippery slope. It was 1960, I was fifteen, I knew no better and trusted in my doctor, and after all they had helped me, hadn't they?

# Chapter Two

For a while, after first seeing my GP and feeling better, life became a bit easier. The main reason for this was that the source of my biggest fear, Uncle Bill was absent. I didn't know why but I didn't care. He wasn't there to hurt and abuse me, so I didn't have to worry constantly that he would be there, asking to take me out. I was powerless to stop his assaults on my tiny body. He was a tall swarthy looking man with dark hair and was very strong; I stood no chance against him. It may just be how I saw him but he always seemed to wear dark clothes, very tidy but dark. When the abuse began, he would threaten me, saying that *no one would believe me if I told*. He was right. I told mum and she didn't believe me. But now, for some reason, this evil man of whom I was terrified, wasn't around and that was more than fine with me.

Life in general was okay, my school work had improved, although I was a long way behind the rest of the class, I think and it was almost exam time. School was a kind of safety, safety from the constant ridicule from Mum and abuse by Bill. I enjoyed being there and would always be the one to leave last at the end of the day. I stayed out of Mum's way as much as I could as

I never seemed able to please her. Whenever I was in her presence, she made it quite clear that I wasn't part of her family as the others were, my brother Tom and my sisters, Ellen, Rosie and the youngest, Anne. It was as though we lived as two families in the same house. Well, when I say 'families' I mean them and me.

I didn't even look like my family, and this was something frequently pointed out by my mother but always dismissed in an unkind manner. *'No, the devil's spawn'*, was one remark that was made by this woman they called my mother; on an occasion when a neighbour had said how unlike the others I was. Both Ellen and Rosie were quite tall and had the same colouring as Dad and so did Tom. Anne was at this point still growing but had the same colouring as Mum, with pretty blue eyes. Then there was me. Frail looking with dark hair, blue grey eyes and not as tall as my siblings.

Mum had always gone out on outings with the others and without me. I would be left to do chores or when my Nan lived with us, I would be told to stay and look after her. Most of the time, I was sad that I was never included, but not when Nan came to stay.

Nana C was Mum's mum; she was a tiny delicate looking lady of whom I was very fond. Her hair was brown with touches of grey at her temples and she had the bluest of eyes. Most of the time now, she was dressed in a nightgown with frills around the neckline and wore a dressing gown made of a kind of brushed cotton, when she was out of bed. She had been quite ill and in hospital, and when she came to us and was confined to her bed most of the time. The back room in the house was partially converted to take a small bed and an armchair and table. Nan lived in there. I had moved the bed over to the window so that she could look out and watch the birds. It was quite a small room and decorated in wallpaper with scenes of woodland. It had a green hazy effect and there were green curtains at the window onto the garden. There was a small fireplace on the centre wall so there wasn't much room for anything else. But Nan never complained. Very soon after she had come to live with us, it was the school summer holidays and so we were all at home. Mum and the others would often go out for the day and I would be left with Nan. But we had a secret.

"Have they gone?" she would whisper, "Have they gone over the bridge yet?" We lived on a short road that led to a small bridge over the railway. The nearest bus route and coach route was the other side of the bridge. I would tell her when I couldn't see them anymore and she would giggle and get out of her bed and join me in the kitchen. We would sit together and she would tell me stories of her life, nice stories about the good times in the war when everyone was friendly and would sit around in air raid shelters and sing songs. We would make jam tarts or little cakes and have to eat them all before Mum and the others returned, making sure the kitchen was clean and how it had been before the family had gone out. Then Nan C would climb back into bed and no one ever knew our secret. This was a good time, *an in-between.*

The family behaved, most of the time, as though they were separate from me, that I wasn't one of them. In my fear and pain, I suppose I became isolated from them in a way and being excluded was just how it was.

As time went on, I felt much better and the headaches lessened, so I continued to take the prescribed medication. But my respite was brief.

One afternoon when I arrived home from school, I went around to the back of the house as I always did. The door led straight into the kitchen which was blue and cream and had a large dresser to one side and the sink under the window on the other. It was small and could only comfortably house two people at the same time. So going in when someone was there was a bit of a squeeze. There he was, my 'nasty', the reason for my fear. Uncle Bill was in the kitchen, leaning on the dresser, talking to Mum. I froze.

He was a close family friend and as I said, when I was little was the only person who showed me affection. Back then, I felt safe and loved in his strong arms. I looked forward to his cuddles. I was very fond of him, until he started doing things that made me uneasy. Now he terrified me. I used to enjoy the attention and the affection but that all changed.

Seeing him in the kitchen brought it all back, vividly as though it were yesterday.

*"Let's get into the back of the car for a cuddle," he had said after a lovely day out with him. "That will end the day nicely." I had no reason to be afraid, I clambered over the front seat into the back and he held me. It felt good. At least he loved me. But then he began to kiss me, roughly, hurting my face. He was touching me all over and then his hand was in between my legs. I knew this was wrong. "No, stop it, you're hurting me!" I cried out but he didn't seem to hear me. He was a big man, a man who said he loved me. But now he was hurting me. I was pushing with all my might to get him off me but it made no difference. His big rough hands were gripping my skinny little body, his fingers poking about inside of my panties. I began to cry. "Stop please stop." I sobbed. After what seemed like forever, he stopped and moved away. He eventually climbed back into the front of the car, laughing and saying,*

*"No one will believe you if you tell them anyway, they will just say you're lying." He then took me home.*

So my respite had been short, only a few months, and now he was back. Seeing him in the kitchen, his dark hair falling onto his forehead brought all the fear back. Pretend had become easier, after beginning the pills, blocking the evil became something I could do, had to do, to survive. Before he had gone away to wherever he had gone, the things he did had progressed to evil things that I knew were wrong and caused me fear and pain. The abuse had taken a more sinister turn and the rapes became more traumatic. And now he was back, in our kitchen like he had never been away. He smiled at me, looking pleased with himself. My head started to pound and I felt cold and shivery. Then the words.

"Can I take Cassie out for a while?" The words came out of his mouth like a kind invitation to a favourite niece. But I knew different. "We have a lot of catching up to do, don't we Cassie?" he continued. I didn't answer. I couldn't answer. I knew what he meant; I didn't want any of his 'catching up'. I felt frozen to the spot.

*Just when I was coping, he came back.*

"Yes, of course you can, Bill," my mother answered, "You'll like that won't you, girl?" She looked at me, daring me to argue. I stared back at her. What kind of mother sends her child out with a monster? She knew what he had done. I had told her.

*"No No! I don't want to go out with you, ever!"* I wanted to shout, but I didn't. I was now left feeling as I had always done. Scared of both of them. Mum and Uncle Bill. Two people who should have loved me.

The abuse had been escalating over the years before he had gone away. Now it was much worse. The thought of going out with this evil man brought so many horrors back into my head; it felt like it would burst open. Memories of a time when I was eleven, when the horrors had become unthinkable, came rushing back into my crowded mind.

*His breathing became heavier; he was fumbling between my legs prodding hurting me, oblivious to my tears. "Please, please take me home, I want to go home!" I sobbed but he didn't seem to hear me. And then the pain, pain like I have never had before, tearing me, awful awful pain. I couldn't work out what was happening. Uncle Bill was squirming on top of me and groaning. Then suddenly I felt the awfulness of him inside of me. Now I couldn't cry out. The pain was terrifying, the fear overpowering, rendering me unable to speak or cry. What had happened? What had he done to me? The pain was horrendous. I wanted to die. I had been raped.*

So with no choice, and the blessing of Mum, I went out with Uncle Bill and the abuse continued. Although the headaches until that day, had gone, that day when he returned, they came back with a vengeance. No pill could ward off this fear and pain. But I did take a tablet, I had to try and rid myself of some of the pain. I knew the headaches did go after I took the tablets, so I took one then. Taking them and being able to at least cope with what was happening to me, was all I could do. I didn't realise the impact that the pills were having; I suppose coping with my life was hard enough.

Nothing had been reported about the use of these 'headache' pills, at least I hadn't seen anything, not in the newspapers and TV was limited in information. This was way before the days of the Internet. Oh how I wish I had had the foresight to ask the questions, to find out more! But the longer I was on the medication, the less inclined I was to ask. I was coping wasn't I? Coping in a home with no love. Coping with the 'nasty'.

I welcomed the numbness that sometimes enveloped me, during the many rapes and despicable sexual acts, that were either done to me or that I had to perform for this man who 'loved' me.

Make believe was something I would do, in my quiet moments, make believe that none of this evil that was happening to me, was really happening. That was enough to help me through. I could 'escape' my life as it was in reality and go to my make believe world.

I used to make up a story, where I was reclaimed by the parents who had given me away at birth. Then my life was good. But sometimes, it seemed, I didn't think at all. For some reason I had times, just after taking the medication, that I felt numb and almost heady, it was a lovely feeling. A safe. As this wore off, and the pain in my head began to return, I knew it would be okay again as soon as I took the tablet. Then the pain would go and I would be okay. Nobody told me of any danger or dependency on these 'headache pills'. My youth was obviously my salvation. I was able to live a reasonably stable existence, at least to those who didn't know me. I still hadn't realised at this point, that my judgement had already been impaired.

I became quite submissive and this was new to me. In the early days of Mum picking on me, I had been able to stand up for myself or at least protest my innocence when accused of something I hadn't done.

*"It wasn't me!" I protested when the doll's house furniture had been left out, trodden on and broken. "I didn't do it." I protested with tears in my eyes. I had been at dance school that morning. My sisters Ellen and Rosie had been playing with the doll's house, not me. "Liar!" Mum screamed. "You're always telling lies. I don't know why I have to put up with this."*

But now, after all the years of emotional cruelty at her hands, I never answered her back. Just did her bidding. I thought that things just didn't matter as much, because I was feeling better so she couldn't hurt me as she had done previously. Each time I took a tablet, I felt more relaxed, more able to almost brush aside what was happening or being said to me. Although the abuse had become worse and more frequent, I had stopped protesting about going out with Bill, never tried to get away or stop his assaults. There was no point. I couldn't win. I suppose was tired and resigned to my fate.

During the episodes of abuse, I often felt almost outside of myself, looking in. I taught myself to switch off. I don't mean I switched off to what was happening, so much so that I didn't make memories. No, that would have been wonderful. But I taught myself to mentally concentrate on something else. It didn't stop the horror or the pain, but it made it bearable.

*How pretty are those patterns on the wall, blue, a lovely colour. Must keep looking at that wallpaper and thinking about lovely. Must, must. I think that's my favourite colour, Blue. Yes it is. The dress Claire's mum bought me was blue and the flowers on her bedroom wall are blue. That's a good place to be at Claire's, I am always having fun. It is safe and warm and her Mum and Dad are kind to me. Yes. Blue is good.*

After starting on the tablets, doing this was much easier. Things were easier to bear. If I felt anything, I just felt numb. Sometimes I felt nothing at all. Sometimes, even in the not-so-scary times, I was almost on the outside of my life, looking in. Almost as though I was watching someone else's life and not actually living it myself. My senses seemed to be wrapped in cotton wool. I just switched off. I wasn't aware that the 'headache pills' were responsible for this, At that point, I don't think I would have cared if I had known. The abuse had gone on since I was very young, since forever. I don't remember when it started, it was always there. This was the only way I could survive, keep quiet, try and think of something else and hope it would soon be over.

Perhaps if I had had more control of my sense of judgement, I would have been able to fight him, but

I'm not sure. Perhaps I would have felt strong enough to tell someone else, but I don't think so. Maybe if I hadn't been living in the fog that was Benzodiazepines, I would have asked the questions, should this be happening to me, is this normal? Without the effects of the medication, would I have been stronger? Who knows? All I knew at that time, was, that now, now that the headaches had stopped, hurt didn't always come into play and I didn't feel so sad or so scared. Life didn't seem real somehow. That was okay with me, because real was bad.

Sometimes, in the evenings, I would begin to feel like I did before I saw my GP, terrified, scared and alone. Once I had taken the pills he had given me, all was well again.

During the early years of the abuse, I was so afraid of the threats Uncle Bill made, afraid that he was right. That what he said, would happen to me. His threats to me when I was a little girl were terrifying and I had never lost that awful fear.

*His tone was menacing, "You can't tell anyone, you know. They won't believe you. They might even take you away to a children's home. In children's homes everyone would want to do things with you, they would all try to kiss and cuddle you, just like I do." I was petrified.*

I knew he was right about telling anyone. After all, I had told Mum and she hadn't believed me so why would anyone else?

Child abuse was never heard of, at least I had never heard of it. At first I had thought it must be normal, that this is what happened to children. But I found out that it wasn't, when I spent more time with my best friend Claire. Her dad, would never have done anything to hurt her. In the senior school, when I was about twelve or thirteen years old, girls spoke about sex. I had realised, that what was happening to me was sex and the way the other girls spoke about it, I knew what was happening to me, was wrong. They never said these things happened to them, so why was it happening to me? I thought and thought about this and came to one conclusion. It must be my fault. I then had the guilt to contend with as well as everything else. But I was too scared to tell.

Soon the headaches had gone completely, thanks to the tablets, especially during the times that Bill was away. I hadn't equated the two things. Before he went away, I was in constant fear of his turning up and insisting on taking me out. I was having flashbacks of the abuse and living in constant fear and apprehension. The pain in my head was sometimes unbearable. But the 'headache pills' had taken the pain away. I still had to deal with the unkind actions and verbal abuse from Mum, but somehow I didn't get so upset anymore. I was almost able to push the insults aside. The numbness I suppose. But I didn't analyse the fact or put two and two together. I was just glad that I could cope with my life better than before.

*"Don't think you're going straight to your room girl!" Mum screamed as I walked towards the stairs. "There is far too much to do here." She was in the kitchen and preparing a meal for my sister Ellen and her new boyfriend. "I have lots of homework to do." I tried to protest, without it sounding like a protest. "Homework?" Mum said in contempt. "That's a waste of time, you're a waste of time; you're stupid now and will still be stupid, no matter how much homework you do. Get here and help with tea!"*

These words would have really hurt me before, but

now they just went over my head. I knew from previous times that there was no point in trying to argue. Help her I did.

Shortly after I was fifteen, my periods started and the sexual abuse changed. The first time after they began, I wasn't as scared of what might happen when Bill took me out. I told him that I was bleeding, hoping he would stop hurting me. How naive was I.

At first he was angry. Angry I could cope with. Good, he will stop now; he knows he can't do these things to me now. But then my hopes were dashed.

*"Well, we'll have to be happy playing games then." he said, as though he were cheering me up with this statement.*

*Happy! Who's Happy?*
*Where's the stopping!*
*I had thought it would stop.*

But it didn't stop. The abuse continued.

# Chapter Three

When I was sixteen, it had been decided by Mum that I would go to college and study nursing. I had wanted to take a different path, but mum wanted me to be a nurse. I had failed at all my O Levels, at school; my concentration was either non-existent or now a-days, clouded in a dense fog. I remember my English teacher looking concerned, just before the exams.

"Are you okay, Cassie?" she asked. "You seem a little vague today"

Mrs Turner seemed worried for me. She was one of the teachers I had a good relationship with. She was tall and very well dressed always wearing jewellery and makeup. I liked her.

"I'm okay," I said. "My doctor gave me some tablets for my headaches and sometimes they make me feel a little odd. But I'm okay really," I said reassuringly. This seemed to satisfy her and as it was the truth, I didn't give it another thought. I had episodes of numb feelings after starting the pain killers; periods of time, when nothing made sense. I did think they could be a result of my taking the drugs but didn't worry about it. My GP had prescribed them so I thought they must've been safe.

I met a girl called Katie, the summer before starting at college and she was going to be in the same Nursing course as me that September. We both did holiday work in an electronics company in the next town. The days at the factory were fun representing another time of 'pretend', but my daily journeys home were still filled with the horrors of sexual abuse. On hearing of my summer job, Uncle Bill had offered to pick me up from work and Mum had agreed this to be good idea.

*For whom?*

*A good idea for whom?*

He had begun taking me to a houseboat a few years before where the abuse had become even more horrendous. Having Katie with me at the summer job and knowing she would be there into college term, helped me keep going. She was taller than me, a leggy blonde, pretty and was very confident and sure of herself. She always wore the most fashionable clothes and turned the heads of boys whenever they saw her. I think her family were quite well off since they lived in a big house in a nearby town and seemed to have exciting holidays.

In the September of 1962, Mum, as usual where I was concerned, had her way; I embarked on the nursing course in a town just a short train ride away. I enjoyed these journeys with Katie and soon got into a good routine. College was good. Life was okay. At home, things didn't change but being away most of the week was good. One problem I had, was that everyone seemed to have boyfriends. I would pretend that I was as keen on boys as the rest of them, but secretly of course, I wasn't. I didn't want that kind of 'love'.

I didn't want to get that close to anyone. But I did have dates and actually began to regularly see a boy who was in college on day release. But, like every other 'friendship', it ended because I wouldn't give in to what he wanted. We had been seeing each other for about a year and he wanted us to have sex. I couldn't do this. Sex was dirty, painful, and scary. I said I couldn't, didn't want to have sex with him or anybody. I didn't tell him the reason behind my feelings, so we ended the relationship.

My *pretend* or *make believe* was with me all the time. Being at college, was fun. I made friends and had a sort of social life that was good, almost normal I suppose. I could *pretend* that my real life was good. I made up stories of family and things we did together. I didn't want to be seen as different. When Katie and the other students, talked about what they were up to at the weekends, I found myself making up stories, telling them of things that never happened.

"We went for a picnic on the beach," I would tell them, and on another occasion, I remember saying "We went to the Isle of Wight on a day trip, it was fun." These were lies, but only just. Mum and the others often went for picnics and took boat trips to the Isle of Wight. The only part that was a lie, was that I never went with them. Was that so wrong? My *make believe*, my *pretend?* They never suspected and I became very good at it.

It was at this time, I realised that the headaches were not a problem now and so I might not need the medication. I didn't think about the fact, that taking the pills was why I felt better. I just thought perhaps I was okay now. I decided not to take them and stopped, but I felt very unwell. I had never heard of withdrawal and anyway, how could you become dependent on 'headache pills'! I tried to stop them, purely because I didn't like taking tablets and the pain had gone, so I didn't need them anymore. After two days, I didn't seem able to function properly, I felt sick and shaky, lost my concentration and the headaches returned. I would phase in and out of concentration, I couldn't cope with college or anything so I took one of the prescribed tablets and felt much better. I didn't really think about why I was feeling so bad, I wasn't aware that stopping these tablets could make me ill.

*But I was ill, unbeknown to me.*

*I was becoming dependent.*

*And that's an illness.*

This happened a few times and every time I tried to stop I would always go back to taking them. I would ring the surgery, they would write a repeat and I would have my supply. No questions, no consultation, no warning. Just collect the prescription and go to the chemist!

"When I stop or cut down on the drugs, I feel really weird, is this normal?" I asked one day when I rang for a repeat. The receptionist said she would ask my GP. When I rang back she said, "Dr Oxley wants you to continue with them, he has signed you another prescription." "Could the strange feelings and the shakiness be the tablets?" I asked. "No, Cassie" she said. "The doctor says you obviously need these pills. Just collect your script and you'll be fine." Conversation ended. I had no reason not to believe her. She was telling me what the doctor had told her. I collected the tablets and took them as told.

About a year after starting college and enjoying the pre-nursing course, I did manage to stop for a little while. Life had become so good, Bill was not around and the headaches had completely disappeared. I just stopped taking the pills. The memories of the first time I stopped taking them had gone from my mind.

The first day wasn't too bad, but then I began to feel sick and dizzy, my arms and legs felt strange and I began to suffer awful nightmares. Dreaming of the past abuse, the horrors were real.

*The car had veered off the road into a field I was about eleven years old, Bill had been away*

*for a while. What was he doing?*

*What now?*

*He suddenly leaned towards me and grabbed my leg - pulling it over to his side of the seat.*

*Cars at that time, didn't have separate seats in the front. It was one big seat, leather and so easy to slide on. Oh how much more difficult would it have been today, with separate seats and handbrakes to struggle with. How much I would have liked this difficult. He started to kiss me roughly.*

*"Oh, I've missed this, I've missed you," he slurred, all the time grabbing at my skirt and trying to put his hand inside of my panties. "Oh stop, stop!" I wanted to cry. But I couldn't. I couldn't make a sound. I was terrified. I hadn't forgotten the pain of the many times he had abused me before. I prayed that this time he would stop before he had hurt me as much as the other times. I prayed that God would stop this from happening. After all I was a good girl, I was confirmed wasn't I? But as through-out my childhood, God wasn't listening.*

*He, the man they called my uncle, grabbed my hand and pulled it into his trousers. No game today, no time. He seemed desperate. Desperate for what? Why was he different this time? Why was he making me touch him in a way that seemed rough and fast and why was he swearing?*

*It was all over in a second. Was that it? Had God been listening? Was it over?*

*I hoped it would it stop now and we would go home? The relief I felt was short lived.*

*Hope was away.*

These nightmares were horrendous and the headaches came back. I felt agitated and panicky, almost like I had no control, like life was happening outside of me. This scared me; I didn't know what was happening. I had never felt this bad. I went to see my doctor.

This time, I felt more hopeful, he had helped me before so I trusted that he would be able to help me again.

"I feel worse now," I said to Dr Oxley who had first given me headache tables, "it's as though I'm not really here most of the time and I had been feeling so good." I thought I sounded okay but I began to shake, "I feel terrified, shaky and wanting to run." I began to cry.

Those kind eyes looked at me, I'm not sure what they saw, but they saw something. "Did you just stop them suddenly?" he said "Did you take less and then stop or just stop?" I couldn't see how this mattered, they were just pain killers, I had no pain and so stopped the pills. "I just stopped them, the headaches had gone, so I didn't need them anymore" I answered, slightly confused.

Again, reaching for his prescription pad, no explanation of my symptoms, he started writing.

"Take these Cassie, they're different from the others and you're clearly unwell, take these and you'll feel much better." At this, he stood up, walked round the desk and opened the surgery door. Once again, I was dismissed.

As I left the surgery, I looked at the prescription. 'Diazepam' it read. That was the name of the tablets. I had never heard of them, why would I have? Trusting Dr Oxley, I began these new pills, I hadn't been told what they were, I didn't ask, you didn't. Although I now knew the name of the tablets, it meant nothing to me. The doctor, hearing my symptoms, gave me the prescription, I took the medication. Life became better again and once more, I was enjoying college. This was an *in-between*, a *happy*.

Life was good during the week. The college had an active rag committee and lots of social gatherings. I even became Chairman of the Entertainments committee. I remember a college dance I organised, we hired a group for the music, they were barely known at this time, the Baron Knights. We were not allowed alcohol on the campus, just soft drinks.

The 60s were supposedly the era of '*Sex, Drugs and Rock n Roll*'. I never saw any evidence of the second. The drugs, at least not the kind that were meant in the song, as for the first, I didn't go there but I did enjoy the third. If it happened, the *Drugs*, I mean, it must have passed me by. I suppose I did take drugs, but these were not to make me 'high', or make me feel good. I wasn't even trying to blot out the memories of the horrors in my life, nothing could do that, I was taking pills for headaches. End of.

I didn't know what Benzodiazepine drugs were; I didn't even know that was what I was taking at first. I never knew that the headache pills were mind-altering and that I could become dependent on them. Would I have taken these pills so readily? I'm sure I wouldn't have. Wasn't my life difficult enough already.

But...

*Nobody told me.*

Another change in me at this time, was my ability to take on a role and become someone else. In a way, I had been doing this for years, in my *pretend*, my *make believe*. If I became someone else, then my real life didn't exist. If I was somewhere else he couldn't touch me. Pretend was much better.

*I stared at the wallpaper and lost myself in the pictures. He can't hurt me here. I won't feel the pain and the horror. I'll hide in here, inside of this big oak tree, then I will be safe. Look at the butterflies, how they perch daintily on the leaves and how the shadows fall on the path in the woods. I'll be okay now. I'm safe here, nothing can hurt me now.*

At college, taking on a role as someone else, I was much stronger; or rather the Chairman of the Entertainments Committee was much stronger. I suppose, taking on this role, filled with artificial confidence from the pills, made me much stronger. I became someone else. At the college on the night of the Baron Knights performance, I noticed a crate of beer being loaded into the back room of the dance hall.

"You can't bring that in here," said a rather haughty voice.

*Was that me?*

*Did I say that?*

"We aren't allowed alcohol on the premises," I continued. Yes, this was me, standing up to a very large bearded manager.

"It's okay girlie," he said. "It's for the boys in the band, not the students."

*Like that was alright.*

*Like that made a difference.*

"I don't care who it's for, it will have to go back into your van," I said, slightly less confidently now, standing there in front of six foot of muscle and hair. "It can't come into the hall or backstage."

I thought I was losing, losing the argument about the beer, when a warm, kind voice from behind the stage curtains, spoke: It's okay, it will go back on board our bus, and we can drink it later, after the show." These kind, reassuring words came out of the mouth of the lead singer of the Baron Knights, Duke D'Mond. He was a gorgeous looking man with the best smile ever and I hoped I didn't stare.

The beer went back in the van.

It was much easier being someone else, in my land of pretend, make believe or just as someone in a different role, than being me. I was able to be stronger and slightly assertive, but I was always glad when someone stepped in to help.

These times when I felt strong, when I was acting a part, were only when I was out of my nasty, loveless life. Oh how I wished I could be like that at home but I couldn't. I hoped, a feeling I still held on to, that the *Cassie* at college would take over the weak, scared, broken *Cassie* who was really me. The *Cassie* I had become after years and years of abuse. I suppose the pills had also played a part in rendering me submissive, obedient and subservient when I was in danger or isolated. As I was when at home.

But outside of home, I could become an actor and pretend. The drawback was, that keeping up this pretence, was really tiring. On top of everything else, my home-life and the sexual abuse, I was exhausted, but I tried very hard not to show it. While at college it was not as bad, but when I got home and had finished the chores that Mum had left for me, I could just about make it up to the bathroom; I would brush my teeth and sometimes, without washing, fall into bed. I wasn't sleeping well at this time; I would lie awake and go over in my head, the nice things that had happened during the day.

*"He really likes you, Katie," I said to the friend I had made at college. "You can see he does the way he looks at you." I smiled at the girl sitting in front of me in the college refectory. She was a pretty girl with long blonde hair. We had become quite close and I had almost told her about my life. Only almost. "Why don't you smile at him and see if he comes over?" I suggested. Katie had liked Terry, one of the trainees at the college for a long time but she was a bit shy. She giggled and turned around to look in Terry's direction. He smiled and came over. "Would you like to come out to the pictures?" he asked her quietly. Katie nodded and they made arrangements to meet the following night.*

*She was so happy and we giggled together after he had gone and talked about what she would wear. I loved seeing her so happy.*

As time went on, the times of the strong Cassie

surfacing became less and less. I had always been quite shy, a bit of an introvert. Living in the background had always been second nature to me. College had brought out the other side. I loved wearing all the latest fashion, although Katie and I made the most of our outfits as money was tight for me. I loved makeup, I suppose this was part of pretending, being someone else. As chairman of the Entertainments Committee, I felt important. I loved the music and the dancing and dressed as well as I could afford to.

Home life was the same. I had never been close to my older sisters, they had frequently been away during my childhood, a summer school I think, and they were a lot older than me.

When I was at college, Ellen had married a country boy and seemed happy but Rosie had left home and married a man my mother loathed, so we lost touch. My brother Tom had joined the Royal Marines and he was often away.

That left my baby sister Anne and me. We were only five years apart, but in some ways, I was young for my age, in others I was way too old. The baby of the family had been spoiled by both of my parents, I wasn't jealous because I loved her. She was about ten when I was at college I think. A pretty girl with brown hair and greyish eyes. Always smiling and always seemed happy. We did spend some fun times together, when Mum was out. Trying on makeup and doing each other's hair. But these were few and far between. Anne liked to dance around to Tommy Steele, a rock singer at that time. He had a Top Ten record, 'Singing the Blues' and we played it over and over again, she loved it. If Mum was home, Anne wouldn't show me any affection or spend any time with me at all. I spent a lot of time, in my room, listening to country music, Patsy Cline was a favourite. I loved ballads, sad music, I suppose I could feel the pain in some of the words and this gave me comfort in a strange way. Perhaps I felt that someone else was sad and lonely too and that meant I wasn't on my own.

But life at college as 'Cassie the Confident', only lasted while I was there. Although the new pills had taken the headaches away again and made me feel able to cope, after a while, they seemed to have taken away any fight I had left. As I walked back through the door of the house I lived in with Mum, I changed. I took and accepted anything that was dished out.

# Chapter Four

I remember going back to my GP once, during my time as a student because I wasn't sleeping very well. The waiting room was empty; I felt very small sitting on the hard green chair in this high ceilinged room. The receptionist called me and I entered the consulting room. Dr Oxley was sitting in the same position as he always was, almost as though he had never left the room.

"I'm having trouble going to sleep," I told him. "I'm tired all the time at college and unable to concentrate."

I was hoping, that this medical man would have asked me if I was worried about anything, but he didn't.

"What time of the day do you take your tablets?" he asked, reaching for his prescription pad. "Do you take them at night or in the morning?"

I couldn't see what difference it made, but he was the doctor.

"In the morning," I said, "it's easier to take them then, before I go to college."

"I'll give you something different, to help you sleep," he said. "Take these as well as the ones you are already taking and increase the Diazepam, the ones you have, to three times a day."

He wrote me another prescription and told me to take the new pills at night. I didn't question, perhaps I should have questioned, but I didn't. After all, he made the headaches go away; he would be able to help me get off to sleep. Wouldn't he?

Again no warnings, no questions, just a prescription.

I took the piece of paper he had given me and went to the chemist. I didn't read it, it didn't matter what it said; I just wanted to sleep. Now I was taking two lots of medication. But it was okay, my doctor gave them to me, so it was okay.

The abuse was continuing most weekends. I hardly saw Claire now and my new friends at college lived so far away from me, that I didn't see them much outside of college. The course campus was in a town about 25 miles from where I lived and most of the students came from a huge area around the college. We only saw each other during the day in term time.

Katie had moved on and had a boyfriend so I didn't spend much time with her now. When there was something on, like a college dance, we would stay on campus and get ready in the changing rooms. Those days were fun. Life was fun, outside of my *real life*, at home.

I started to take the new pills and one morning I felt so awful, I called downstairs that I wasn't getting up. I felt giddy and sick and my head was pounding. It was an 'outing' day with the 'nasty'

"You come down here now!" Mum shouted. "Get down here. I want the shopping done before you go out with Bill." She continued to shout, "If it isn't done, you won't go!"

*Won't go?*

*Won't go, she sees 'not going' as a punishment?*

*Won't go is good!*

"I don't feel well," I replied thinking, not going, is okay with me. "I feel a bit sick."

44

"Have you actually been sick?" she enquired. For a moment I thought perhaps she cared. I *hoped* she was concerned, but that little word *Hop*e, had let me down many times.

I hadn't 'actually been sick' but felt very nauseous.

"No, I haven't but I feel like I might be," I called down, sounding, I thought, slightly fragile. But if I did sound fragile, she didn't notice.

"Then get yourself down here now, I feel sick most of the time having to look after you, so get down here now!"

*She's getting angry.*

*Mustn't make her angry.*

I went downstairs. I felt a bit giddy and not quite right, my head started to hurt. I suppose the new tablets were distressing me, I also had a pain in my head.

"I think my headaches are coming back." I told this woman standing in front of me with her arms folded, "I feel quite poorly."

"If it's not one thing it's another with you. The doctor gave you the pills for headaches, so take one of them and get on with the shopping."

I tried to say to her, that I was told to take one, three times a day and I had already taken the morning one.

"They're only headache pills, so take one now and stop moaning," she said. I wonder now, if she had known what they actually were, would she have made that statement. Sadly, I think, yes she would have. This fitted in with her, just getting me able to do the shopping, was all she was interested in.

I took another tablet.

Many times after this, if I felt unwell or couldn't do things Mum asked of me, she would suggest I took an extra tablet. I was taking the Diazepam, 'the headache pills', three times a day now and the new tablet in the evening. I never argued with Mum, I couldn't. She would always win and I did anything for a quiet life. So when I couldn't cope or things were really bad, I took another tablet. They were only painkillers after all. Mum said it was okay and Dr Oxley had prescribed them, so they must be okay. Almost immediately, I would feel calmer, the pounding in my head would stop and I could cope with whatever life threw at me.

Because taking an extra pill made me feel better, this became the pattern. Very soon, I didn't mention how I felt when things were bad; I would just swallow more of the medication, to enable me to cope. I didn't have to worry that I would run out of pills, I only had to ask and I would be given more.

Shortly after this time, Bill went away again. I thought that life might get better without him around me but my mother's treatment of me was the same, sometimes worse. It was as though she had begun blaming me once again, for what, I wasn't sure.

I became very close to one of Uncle Bill's sons, Steve, and during the time his father was away, we began dating. Bill had four sons, and Steve was the second to youngest. We had known each other all our lives, all our growing up days but had not seen each other for few years. We met again when I was sixteen at a family party. Steve was tall and dark haired. He looked wistful and a little sad. I was sitting at the side of the room and was wearing a pale blue dress, one of Katie's cast-offs. My hair was up in a pony-tail as was the fashion. I looked over at this handsome young man and was instantly attracted to him. I wondered at how the scruffy boy I had known, could have changed into such a good looking young man. He came over and spoke to me, his sparkly eyes smiling with a warmth I wasn't used to seeing. I felt shy at first but once we had begun to talk, he made me feel very relaxed and the evening became magical. As a boy, the same age as

Tom, he used to tease me as boys do. But here he was, treating me as though I were special.

"Would you like to come out with me?" he said softly. "We could go for a walk on the hill if you like".

Like? Like? Yes I would like. The 'hill' was a beauty spot where courting couples used to walk. A romantic, beautiful place and he wanted to take me there! *How good was that!* I had never for a moment thought he would be interested in me. I had never wanted any boy to be interested in me. But this was different. The feeling I had that night, the feelings that came very soon after our first date, was something I wasn't prepared for but it felt right. It was to be the first of many wonderful times. We would go to the local castle and walk for hours around the water that surrounded it.

Sometimes he would come round to my house, Mum seemed okay with this; we would sit in the best room and play records on my Dansette record player. Our house had two rooms downstairs apart from the kitchen and the family used the back room for meals and anything else. The front room was only used at Christmas or if Mum had company, this was called the 'best room'. In it there were two easy chairs and a huge sofa that could be made into a bed, seldom used as we didn't often have people to stay. The windows were dressed in beautiful heavy drapes and there was a small coffee table to the side of a lovely old fireplace. The whole floor was covered in fancy carpet, not heard of in the 60s very much.

So to be allowed to use this room, was almost an honour for me. I think it was done to impress Steve, as Mum and his mother didn't get on. Spending time in the 'best room' with Steve were the best times. Suddenly the house seemed safe, for the first time in my life.

One time when I couldn't see him, for a week, I realised how much I had missed him.

When I saw him a few days later he surprised me. "I've missed you so much Cassie, I want us to be together forever." He said he loved me and I knew I loved him. It was wonderful, he was wonderful; this was love in a way that I had never known. It was good and clean and right. How lucky was I!

Perhaps we were both looking for the same thing, in our own private pain; perhaps we had seen something in each other that drew us together. I don't know, but we fell in love. He was a few years older than me, like Tom, my brother. He made me feel loved, protected and safe. This was an *in-between* time. In between, the abuse, the emotional cruelty that was my mother, *in-between* the loneliness that was my life.

When Uncle Bill returned, from wherever he had gone, at first I managed to avoid him. I was studying every evening, at college during the days and seeing Steve at the weekends. I suppose it was difficult during this time, for him to get me on his own. This was an added bonus to my happiness. I hadn't realised that the affair between the two people who inflicted hurt on me, the woman who was my mother and the man they called my Uncle, had been rekindled. I hadn't realised this at first and I didn't care. I suppose that was selfish, but I didn't care. They were both leaving me alone.

I had begun to cut down on the tablets, cut out the new ones and cut down drastically on the 'headache pills'. I felt a bit strange at first, shaky and a bit sick, but was so happy and in love that I managed to cope. When I was feeling shivery or agitated, Steve would hold me, cuddle me and tell me everything would be okay. I never told him about the pills. I don't know why, I just didn't. Should I have realised that these strange feelings only ever happened when I cut down or stopped the medication? I was beginning to think, that my feeling odd, kept happening, when I tried to cut out the pills, so I suppose I should have. But I didn't, nobody told me to be aware of symptoms such as these. Steve helped me during the worst times. But at night, at home, I was on my own, then it was bad. I couldn't sleep very well. To help with this, I would lie in bed and relive the times Steve and I spent together. We had kissed and cuddled but nothing else. That was what we both wanted. That was enough.

Sometimes, when the headaches were really bad, I would take a 'pain killer'. But most of the time, I would look at how life could be in the future, a future with Steve. I would try and imagine us in a little house together, with a family of our own. When I felt shaky, I would hold on to the blanket on my bed and imagine it was him. Somehow I managed a few hours' sleep. But it didn't matter. I was loved now and nothing could spoil that for me.

Life was easier, my future would be good, I had a wonderful boyfriend who loved me and I would stay with Steve forever. I was enjoying college, and the abuse had stopped. A *happy,* my future looked wonderful.

# Chapter Five

During the first year of the pre-nursing course I went away for work experience. Although I was upset at leaving Steve, Katie was going to the same hospital. This didn't work out very well for me. I was found unsuitable for the work on a male orthopaedic ward where I became upset at the remarks of the male patients. They were probably just trying to be funny, but I didn't handle sexual innuendos very well because of the abuse I'd suffered. As a result, I was moved to a children's ward but became very upset when a young patient died. I had also stopped all the medication at this time but didn't realise, that the withdrawal was also affecting me. Leaving me vulnerable and a bit shaky, a bit panicky But, I had to succeed at this placement.

I had to.

*I can't fail again.*

*I can't let her down.*

*She will never forgive me.*

All of my life I had never been able to please Mum. I had failed the 11-plus exam when I became ill half-way through. I hadn't taken the re-sit exam, my choice and against her wishes and so didn't go to the Grammar School that she had set her heart on. I also had failed all five O Levels, with so much going on in my life, I hadn't been able to concentrate. And although I had re-taken three at college by this time and had passed, there had been no acknowledgement of that. So I couldn't fail this placement. Even though nursing wasn't my career choice.

After two weeks and several moves of ward the matron of the hospital, who was very kind, said she felt that I could make a good nurse, but not yet. I needed to mature a bit.

*Mature!*

*How mature did I have to be!*

*Wasn't having sex mature!?!I've been 'mature' for years.*

But that isn't what she meant by using the word.

Sexual Abuse isn't mature, as a victim or an abuser.

She encouraged me to ring Mum and explain. I tried to call home three times. I felt so poorly, trembling and panicking until I felt sick to my stomach that I had to abort the mission until I felt strong enough to cope with Mum's anger. Eventually, with shaky hands and an even shakier voice, I rang.

The call was met with anger and hostility and her slamming the phone down.

I was miles away from home and she slammed the phone down on me. Leaving me scared and alone. The pains in my head came back with a vengeance.

*Was I surprised?*

*Did I expect her to understand?*

*Of course I didn't. This was my normal. Again, I was on my own.*

The one thing that kept me going, made it easier to cope, was knowing that Steve was waiting for me. Yes, I was scared, upset and alone in this big city. But back home he was there for me, him and our love. He would make everything better.

*Then I would be okay.*
*Then I would be safe.*
*Then I would be loved.*

On my GP's advice, I carried the headache pills with me, in my bag and although I didn't want to, I took one. I had very few left and was determined not to get another repeat. But now I took one of the few, just to get me through this, to enable me to function. I vowed I wouldn't take anymore, *just this one*.

I went home. Little did I know, that this failure would lead to one of the most devastating times in my life; that it would lead to my whole life changing forever and my heart being broken.

On my arrival home, a failure again, I was met with the cold shoulder from everyone. Ellen and Rosie were working by this time, but were in the house, off-duty when I arrived. My brother Tom was away on duty in Aden. My baby sister, Anne, was in the sitting room with Mum, she was Mum's strongest ally. When the woman they called my mother wasn't talking to me, no one else dared.

I wasn't feeling very well, light-headed and swimmy. I thought it was just the upset from the nursing placement and the reaction of my family. It never once occurred to me that I was 'missing' the 'headache' pills. I had a really bad headache on arriving home but thought everything would be okay when I saw Steve. I caught a bus to his house and ran as fast as I could up the hill from the bus stop, his house was a long way from the end of the road. I ran up to the front door and knocked. At first, his mum Gwen, a tallish quiet lady who never usually had very much to say, wouldn't let me see him.

I didn't understand, he loved me; I loved him, so why couldn't I see him?

After a while, I heard him tell her to let me in and I hurried into their sitting room. A lovely warm welcoming place where the boy I loved and I, had spent many happy times. I had always liked his Mother but would often feel she was trying to avoid me when I visited. I know she didn't have anything to do with my Mum and thought that might be why she was sometimes a bit odd with me. She was never unkind, just a bit distant I thought. Everything looked the same, the armchairs in their pale pink covers and the matching sofa. The long deep pink curtains were still at the windows and the tiny fireplace with a vase of roses on the hearth. Everything was where it had always been. So what was wrong?

What happened next broke my heart, broke it in a way that hurt more than anything else in my young life. After a traumatic meeting with the boy I loved, through tears from both of us, he ended it. He took away all the hopes and dreams of our future together in a few words.

"I can't see you anymore" he said, "I have to break up with you. I do love you but I have to end it. I'm so sorry."

I didn't understand. If he loved me why was he doing this?

"Please tell me what's wrong! If you love me, why are you finishing with me?" I sobbed, trying to hold on to him.

"I can't tell you. I won't tell you," he said; taking my arms from around his neck, he ran from the room in tears.

After a while, sobbing and calling to him to come back downstairs, trying to hang on to my dream, I was asked to leave, I had no choice. I left.

With my mind in confusion and turmoil, I sat outside of his house for what seemed like hours, before getting a bus back home. I looked back at the house

I had loved so much and it had changed. It seemed hostile, unfriendly and somewhere I didn't know. I felt so lonely, so bereft, so confused. The pain I was feeling was a physical pain in the pit of my stomach.

The only thing I could do was to go back to the house where I wasn't wanted. I walked slowly to the end of the road and took the bus home. The panic that had begun to creep into my body, was coming back. Shaking and crying, I went straight to my room and curled up on my bed. The pain in my head was so bad that I wished I had one of the pills my GP had given me, but then I remembered how bad I had felt, when I had stopped taking them, when I first went out with Steve. I didn't want or need to feel any worse than I did at that moment. So, I had a headache. So what! That was nothing compared to the pain of Steve's finishing with me. There was nothing I could do. No pill would make this feel better. Once again I was powerless and the loneliest girl in the world. The only good thing in my life, my relationship with Steve, was gone.

The next few weeks were awful, I had periods of sheer panic, the pain in my heart was real pain, and I had a constant headache and a heavy feeling in my tummy that wouldn't go away. At times I felt that life was hopeless, without Steve's love, I had no one to show me any affection. I was sure, that any time, Uncle Bill would begin to come round again and I would once again be lost in a life of sexual abuse and fear. I thought of going to see my doctor but was sure he would just give me more pills. Yes, they helped, but I knew that nothing really helped me, the medication just made it possible for me to survive. It wasn't the answer, I knew that, but I didn't know what the answer was.

A few weeks later, during a phone-call from the hospital where I had 'failed' my placement, the Matron had told Mum that I would make a good nurse, one-day. Although I wanted to study journalism, Mum was insisting that I went back to the nursing course. I decided to talk to my Dad about changing direction at college. Dad was a gentle man, used to doing whatever Mum told him to do. Not because he was weak, but because he loved her. She had always, throughout my childhood, treated him with ridicule, unkindness and distaste. He, like me, was often at the end of her vicious tongue and the object of her anger and fury. He would do anything to please her, anything for a quiet life. Mum had showed no concern about my heartache at splitting up with Steve, she never mentioned it, or even of my being so unwell, I had never expected her to.

I spoke with Dad and he agreed with me, that changing the course to something I really wanted to do, seemed the right solution. While we were talking, Mum came into the room. I told her that I had decided to change courses and do a course in journalism. I told her that Dad had agreed with me on my choice. She looked completely shocked. She was angry and seemed horrified.

"What right do you think he has to agree with you?" she bellowed looking over to my Dad with a smug expression on her face. "He has no rights over you, only I have!" she spat. She was smirking one of her 'I'll show you' looks.

She had made similar jibes earlier in my life, when I hadn't wanted to re-sit the 11-plus and perhaps gain a place at the Grammar School. She had made spiteful remarks saying he had no rights over me. I didn't understand, then and I didn't understand now. "He is my Dad, of course he has rights," I said softly.

At this point she was seething, I was questioning her.

How dare I? I had just failed her again and here I was questioning her! She was angrier at this point than she had ever been.

"Ask him!" she continued screaming and pointing at my beloved Dad. "Ask him what I mean!"

I looked over at this poor gentle man who had agreed with me, there was a look in his eyes that I will never forget. He was in bits. I was in bits. Both of us hurting and almost in tears. I didn't want to add to his pain, I didn't want to ask him. Perhaps I was scared of what he might tell me. But I did. How I wish I hadn't. But I did.

"What does she mean Dad?" I cried, not wanting him to answer but wanting to know what she was talking about. He was trying to hold back tears, this confused and scared me.

I tried to reassure him that he had every right to help me, that he was my Dad.

That's when it happened. When my world, the world that I thought had sunk as low as was possible, my hurting confused world, came crashing down around me. He told me very quietly, through his tears, his voice almost a whisper, as if he didn't want to speak these heart-breaking words. As if he didn't want me to hear. He told me that he wasn't my biological father. That he had no rights over me because he wasn't my real Dad.

The room was silent, I looked over at Mum; she had a curious almost triumphant expression on her face. I felt faint, sick and dizzy. If Dad wasn't my father, then who was? A tiny voice that came from somewhere deep inside of me, a frail frightened voice, asked who my real father was.

I wasn't ready. I wasn't prepared for the horror of the revelation that came out of the mouth of the woman who was my mother. Like a knife that pierced my heart with its force.

"Bill" she screamed at me, "Bill is your Father!"

The shock of what I had just heard was like a thumping in my head. I felt as though someone had slapped me very hard. I was reeling and feeling very unsteady. Bill, my Godfather, the man who had raped and abused me for the whole of my life, was my real Dad?

*No, this can't be true; this can't be happening* I thought, trying hard to deny the truth of what I had just been told. He couldn't be. The man in tears in front of me, he was my Dad. The man who was never allowed to show me any affection, but who I knew loved me. He was my father. Not the evil monster of whom I lived in fear and dread, every day of my life. He wasn't anything to me except my abuser.

I suppose I was struggling with life without the help of the 'headache pills'. I was still hurting after Steve had called our relationship off. The shock and confusion around this was still very much with me. Life couldn't get any worse for me could it? Then, like a bolt of lightning, the realisation struck me. The sound of rushing and crashing inside of my head was overpowering.

*This can't be true.*

*This isn't happening.*

*Somebody make this go away.*

But the realisation stayed. If Bill was my father, then Steve, the boy I loved, the boy I had planned to spend my life with, who had so recently broken my heart, was my brother. I ran out of the room and was violently sick.

The next day after a sleepless night, things started to make sense. Steve had been told the truth and been told to tell me. But he couldn't. The people, who were my parents, had obviously told him to break it off and to tell me the reason for breaking up. What cowards! They had made this problem; they had allowed us to become so close that we believed our future was together. But they didn't have the courage to tell us the truth. Any more than Mum had the courage to tell me, that the man I had always thought was my father, wasn't. No she made my poor Dad break this earth-shattering news to me, as she had made Steve break my heart, for her. It dawned on me now. Bill used to say he had the right to do what he wanted with me. This is what he must have meant. But he had no right.

By this time I was having periods of shaking and my heart was racing so fast, I was terrified it might stop. I became agitated and shivery, unable to stay still for more than a few minutes. It seemed the whole of my body was suffering physical and emotional pain and I was finding it hard to do even the simplest of tasks. My heart was broken, my world had fallen apart with this revelation about my birth right and the only person who loved me was gone. Life was now unbearable.

For the rest of the summer I struggled through, lost in my heartache. I was so pleased that we hadn't been lovers, Steve and I. Sex hadn't been on the agenda. But the realisation that Bill had had sex with me, his own daughter, was horrendous. Thankfully, I wasn't aware of the word incest. I am grateful for that lack of knowledge. I felt the shame of the two people who had conceived me, I felt ashamed of all the pain they had caused. I took on all the blame, something I was used to. I was always told I was to blame for everything that ever went wrong, and that it was my fault that Mum was unhappy. So this new blame was nothing. I was the one who felt guilty, I didn't realise then, that Steve, Gwen and my Dad as well as me, were all the victims in this awful drama.

A few days after this shocking discovery, my life seemed empty but at times my head was so full. It was as though it would split open if I had anything else in it. I had made an appointment with my doctor. I had been having trouble with heavy periods and my Nan suggested that I saw him. As I said, I spent a lot of time with my Nan C and we had become very close. Perhaps she realised that I needed help, perhaps she suspected something. I had told her about my bad periods, maybe she saw this as a way of my getting help. I don't know but I felt so down, so unhappy and so I took her advice.

Once again, I found myself in the cold waiting room, waiting to see the doctor with the kind eyes. I hadn't had any more of the tablets that he had given me, the headaches were bad again now but I put up with them. I had felt strange when I stopped taking the last medication and was a little concerned that it was the pills.

"Hello Cassie, how are things?" he said kindly.

*Things.*

*Does he really want to know about my 'things?'*

*I thought, shall I tell him?*

I was so confused about my life, so hurt and unhappy. Tired from pretending that everything was fine, hurting from the happenings of the past few days.

*Perhaps if I tell him, my 'things' will get better.*

*But will he believe me?*

*If he asks me, he might be able to help me, protect me from Uncle Bill.*

*So perhaps, if he asks, I'll tell him.*

My mind was jumbled with these thoughts. I couldn't hold it together and I broke down, I thought he sensed something, I thought he would know.

*Couldn't he hear my heart aching?*

*Couldn't he see my fear? Couldn't he see that I was different now after everything that had happened in my young life??*

But he couldn't see because he didn't look at me. He only heard the symptoms that he had begun to expect.

"I notice you haven't had a prescription for a month, so you haven't been taking your medication?" he enquired.

"When I stopped taking them, I felt so ill," I said, reluctant to have more pills. I wanted to talk, to make some sense of my life. He was already reaching for his pad, ready to prescribe me some tablets. I wanted to tell him, I really wanted to. But how could I? I had told the one person who should have helped me, she didn't. But I was so close, with a tiny bit more persuasion or kindness; I think I would have told. But I was scared, traumatised by the abuse but more recently by the revelations about my parentage and the heartache over Steve; that I couldn't tell. Dr Oxley seemed caring, perhaps he sensed something else was wrong, but if he did, he didn't push it. Anyway, he wouldn't have believed me, and he didn't ask, so I said nothing. It was just my heavy periods and the headaches, I said.

He seemed quite happy to leave it there.

"I want you to go back on the tablets, not the same ones that made you feel poorly, but some new ones that will lessen the period pain and take away the headaches." He was writing while he was talking.

*Why don't you look at me?*

*Doesn't the pain show in my face?*

I thought anyone could see it; I was carrying it around like a heavy load.

*Why couldn't he see?*

Perhaps he wasn't the person to tell. Perhaps Doctors didn't ask such questions. So I said nothing.

"These are different, stronger," he said. "They will make you feel a whole lot better." With that, once again, he escorted me to the door, albeit, kindly and showed me out.

I think I thanked him, I don't know. I had again, lost an opportunity to tell someone how my life was. I almost did, I was almost there; almost ready to tell him how I lived in the fear of Uncle Bill and Mum. But I didn't. Once again, clutching a prescription that was going to make everything alright, I made my way to the nearest chemist.

# Chapter Six

As time went on, once again, I began to feel better. The headaches had stopped and as a bonus, my periods became less heavy. So he must have been right, my doctor, he said I would feel better and I did. Benzodiazepines had, apparently, been talked of as wonder drugs, there were researchers who had raised concerns about them, but millions of women had been prescribed these pills on repeat prescriptions for years. I was one of them. I don't remember reading anything in the press about warnings, I suppose it was only the medical profession who had this information. People like my GP.

Mum had her way, well, sort of. She had insisted that I went back to nursing but was persuaded by the principal of the college to allow me to change my course. Not to the one I had chosen but to a medical receptionist course, a government pilot scheme. As usual Mum hadn't asked me, but I was okay with this as I enjoyed being at college and it would mean I could continue to see my friends. I went back in the September of 1963, I was seventeen years old. I was still hurting from the revelations of the summer and grieving for my lost love. I had been told to stay away from him and his family and I did.

*What could I do?*

*They all hated me, didn't they?*

*Mum had told me that they did.*

I hadn't seen Bill for a year now, so life was being kinder to me. I was managing day-to-day things, coping with the mental cruelty of Mum, with the help of the pills.

I was so good at hiding the things about me that had been harmed by the previous years; nobody knew there was anything wrong in my life. I loved college. While there, I was 'Cassie the fashion queen' and was still on the Entertainments Committee. I didn't have much pocket money but I was able to shop in second hand shops, it was the time of Carnaby Street fashions that said, *'almost anything goes'*! With the help of Katie, I was able to adapt things to look 'cool'. I am sure sometimes, we, Katie and I, looked outrageous in our improvised fashion. Memories of my childhood and days out with my best friend Claire, came back into my mind. We would dress up in our, or rather her, best clothes and go into town for lunch. We possibly looked a bit outrageous then, but we thought we looked good. I had many good memories of times with Claire and her family, where I pretended to be one of them, that her Mum and Dad, were my parents. This was a *happy*, an *in-between*. And college was a *happy*; I had fun, especially in Rag week when pranks were played on the new students.

But there was one moment, when the past came too close for comfort. I was kidnapped during one of these 'fun-times' and taken by car to a remote spot on a hill. There I was ceremoniously dumped by the other college. It was okay, someone would find me.

Suddenly I became scared.

*I don't like it here, it's scary. It feels like it did in the woods, where Bill would take me. It's like when he went back to the car, to collect things he needed for the sexual games he played.*

I began to get panicky, felt shivery and weak. Then suddenly a car came over the brow of the hill, it was a mate from college and I knew I was safe. They often showed themselves, these fears and terrors of my past, they would rush back in and scare me. Usually when I least expected them to. This was also the beginning of a new fear, the dependency beginning to show itself. At first, on new medication, I was fine, but after a while, the pills wouldn't block everything out and the panic attacks would come, slowly and mildly in the beginning, but come they would, all the same. If I felt well enough to miss a pill, thinking I was okay, the fear would slap me in the face to remind me that actually I wasn't.

I spent the next few years at college and as well as having fun, I worked very hard. On graduating, I got a job with a large medical practice in a nearby city. There were four doctors and I was responsible for all the clinics, the administration and writing repeat prescriptions. I was so happy to have at last succeeded in something. And although there was no praise from Mum, I didn't care.

It was in this job, that I became aware of how many people were on the same tablets and me. I suppose this should have warned me, but it didn't. I just thought that if the doctors at my place of work and my own GP were all prescribing the same tablets to lots of people, then they must be safe.

*They wouldn't have been doing this otherwise, would they?*

I was writing the prescriptions, the GPs were signing them and people like me were taking them.

*That's alright then!*

I continued to take the 'headache pills', then continued to get repeat prescriptions as I had for years, no consultation, no request for my being seen. So no one was worried about how these pills might affect me, why should I have been?

I had joined a theatre group just before starting this job, I hadn't seen Bill for quite a while and I really thought it had all stopped. That the sexual abuse was in the past. That I was free.

*How stupid was I.*

*How stupid was that!*

I was eighteen and had begun to see a lovely young man, an actor. It was very much a surprise to me when he had asked me out, but he did, and it was wonderful. Although I had lived as an adult, being sexually abused, having sex as adults do and carrying out the chores of a woman in Mum's house, inside I was a little girl. A child with the dreams of happiness. I had lived a good life and had been a good girl, if I didn't consider the outings with Bill as me being bad. I had even joined the church choir and been confirmed thinking that if I became one of God's family, I would be safe. I prayed, oh how I prayed, that God would keep me safe. But God didn't seem to be listening to me.

When I met Alistair, the actor, I hoped that things would change. Without Bill on the scene and getting close to a young man who seemed everything Bill wasn't, I thought life would now be better, okay. He was the original tall, dark and handsome that you read about. Charming and full of confidence, every girl's dream. He dressed in a rather eccentric way, corded trousers and waistcoats, sometimes wearing a silk scarf loosely around his neck. Very arty looking. His family apparently were quite well off and they lived in the 'better' part of town. None of this mattered to me but I knew it would to Mum.

*Perhaps now I will be happy, perhaps now I would be loved.*

I still had my times of pretend, times when I made believe that my childhood had been good, free from abuse and loved by my Mum. I worked very hard at keeping the past away and keeping busy, this helped me keep my reality, my life at home, from spoiling my every day, these were my *in-betweens*. In the theatre group where I was to play different characters on stage, I was in my element. I was good. Why shouldn't I have been, this was normal for me, acting a part, so, yes, I was good. I was taking the medication prescribed by my family doctor and getting any amount of the pills that I needed. I did sometimes worry about taking them but I knew from experience that life without them was so much harder than life with them. I would stop taking them one day, I knew I would. They weren't addictive; my doctor had told me they were safe. I had asked about the  symptoms I had when I stopped the medication, if they were because I had stopped them, asked if the tablets made me feel that way. I was always reassured that they weren't. That it was me .At this time I hadn't questioned the prescriptions given out at my work place, I hadn't been in the job very long. Back then you didn't question doctors and I was already quite subservient so didn't keep asking. Why should I have been worried, he wasn't.

On one occasion when Alistair was walking me home, past the river just outside of where I lived, he stopped and turned to face me.

"Do you know how I feel about you Cassie?" he said, smiling at me. I didn't answer, what could I say? I knew I was falling for him but never imagined he felt the same way. "I have fallen for you hook line and sinker," he said laughing. He grabbed my hand and I had tears in my eyes. We laughed and hugged each other, dancing around in the moonlight.

*Will I be happy now?*
*Is God finally listening?*

This was a beginning of a happy, a time of love and romance. This time, this love was allowed, it would be a *happy*.

One day on arriving home, he was there, in our house, Bill, my abuser. He and Mum were drinking tea like it was the most natural thing in the world. Even if he hadn't abused me, hadn't damaged and terrorised me for years, how was I supposed to be, how was I supposed to act when he was around? He was no longer the man who was my Uncle; he was my father. This was still so raw for me, so painful and difficult for me to deal with. I spoke as few words as I could get way with and avoided him wherever possible. He didn't at first, manage to get me on my own, I made sure of that. I was so afraid, all the bad memories, all the fears of the past came flooding back, the times he abused me in the car, in the woods, on the boat. I couldn't let this happen again.

A while later, finding me alone, in our tiny kitchen, he stood in the door way, preventing me from leaving the room.

"Come on Cassie, let's go for a drive, we can have fun," he said.

*Fun?*
*Fun?*
*It was never fun.*

I knew what that meant. Fun with him was the one thing I never wanted again.

"I'm not coming with you!" I said firmly "If you try and make me, I will tell Alistair." I never really thought this through, I was panicking.

Bill laughed. "What will he think of you if you told him? He'll wonder why you didn't stop it, why you didn't tell someone if you didn't like it." He looked so pleased with himself. Safe in the knowledge that he was right. How would it look to anyone who didn't know me? Anyone who thought that Bill loved me and that I loved him? A loving uncle who wanted to spend time with his favourite niece. What if Alistair believed Bill and thought I had enjoyed all the sex and games? So once again, he had won. He continued to say that he would tell Alistair that I had a sexual relationship with him, this man they called my uncle and that I had been the instigator. He would do this if I didn't agree to go with him and have sex. I was so ignorant of the law, so afraid of his threats; I believed everything this evil man said.

*I had told, hadn't I?*

*I had told Mum and she didn't believe me.*

*How was anyone going to believe me?*

I went with him. The abuse continued.

During the summer of 1963, a friend of Uncle Bill tried to sexually assault me. He had been doing some work in our house at the time. I began to think that I must have given out some kind of signal that meant I was fair game to men. He hadn't actually touched me, but after I managed to get away from him, as he was leaving, he said that Bill had given his permission.

*What was I?*

*Some sort of toy to hand around?*

I had told Alistair in a moment of panic and he had made me tell Mum. The result of this, was a long drawn out court case and horrible interrogation by his defence. This wasn't an act of love on my mother's part but one of revenge. Unbeknown to me, the man who had tried to assault me, had been having an affair with her and had called it off. I discovered this much later in my life. Ellen had known about their 'friendship' and told my Dad, I overheard this conversation. He did nothing. He wasn't a weak man but he loved his wife and I believe she could have done anything and he would have just accepted it. His love was so great. But back then, for a moment I really wanted to believe she was making me go through all of this, the court case, the newspaper coverage, because she cared. Again I was wrong. It didn't take very long for her to resume her dislike of me, soon after it was over, she didn't need to act and she had had her revenge, on my would be abuser by taking him to court. This left me traumatised and I felt drained and depressed.

I rang my doctor and Miss Pringle asked me what was wrong. I briefly told her about the assault and the court case, she said to ring back, later that day. I must have sounded upset, scared or something because she seemed concerned. I rang back and she told me I was to increase the tablets by doubling the amount I was taking in the morning and again double the night time ones. I did ask if she was sure, didn't Dr Oxley want to see me? She reassured me that this was what the doctor had said and I didn't need to be seen. Feeling so upset by everything, I did what I was told.

Following this awful time, life became better. Alistair and I became engaged much to the delight of Mum, seeing a daughter marrying into a very respectable and wealthy family. We had been going to wait, but in the November of 1963, we had both been devastated by the death of President John Kennedy, a man we both admired; we decided not to wait because we didn't know what life had in store for us. Even though I was only eighteen and Alistair was only twenty-one, we became engaged.

But my dreams were shattered, it didn't last. He turned out to be the same as all the other men in my life, except my beloved Dad. When I said Alistair couldn't have sex with me, before we married, he became angry and I called off the engagement. It took a long time for

Mum to forgive me. I had let her down again. Once more I was on my own, still suffering horrendous abuse and still taking the tablets. Life was not good.

# Chapter Seven

After my engagement ended I dated a few boys but soon realised that sex was the main thing on their minds. I would go so far, but when I wouldn't have sex, these relationships ended.

In the summer of 1965 my best friend Claire got married and I was the maid of honour. It was a wonderful day and it made me so happy to see her looking the beautiful bride. With her blonde curls and sparkling complexion, she looked like a fairy princess in her beautiful white gown. A few days before the wedding, I had a fall and on the day itself I awoke really poorly, giddy and sick and in a lot of pain. My knee was hugely swollen and inflamed and Claire's dad took me to the emergency department at the local hospital. They wanted me to have complete rest but I explained that I wouldn't miss the wedding for anything. They gave me some strong painkillers and antibiotics and told me to go back to my GP on the Monday.

At the reception, I remember someone gave me a glass of brandy as I was feeling unwell. I didn't think about it, I drank the tiny glass of sweet liquid, so wanting not to let Claire down on her big day. I began to feel very strange and had to go outside because I needed air. The bridegroom Paul, was a Naval Officer and many of his mates were there. One of these, a naval medic, asked if I was taking anything else. I told him about the headache tablets and on asking what they were called, I showed him the bottle. He explained that the combination of the pills and the brandy had made me feel unwell and that the pills prescribed by my doctor were interacting with the painkillers or antibiotics. I thought he looked quite concerned after seeing the name of the prescribed medication, and seeing how many I was taking. He suggested I went to hospital. I assured him I was okay and would see my doctor on the Monday.

After the weekend, again I found myself waiting in the room with the high ornate ceiling to see Dr Oxley. I really wasn't feeling well now. My leg was swollen, red and angry and I was feeling nauseous and feverish. When it was my turn, I limped into the consulting room.

"Hello, Cassie," greeted the doctor cheerily, "looks like you have been in the wars".

I explained that I had fallen over the garden gate after working in a café, helping Mum, as it was dark when I arrived home. Someone had put the bolt on the tiny garden gate, I had pushed it and it had stuck, I fell onto the concrete path.

"When I went to the casualty department, they had given me some strong pain killers and these antibiotics." I showed him the bottle. "A friend at the wedding reception said that I was feeling worse because these tablets had interfered with the tablets you gave me for headaches."

I only mentioned this because I thought perhaps he could change the painkillers so that this didn't happen. "He also said that these drugs were dangerous if taken over a long time and I have been taking them for years."

I just repeated what the young medic at the reception had told me.

"No, you don't have to worry," said my family doctor, "Chlordiazepoxide tablets are very safe with anything else you are taking, there is also no reason to worry about being on them long term, they are very safe." He sighed and sat back in his chair "If you are ever able to come off them, which I doubt, it will be easy, you won't have a problem"

I hadn't known the name of the pills he had changed me to, didn't think it was important. He wasn't worried, after all he would know, he was the doctor!

"You probably feel so poorly because the wound has become infected, you'll feel better in a few days. Keep the leg up and rest."

Keep my foot up and rest! Fat chance of that living with Mum. But he had put my mind at rest about the medication. He was right, in a few days, the symptoms decreased and I felt better.

After the wedding reception, I had popped into the café where Mum was working, even though I felt so ill. It was only a short distance from the reception venue and so I would have been in trouble if I hadn't gone in. The son of her friend Dottie, who owned the pub next door to the café, was there and we chatted for a while. He was a tall sporty looking guy and I knew he played football and cricket for the local town. He had fair hair and green grey eyes, a nice looking young man I thought. A few days after this, he asked me out and we began dating and soon, life in general was fine again.

I was working in the group medical practice and was very happy being treated as a colleague and friend by the doctors. One of my duties was to write the repeat prescriptions. I had noticed when I first started this job, that lots of people were taking the same drugs as me, lots of people with headaches then, I had thought.

After overhearing a conversation between two of the partners, I realised that the tablets I was taking were antidepressants.

I mentioned this to one of the doctors and he asked how much I was taking. I was actually taking 40mg twice a day now, or 20mg as and when I needed them and 5mg of the night time tablet. He seemed horrified and explained that these tablets were very strong and shouldn't be taken with anything else. When he asked if my GP had explained these dangers, I said no. Because he hadn't. Nobody had. He suggested that I try and stop taking them and ask my GP for something else for the headaches.

I was shaken by what he said and tried to cut them down, but I couldn't. I had to stay well enough to get to work, a job I really enjoyed and had trained for at college. Every time I tried, I had severe shakes and the headaches came back worse than before. I went back to see my GP and he reassured me that these pills were very safe. I had known Dr Oxley for far longer than the doctors I worked for and he knew me. I had been feeling much better after the knee had healed and I wasn't taking the antibiotics and strong painkillers, so I believed him. I wasn't taking anything else now, so I would be okay. I was still on the Librium, as I had found to be the new name for the new tablets, Chlordiazapoxide, I had begun a while before Claire's wedding. No one mentioned anything about dependency, or long term side-effects. My family doctor assured me they were safe and that I needed them. I continued to take the tablets.

The romance with Edward blossomed, even though I fell out with Mum, because she suddenly decided that a son of a publican wasn't good enough for her daughter. The daughter she cared so little about. She threw me out of the house. Dottie took me in and between us, we planned the wedding. I missed my Dad and my little dog Bobbie. I had him since he was a puppy, had walked him, and looked after him. As expected on this occasion, to suit Mum and I believe to hurt me, Bobbie became 'Mum's dog' and she wouldn't let me have him. So missing him was hard but otherwise life was good. Edward's parents, Edward Sr. and Dottie were lovely people. His mum was rather plump with grey curly hair and it seemed, but I know she couldn't have, that she always wore an apron, paisley and soft coloured, over her day dress. Edward Sr. was also plump and silver haired, always smiling. His clothes were always clean and tidy. They had seemed to like me straight-away.

Edward, being tall and thin, was nothing like either of them. They were a lovely close family. He had been understanding about my feelings about sex before marriage, he hadn't asked why but had respected my decision to wait. Bill was off the scene now, as he had fallen out with Mum, I was safe. Safe from him and the abuse and safe from Mum I thought. She tried her hardest to ruin things for me, even tried to stop the wedding but with the help, love and support of Edward and his family and the love of my brother Tom and his wife, she failed. I was married on my twenty-first birthday on the wettest November day ever. I think I loved Edward, well I know I did, in a way. Just not the right way. I had stupidly thought, that once we were married and I had his ring on my finger, life would be good. I would be able to love him in the way a proper wife love's her husband, after all, he loved me. I never thought it through. I didn't realise how much damage the sexual abuse had done to me, how it had affected my ability to be that proper wife. I thought I was past all of that now. Living in a new life, with a man who was good to me. I thought at last I was safe, but I wasn't safe, I had a new fear now, one I hadn't anticipated. The fear of making love, to my husband.

We had bought a little bungalow in the town where we lived but decided to have a break before actually moving in.

We went to a local seaside town for a week's honeymoon. It was a beautiful old fashioned hotel and although the weather was still wet when we arrived, it was the least of my worries. Our wedding night was awful, Edward tried to love me, tried to show his love for me. I couldn't respond. I tried to but I couldn't. I screamed and became hysterical. It must have been awful for my new husband who I know loved me. Our marriage wasn't consummated during this time.

After the honeymoon I went back to my GP. He still didn't know about my childhood, my young adulthood and the abuse. I hadn't told him. I explained how I couldn't let Edward touch me and again, he prescribed a drug that would help me. This one, he said, would take away some of my inhibitions. Again, after being dismissed by my GP I began another regime of medication, trying to save my marriage.

Bill had found out my address and called round one day when I was alone. He had tried to assault me and after I stood up to him, he laughingly said that I couldn't tell anyone now about the abuse because no one would believe me. He threatened to put all the instigating and blame onto me as he had threatened before. The way he said it, sounded plausible and I was terrified that he would be believed. I was ignorant of the law and so I believed him. The Cassie who had been so badly hurt by him as a child, once again surfaced. I felt as broken then as I had when the abuse had begun all those years ago. He threatened to come back and resume the 'games'. I remember standing, frozen to the spot at the door to the little house Edward and I shared. I was terrified, I knew he would come back, just as he promised and felt so scared I was shaking. After he had gone, I took some pills to help with the shaking and ensuing headache and felt calmer. I couldn't let my husband see me like that, I needed to be calm.

Edward and I talked a few nights later, I hadn't told him about my unwanted visitor. I couldn't tell him, I was too scared. But we talked about our marriage and my 'problems' with being unable to make love. I knew he couldn't be expected to wait forever for our marriage to be consummated, so I agreed to talk to my doctor. I hadn't really understood what was wrong with me.

Of course I knew that sex had become a dirty word, something to fear more than death itself, but I wasn't aware that the abuse and Mum's treatment of me, had always been the reason I was getting the headaches. Although I did know it was why I wouldn't let Edward near me, I still hadn't accepted that the need for the tablets, was the horrendous sexual abuse and the cruelty of Mum, things I had suffered all of my life.

Sometimes, just as we began to cuddle and kiss, it wasn't my husband in front of me; it wasn't the lovely man who loved me. It was him, Bill. It was his face that was looking down on me menacingly. I would scream and push Edward away; fighting him when he tried to love me and reassure me that everything was okay. I couldn't tell him, this; I hadn't told him anything about the abuse, so how could I have told him, that every time he wanted to make love to me, I saw my abuser in his eyes? But I wanted our marriage to work, so once again, I went to see Dr Oxley.

I stood outside of the surgery for quite a while, not wanting to go in. Not wanting to talk about my life as it had been so far, not wanting to go there. But I did want things to get better, I loved Edward in my way, I wanted to succeed at being his wife, so eventually I made my way into the waiting room.

It was the January of 1967, I had been taking a new medication, still a Benzodiazepine drug, but a new one called Valium, since the tablets were changed just after I was married. I wasn't aware that the medication Diazepam, that I had been on before, was now called Valium, I didn't recognise the pills as these were blue, different from the original ones. Apparently, I was told, when I rang for a repeat, that the doctor had found a better form of treatment for me, than the one he had just started me on and was given a prescription for Valium.

So here I was, on a cold January day, once again, sitting opposite my family doctor, asking for help.

"What's the problem Cassie?" he asked, looking I felt, slightly annoyed. "You're married to a lovely man, have a job you love and your own little house, but here you are looking sad and worried." I didn't know what to say.

*What does he want me to say? Is he asking if I suffered nightmares, that's why I couldn't sleep?*

*Is he asking me if I have problems that are giving me headaches? Is he asking if I have been abused?*

No, of course he wasn't. Why should he, I never hinted at that, ever. I couldn't have told him, could I?

"I still can't sleep," I found myself saying, breaking the silence that was filling the room expectantly. "I've tried many times to stop the tablets but feel so ill, I go back on them."

"It isn't the medication Cassie, that makes you feel that way when you try and stop them. I have told you this over and over. It's you. There is no reason why you can't stop them, just like that, but I feel you need to take something, to help you cope, in your everyday life."

*What did he know of my life?*

*Did he ever ask?*

*Did he ever try and find out the reasons for my life being so hard that I needed help?*

No he didn't, ever.

I could see this going the same way as every other time I had come to see him, write a prescription, 'keep taking the tablets' kind of treatment.

"I can't sleep with Edward!" I blurted out, not wanting to, not wanting to expose this to anyone, but also not wanting to take more pills. "I have tried but I can't," I said quietly almost in a whisper.

He looked at me, the doctor with kind eyes; he looked but didn't see. "By sleeping with him I presume you mean have sex?" he said, slightly exasperated. "What happens when you try?" he asked.

"I end up screaming hysterically and Edward gets upset," I said almost crying. "I can't do it, I just can't."

*Now I had told, now he would ask. I had hinted, hadn't I? I had said how it was.*

*Now he would ask why. Wouldn't he?*

The same reaction, the same reaching for his prescribing pad, Dr Oxley was doing what he always did. Writing me up for some more medication. I thought he would ask, perhaps I thought he knew. Hadn't I said enough? Enough to make him understand that sex was a no go for me. But if he did know, if he had heard me, did he not want to know why?

Tablets wouldn't make it better. Pills wouldn't take it away!

"You need something different," he said, still writing and not looking up at me. "I think you will always need something, some people do," he said, like it was quite normal to need to take tablets to survive life. "I want you to continue with the Valium 10mg twice a day, the new medication, Tryptyzol, 10 mg three times a day and Amytal, to help you sleep, three tablets at night. You will feel much better on these and they won't affect you, the way you said the other tablets did, when you eventually stop them, if that ever happens." He spoke quite calmly, as though he had solved all my problems with the flash of a pen.

*'Won't affect you, the way you said the other tablets did'?* I said in my head, he doesn't believe me! He said that as though, only I thought they affected me, made me feel ill when I tried to stop them. Was it me? Did they really make me ill? I doubted myself now. He was the doctor, he had never believed me, when I had said how ill I felt, when I had either cut down or stopped the medication he had given me. This was proof. His words, 'the way you said the other tablets did' echoed over and over in my head. He's the professional, he must be right.

I left the surgery, prescription in my hand, feeling inadequate, pathetic. I would always need something, that's what he said, perhaps that's what people like me, abused and unloved as a child, perhaps that's how they all survive. He was the doctor, I had to believe him, trust that he was only looking after my welfare. But he never told me, how these pills would make me able to be a proper wife. Did he think that I would suddenly feel so well, that my past would disappear into oblivion? He still didn't know what 'my past' was. I had come so close; I thought I had told him enough, enough for him to ask me about my not liking sex, not being able to make love. But he acted like it was normal for some people. I had to trust him. I had to try the new regime of medication and hope that it worked.

A few months went by, Bill had not come round again and I was not seeing Mum. Life as a married woman was good in some ways. I enjoyed playing house, I had had enough practice, I enjoyed Edward's company but we still hadn't made love.

"Cassie," he said one evening when we had sat down for the evening, in our little home. We had made that right at least. Our home. The sitting room was a cosy but well lit space with gold carpet and regency gold and cream curtains that I had made myself. The furniture was very 60s, green with wooden bits on the ends of the arms and I had bought green, gold and brown cushions. Very modern and we loved being there. "I'm not pushing the issue, but do you think a specialist in sexual problems, might help you?" I could see that this was hard for him, difficult to bring up the subject of sex. He had been so patient and I knew he loved me, but I also knew it wasn't right to make him suffer for my issues, my past. "I don't know why you find it so hard but I know that you do, perhaps if you talked about it to someone who knows about these things, you might be able to love me, in that way." He was being so kind, so caring and of course I needed to get this sorted. I agreed to go and see my GP the next day. This time I would tell him. This time, I had to tell him. I knew Edward loved me but I also knew he might not wait forever. My past had to be dealt with; I had ghosts to lay and a future to build. This time, I would tell.

# Chapter Eight

The familiarity of the waiting room, did nothing to calm my nerves. I had to tell my family doctor why I found sex so horrendous. Why my marriage to a wonderful man, had not been a true marriage, that we hadn't made love. I had to tell him. I would tell him, there was no choice. I looked around at the other people sat waiting, again scared they could see through me.

I felt as I had all those years ago, when I first went to see my GP aged 15, sat there in the waiting room.

*Do they know?*

*Can they see?*

*Does the shame of my life show?*

I couldn't see how it wouldn't show, it seemed so huge, so dirty, and so heavy; they couldn't possibly miss it. I stared at the floor.

This time, no Miss Pringle. My GP with the kind eyes, opened his door and called me into the room that was now familiar to me. Nothing had changed and I took my place in front of the desk.

"Hello Cassie," was my greeting as I sat in front of Dr Oxley. "Back again." It wasn't a question, just a fact. Yes I was back again. He didn't look at me, he didn't even gesture to the chair that sat their expectantly. I knew the drill. Sit down and wait.

"So what's the problem today?" he sounded tired. Tired of me? "What can I do for you today?" He still didn't look up from his desk, where he had sat, pen poised.

"I don't think the tablets are working," I said, not knowing how to start, how to begin to tell this man who didn't seem interested, that my marriage was in jeopardy and I wanted to save it. How to tell him that I couldn't have sex, with a man who loved me, because sex had happened to me for years, at my father's hands. The sexual abuse had always been there, for as long as I could remember. How could I put into words the horrors of my life up to now, and how I have always been too scared to tell? Where would I start? Where do I find the words?

"I'm not feeling any better, nothing has changed, and I still can't let Edward touch me." I heard myself say almost recoiling at saying out loud something so private and embarrassing.

He sighed. "I don't know what you expected Cassie, the tablets won't do it all, it's up to you, you know," came the reply from this medical man. "You just have to try."

*Try! Try!*

I have tried, oh how I have tried, I wanted to scream. But I said nothing.

*Tell him!*

Tell him screamed my silent heart. But I said nothing. Not able to talk to this doctor with the now not so kind eyes, not being able to feel safe enough to tell him, I began to cry. "I don't want my marriage to fail," I said, almost as a whisper, "I want to be able to love my husband, but I can't."

I slumped back into the chair. Perhaps then, if he had asked the questions, asked me what it was about making love or having sex that upset me, perhaps then I could have told him. I was so close to breaking, breaking my silence, risking whatever life threw at me, that I would have poured the whole horrible secret out. But he didn't.

I got the feeling that my time was up. He seemed annoyed now. Not kind, not caring but aggravated. He had given me the tablets hadn't he and I should have been better, but I wasn't. I didn't want any more pills. I knew that wasn't the answer. Yes, they helped me cope; yes they took the pain away, the physical pain anyway. But I needed to talk, to tell someone how I really felt and he wasn't listening. I couldn't let it end there, I summoned up every ounce of courage I had and spoke; quite firmly I thought.

"We, that is Edward and I, wondered if I could see a specialist in these kinds of issues." I asked so afraid he was about to write me up for some different pills and send me away. "Do you think that would help?"

"I don't know" came the reply. I hoped now he would ask me, encourage me to talk. I couldn't just tell him. It was just too hard. I needed encouragement; I needed to feel safe in confiding these dark secrets. Anyway, would he believe me? Would he, as Bill had said, think I was to blame? My determination to tell him the reasons for my inability to consummate my marriage, was waning fast.

*Please make me tell.*

*Please let me open my boxes and set free all of the evils I have suffered.*

"I suppose it might help you, if a psychiatrist can find out why you are frigid, then I suppose it might help. But I think it is a long shot."

*Frigid!*

*Frigid!*

*What a horrid word.*

I didn't feel frigid; I felt damaged, scared; alone and lost. But not frigid. "I'll write for an appointment for some treatment, you'll receive a letter to go and see someone. Until then, keep taking the tablets." With this, he handed me a prescription and stood looking towards the door. Another dismissal. I felt a bit shell shocked.

What happened there? Why didn't he ask me? I suppose I could have just told, but it wasn't that easy. The longer the consultation went on, the more disinterested he seemed and the less I was able to say. So he didn't ask and I didn't tell.

A few weeks later I was sent an appointment for *Abreactive Psychotherapy*, whatever that meant. The letter said I was not allowed to drive and had to be accompanied. Dottie, Edward's mum said she would take me. She didn't drive either, so a car was sent to take us to my appointment. It was at a clinic in a lovely country house a few miles from where we lived. The grounds of the house were beautiful, it was April and the late snowdrops were shivering in the cold breeze, the daffodils were just showing their bright yellow heads. I was glad I had taken Dottie's advice and put my heavy coat on as it was a cold crisp day and I was feeling very nervous. I always felt colder when I am nervous.

*Now I would talk to someone about my life. Now it would be okay.*

We rang the bell at the entrance of the house. The main door was framed by large white stone pillars and stonework, very old, I think. A lady in a tailored black suit opened the door and showed us into a grand entrance hall. There were pictures on the walls, many landscapes and beautiful forest scenes. The very smart lady in black, with dark hair swept up in a high bun, on the top of her head, showed us into a huge room, and asked us to take a seat. There wasn't much furniture and just a few magazines. The windows were high and had heavy red printed drapes, quite a lovely room really, if I wasn't there to see a psychiatrist!

I don't think we waited very long before a voice at the door called. "Cassie Payne?" I was the only young woman in the room, so I was confused as to why the nurse looked all around enquiringly. I stood up and said I was Cassie Payne.

As I left to go with her, Dottie touched my arm, "You'll be okay love, I'll be here when you come out." She was a very motherly lady, something I was just getting used to, and I was beginning to love her as a real mother. Her concern for me gave me strength and I believed I would be okay.

This serious faced very curtly spoken lady in a suit, beckoned to me to follow her into the next room. I had taken an extra pill that morning as the panic had started. Dr Oxley had told me that it would be okay to do this on the day and any time I felt panicky or agitated. So I had.

The second room I was taken to had a couch and a large armchair. Apart from a clinical looking trolley, and a weighing machine, the rest of the room looked warm and comfortable. This time I was handed over to a nurse. She didn't tell me her name and didn't look at me.

"Dr Goddard will be with us in a moment," this nurse said; looking at the trolley that was now by her side. "I will have to weigh you first."

*Weigh me?*

*Why would she want to weigh me?*

After confusedly stepping on the scales, she wrote my weight down on a form and asked me to take a seat.

"Will the doctor give me some more pills?" I asked this nurse who seemed reluctant to meet my eyes. "Will he ask me lots of questions?" I hoped he would; at least ask me the right questions.

*How else will he know?*

*How else will he be able to help, me unless he asks the questions that make me tell him?*

*Will he believe me?*

I was scared now. Yes he might ask me, but the thought that I might tell him of the horrendous abuse by my birth father, and that I might not be believed, scared me to death.

"Let's just wait for the doctor," the nurse said abruptly, "He will explain everything."

I was shut up. Wasn't it bad enough that I was here to bare my soul? Now I was told to wait. So I waited. The nurse suggested I lie on the couch; she said I would be more comfortable. The doctor in this lovely house with beautiful gardens, entered the room. Dr Goddard was tall and elderly, and reminded me of my violin teacher at school. He was dressed in light coloured trousers and a navy blue blazer with a badge on the pocket. He walked over to the couch and took the armchair next to where I was lying.

"I'm going to use Abreactive Psychotherapy which will involve me giving you an injection," he said thoughtfully, as though he were making it up as he went along. "It will relax you before we start." He didn't use my name and spoke as though he was only just deciding, on seeing me, what to do. He reached over to the tray that was on the trolley. By this time, the tablets were wearing off and I was starting to get fidgety and nervous. Start what? Start talking, asking me the questions that would help make everything alright?

*He'll tell me what happens next, once I have had the relaxant.* I thought. I was about to ask what this therapy was.

But before I had a chance to say a word, he put the needle in my arm. That's all I remember.

"Drink this, it will help you feel better," said the nurse who had called me into the room. She was holding a cup and saucer. Drink? What happened to the doctor?

*Where is the doctor?*

*Where did he go?*

I took the cup of tea she was offering to me and just sat and waited. I don't know what I was expecting, but whatever it was, it never came. I was feeling slightly dizzy, a bit disorientated. "Where is the doctor?" I asked confused. "Is he coming back to talk to me?" The nurse was tidying the room, like she felt uncomfortable in my presence. She didn't answer so I asked again. "Is the doctor coming back soon?" I was confused and a little scared by this time. "Drink your tea Cassie, you'll feel so much better, I'll call your Mum in for you."

*My Mum?*

*Don't call my mum!*

*She isn't here; is she?*

I was suddenly terrified, who had called her? But before I had a chance to speak; Edward's mum came into the room.

Dottie wasn't my Mum but I suppose the nurse had assumed that she was because she behaved like a normal mother would, caring and concerned. No, she wasn't my Mum, but I was so glad she was there for me. She came in and as soon as I saw her I felt better. "How are you love?" asked my warm hearted mum-in-law. "You were gone ages and I was a bit worried." I was confused; it was only a couple of minutes since I walked into this room. When I voiced this, she said I had been in there for over an hour. "The nurse said you had been to sleep and the tea is to help you wake up."

Asleep? I was asleep? What good could that have done if I had fallen asleep? I wanted to talk. Dottie reassured me that the doctor must know what he was doing. I drank the tea and then began to feel a warm calm feeling inside.

*It will be okay, whatever happens next, everything will be okay.*

The nurse came back into the room where Dottie and I were waiting and handed me a card. "Doctor will see you in two weeks," she said, showing me the door. "Is that it?" I exclaimed, "Am I not going to see the doctor again today?" The nurse actually looked at me for the first time, smiling. "No, that's it, you can go home now, the car is outside." It obviously wasn't unusual, this strange visit to the psychiatrist, say hello to the doctor, he sticks a needle in your arm, you have a cup of tea and then you go home.

*How can that help me?*

*No questions, no answers.*

*No talking!*

I suppose I should have asked. I should have asked what had happened to me, but I didn't. I suddenly felt calmer than I had ever felt in my life. I didn't want that to stop. Once again, I trusted the doctor. Dottie and I went home.

The feeling of calm stayed with me all evening, I began to feel better, happier and more hopeful. I continued to go for this 'treatment' for eight months, I did wonder what had happened during the 'therapy' but was feeling so much better, I believed that must be what happens. I stopped wondering about what I said, if anything and tried to get on with my life and marriage. After each session, once I was home, I felt relaxed and happy. It was on one of these evenings that our marriage was consummated, I had been having the treatment for about seven months by this time. Edward and I had spent a nice day out by the sea and then watched a film on television.

We still lived in our tiny bungalow, two bedrooms, a sitting room, kitchen and bathroom. Our bedroom was pretty, I had made regency striped pink and cream curtains and we had a pink candlewick bedspread on the bed. Candlewick was very 'now' back in the late 60s. Edward's aunt had given us a bedroom suite for a wedding present and this completed the room. The bedside lamps, another wedding gift, made the room very cosy and gave it a soft warm feeling.

It was in this safe, comfortable bedroom that I was determined I would try and consummate our marriage and I did. I didn't enjoy it, but it wasn't horrendous. Edward was kind and gentle and did his best to make me feel loved and safe. I didn't take my sleeping pills that night but did take another anti-anxiety tablet after our evening meal. This made me feel calmer and so helped. So now I was married properly. No shame, no guilt but still didn't feel right.

After about ten sessions of this therapy, I asked to talk to the doctor. I never saw him now, the nurse gave me the injections and then I was drinking tea. It took a few times of asking but eventually he agreed to see me. I asked him what it was that I was being given, what he was injecting into my arm. After all, it was my arm, my body, I felt I had the right to know.

"It's like a truth pill," he said as though it was quite normal. "I ask you questions about your concerns and you offload them onto me. Okay?" At this, he sat back in the chair smiling. That was alright then.

*No! No! No!*
*It was anything but alright!*
*Anything but okay!*
I was terrified, what had I said?
*Had I told him?*
*Did he know?*
*How much had I said?*

I had to try and reassure myself, in my head, that this is what I wanted, wasn't it? To tell someone and then feel better. I asked him what I had talked about. Surely he should have told me, talked about any disclosures I might have made? How did telling him help me? I needed to make some sense of my life of why these things had happened. To be told that I was not to blame. I needed reassurance that sex was okay; I needed the guilt, the disgust and the horrors of my past to be wiped from my mind. Or at least I needed to be free from the feelings that I had, that were now ruining my present.

"What did I say?" I asked, aware that my voice was so quiet he would possibly ask me to repeat the question. But he didn't.

"You miss your dog." Dr Goddard stated, "You miss him a lot, that's all you've said."

My dog, I missed my dog. I was utterly confused and unbelieving. Of course I missed my dog, Bobby. Mum wouldn't let me have him when she threw me out, another opportunity to hurt me, but that can't have been all I said. It can't have been. He said I 'offloaded' my 'concerns', how could I not have told?! I had come to see this doctor, this specialist, in order to feel better about sex. I was prepared for this being really difficult for me, to talk about my childhood demons, but I was determined to see it through, to save my marriage. My whole life had been full of horrendous sexual abuse, secrets of the worst kind, and threats of an even worse fate if I told anyone. I had lived with this fear and horror for all of my life. How, if I had been given the 'truth' drug, had I not told? I couldn't take this in.

Yes, I had managed one act of intercourse with my husband but any subsequent attempts of making love, had ended the same way as always. Me in hysterics and floods of tears. It hadn't worked then had it??

I sat there confused. So had I told? It didn't sound as though I had. But if I had told him, did I say who was hurting me? Did I say it was Bill, my birth father? If this was it, if telling left just this, I prayed that I hadn't told now. I was desperate not to have told.

I looked straight at the man sitting in front of me, I was praying so hard inside that he didn't know it had been Bill who had caused me all of this pain and fear. Afraid of having told everything and praying that what this doctor said was true. I quietly asked again. "That was all I said?" He reassured me that missing Bobby was all that I had said.

Thank you God, at last you were listening!

Dr Goddard was going on holiday and said he would see me after his month away, if I wanted to see him again. What was the point? Nothing had changed. I didn't think being able to make love once in about eighteen months could be heralded as successful. We left it open. I was to ring if I wanted another appointment. I went back to the waiting room and told Dottie all was well and we went home.

I had cut down on the tablets after a few weeks of the treatment because I had felt much calmer; this was a plus to having to endure these sessions. I hadn't noticed at first, that my period was late, I hadn't had much of one for a while but I thought perhaps the Psychotherapy had interfered with it. I was never regular so I wasn't concerned.

One morning just after Christmas I felt a bit strange.

I can't be, can I? It only happened once. But I knew.

In January 1968 it was confirmed, I was pregnant, about five weeks. At first I was ecstatic, my own baby, someone to love and someone to love me. The one time I had managed to have sex with Edward, had given me this wonderful gift. Children had never been discussed as sex had been a 'no go' area. I didn't know how he would take the news. I wasn't worried about telling him because I knew he loved me.

As soon as my GP had confirmed my pregnancy, I told Edward one evening after he had finished his meal. I was sure he would be okay and maybe happy about us starting a family. However, he wasn't overjoyed or excited, just a little confused. One act of making love and I was pregnant. I suppose it was a shock but I soon discovered that babies weren't on his agenda. He wasn't unkind he was just taken aback. So we didn't mention it again. His reaction at first put a damper on my excitement but very soon I was concerned about other things. What about the truth drug? Could that affect the baby growing inside of me? Working it out, I had only had one injection since the night we made love so I hope it was okay. But I was worried about the tablets so I stopped everything.

I didn't see any point in going back to see Dr Oxley, after all he had said there was no problem stopping these pills so I stopped them. At first I just felt a bit shaky, but then the terrors began. I was hot and shivery one minute and then cold and clammy. For no reason I would suddenly feel a fear that overcome my whole being. I would run from room to room and then out into the garden. Eventually it would pass, I would go out into a tiny garden and breathe in the fresh air. Then I would concentrate on planning for my baby. I had to be strong, I didn't need these pills I was happier than I had ever been except for fearing that my abuser might return. I would do anything for my baby's safety, I had already cut down, before the pregnancy and now I stopped.

I also couldn't sleep and the nightmares came, sometimes so badly that I would get out of bed and sit in the room off the bedroom, on my own and try concentrating on the future. The three of us, Edward, me and our child. I thought he would come round and everything would be okay. Just as I had thought it would when I married. The withdrawal was bad but I knew I could do this.

Even with the withdrawal, I blossomed in the early days, I had evening sickness, not morning, but it soon passed. I would tell myself, so I was sick, so what! I was to be a mum and I would be the best mum in the world. I would suffer sickness for the whole nine months if I had to. The only blot on my landscape; was the thought that Bill would return and someday hurt my precious child. I tried not to think of it, but without the medication that kept me calm, sometimes I became terrified. I had to be strong, I wouldn't let this happen. I would die first.

Although my abuser had not returned I knew it was only a matter of time before he did. I was afraid now, not just for myself but for the child I was carrying. His grandchild. I tried not to acknowledge this fact. This child was to have nothing to do with him if I had my way.

# Chapter Nine

Pregnancy was good; I attended every ante-natal and doctor's appointments. The withdrawal was wearing off but the dreams were still coming, but I concentrated on my baby. At one of the clinics, the midwife asked me to make an appointment to see Dr Oxley.

"But I feel good," I said confused. "Why do you want me to see him?"

"You mentioned that sometimes you don't sleep and you look worried. I think you need to talk to him ,worry and lack of sleep isn't good for your baby" she seemed concerned. "Although you look very well Cassie, you do still look tired. Talk to him, tell him how you feel." I couldn't argue with that. Not having the pills and suffering nightmares, yes I was tired.

*Talk to him?! I tried to talk to him before. I'm okay now, well, almost except.....*

I made the appointment and once again found myself in his consulting room, in front of my family doctor.

"Are you coping Cassie?" he asked, this time looking straight at me. "How are coping with being pregnant?" I didn't know what to say. Being pregnant was like winning the pools! I was happy, excited; full of love and looking forward to the future with my own baby. What was I supposed to say?

"I'm really well and happy," I told the doctor, who this time was sitting in front of me and still looking at me, waiting for me to talk! He hadn't seemed interested before. "I am so looking forward to having my baby." He continued to look at me. What was he seeing?

*Is he going to ask me now, all the questions I had wanted him to ask?*

*Can I tell him now?*

*No.*

*No, I don't want to.*

I wanted to try and forget all the horrors of my early life and pretend it never happened.

*It's too late now.*

*Don't ask me.*

*I don't want you to ask me now.*

"The midwife tells me you're not sleeping, is that right?" He continued, "It's too early for baby to be keeping you awake; you're only about eleven weeks' pregnant". I knew it wasn't the baby. I knew it wasn't that Edward didn't seem interested in my pregnancy. It was much worse than that. I was getting dreams, nightmares; I thought it was because of my fear of Bill returning. But I had stopped everything and the side-effects of not having the pills always gave me bad dreams. "Whenever I stop the medication you gave me, I have night terrors so I am hoping they will fade in time," I told this now interested GP.

He sighed. "In a few weeks, I can put you back on some pills that won't harm your baby. I think you need them," he said in matter of-fact manner. "Although it isn't the coming off the tablets that is causing the nightmares, it's just you."

*Just me.*

*What does he mean, just me?*

If he knew it for sure, that it wasn't the tablets; why didn't he ask if I had any other worries? Why didn't he encourage me to talk? I was a little annoyed, although I didn't want to go there, he could have asked. I assured him that I didn't want to go back on the medication, I was pregnant and happy, and so I wouldn't need them. Although this was true, I was so scared of the horrors returning, Bill coming back into my life, into our lives, my baby and me, I didn't really think that the nightmares would ever go. This time, I left without that little piece of paper and that felt good.

Then it happened, a phone-call from Mum, saying that Bill had had a stroke, was in a coma. He wasn't expected to live.

*Oh Yes! Yes!* My heart cried. I would be safe, my baby would be safe. She asked me to go and see him. How could I go and see him, *was she mad.* Go and see the man who had abused me for all of my life. Go and see him?

*No No, I couldn't I wouldn't.*

But I did.

I was very tempted to take one of the pills I had, very tempted as I knew they stopped the panic, but I was pregnant, so I didn't. But I was tempted.

When I reached the hospital that held the man who was my father, I wished with all my might, that I felt stronger. Strong enough to be able to walk in, give him the love that Mum had sent and leave. But I couldn't. Without the medication, I still had the fear that surrounded and enveloped my childhood. Just as I hadn't been able to refuse Mum's wishes, that I went to visit the man she professed to love, the man she had not protected me from, just as I couldn't find the strength to say No to her, neither could I find the strength to just give him her love and leave. When she had first told me that he was dying, I wanted to tell her that I was pleased. That at last, I was free from his sordid horrendous abuse forever. I wanted to scream YES YES! From the rooftops, tell the world how happy his death would make me. But I didn't.

The following morning, I rang work and said I had to visit Mum as she was unwell. They didn't know anything about my family. I had left the group practice in the city and was working for two doctors in the town near where Edward and I were living. I made my way reluctantly, with no idea of what I was going to say or do and caught a bus to the hospital , where Mum had told me Bill was a patient.

It was large old hospital, it had started life as an army medical centre during the war but was much bigger now. The entrance was huge, red brick and a bit scary. I asked a porter where the ward I needed was and walked up the stairs he had pointed to. I stopped before entering the door which was open. I felt shaky and cold, hospitals were usually warm, but I felt an icy shiver running through my body. Flashbacks of this large evil man who had caused me so much pain, came into my mind. I consciously pushed them away. I had to face him, had to do this. If I could face him and tell him what he had done, perhaps then I could let go of the fear he instilled in me, all of my life. I walked through the clinical doorway and suddenly was standing in a cold hospital room, where an old man lay under white sheets, looking to all the world, like he was a picture of innocence. But I knew differently. He wasn't innocent. That's what I had been. An innocent child before he sexually abused me over and over again.

*So, he was dying.*

*So what!*

I had had to tell the nurse who was looking after him, who I was, that I was his goddaughter. I had to think fast, so that no one in Steve's family knew I had been to see him. "There has been a family rift and I would rather Bill's family didn't know I have visited." I was assured that they wouldn't be told. I felt like I was still colluding with him, keeping him safe from the truth, protecting him. But I wasn't. I was protecting them and I suppose me.

I sat beside the bed that held the dying body of this much feared man. He looked so frail, so small.

*So wicked.*

*So evil.*

Because he was dying didn't take all my feelings away. It didn't change a thing. He was still my abuser. And he was dying. I hadn't been strong enough to refuse Mum her request, or strong enough to give Bill her love. But I found a strength from somewhere, to come here. I don't know from where.

Suddenly I began to cry, something that I hadn't been able to do for a long time. I'm sure the hospital staff saw tears of grief, but they weren't. I suppose I was grieving, but not for him, not for this evil being, lying in this cold hospital bed. But for the childhood that had been mine, grieving for my lost innocence. But mostly, these tears were tears of relief. I sobbed tiny sobs and opened my heart to the pain this man had given me for all of my life.

I suddenly found a strength I didn't know I had. I was carrying a new life inside of me and I drew the strength from this. I knew from my brief nursing training that hearing, was the last sense to go, before a person died. I had never been allowed to tell of my childhood. I only ever spoke of it once, to Mum and she hadn't believed me. I spoke now. I told him how he had taken away my innocence and my childhood. I told him *He* was the cause of my fears, my nightmares, and my pain. That he was the reason that I hadn't been able to cope with life, because of his abuse of me. My marriage to Edward had almost been ruined by the evil Bill had subjected me to, the evil that had rendered me hating and despising the act of sex.

I also told him that I would never forgive him. I know that I should have forgiven him, God would have wanted that. But God hadn't listened to me when I prayed so many times for his protection. Why should I give God a second thought? With this evil man's death, I would be safe. But more importantly, so would the child I was carrying. No, these tears were not all sad tears; I was washing away the pain and looking to the future. My abuse would soon be over for good. I could start again.

As I left the room, I felt a huge sense of relief. He couldn't hurt me anymore. It was just a matter of time now and I had an abundance of that. He had very little. I felt no compassion for this dying man. Only relief and a sense of being free. Free from my past and its demons.

The following day, that freedom came in a phone call, saying that Bill was dead. It was over, over for ever. Now my life would be good, I was safe. The *evil* was dead.

# Chapter Ten

As the months went on I blossomed, I could have written the precise pregnancy book as everything went according to plan. To say I was happy was an understatement. For the first time in my life I felt free, a freedom so precious that I gloried in it every day. I didn't have the worry that Bill would come round again and try to hurt me. He could never do that again. The other *safe* I felt, was that now I was pregnant, I didn't have to make love, have sex. I no longer had to hurt Edward or reject him, I had said that it wasn't safe during pregnancy and he respected this.

I did have shaky times but thought that this could just be the pregnancy. I didn't think it was not having the medication that had begun to rule my life. I didn't take anything during these times. I wouldn't even take an aspirin in case it harmed my unborn baby. Sometimes I did feel the same way I had previously, when I stopped taking the medication, but I fought it. It wasn't too hard, the thought of the future, me and my very own child, I could fight anything.

Edward still didn't seem able to accept my condition and wouldn't talk about it. This made me think he thought, that by not acknowledging it, made the pregnancy not real. He wasn't unkind. I don't think he could have been; he was such a nice man. He just wasn't ready to become a father. So I didn't talk about it either. So, in a way, my being pregnant, became almost like a secret. Another secret but this time a good one. If I bought things for the baby, I put them straight into the little chest of drawers I had in the nursery. The second bedroom of our bungalow was at the front and had a lovely sunny feeling. It would be the nursery. I painted the walls a pretty lemon. I was sure I was having a boy but didn't really care. Lemon was okay for whatever sex baby was. Dottie bought things for her first grandchild and was as excited as I was. She said Edward would be okay as soon as the baby was born. I believed her and hoped she was right.

"Don't worry Cassie," she would say reassuringly. "Edward will come around in time, you'll see." I believed her; I wanted to believe her so I did. We had called the 'bump' Fred, so sure he would be a boy. I never thought of a girl's name because I was so certain 'Fred' would be a boy. The only worry towards the end of the nine months was that at one of my antenatal appointments Matron seemed concerned. The midwife on duty had called in the Matron of the nursing home where I was to give birth.

"I think I will have to turn the baby Cassie," she said as though this was the most natural thing in the world. "He appears to be in a breech position."

*Was this serious?*

*Did she say turn him?*

*How would she turn him?*

I wanted to ask these questions, I also wanted to know if it was because of anything I had done. At the back of my mind I had been a bit worried about the 'truth serum' I had been given in the months before I became pregnant, could this have caused this? "Some babies do this," Matron continued before I had a chance to say anything. "I'll just manipulate him back into the correct position for birth. It won't hurt." She was right, it didn't hurt but as soon as I walked out of the clinic, I felt a lurch in my tummy. Fred had turned himself back!

I was due to give birth on the thirty-first of August but he was late, quite normal for first babies I was told.

My waters broke on an early Saturday morning, seventh of September around six-thirty in the morning. The beginning of the labour was textbook, and I wasn't scared. This was such an exciting time I had no fear at all about giving birth. I was still in labour all through Sunday and then Monday arrived and I was beginning to feel poorly. Something was wrong, I knew enough to know that.

Apparently, turning the baby had made him try and get back into the position he had originally been in and he had become stuck. 'Transverse', they said. All of a sudden my GP was in front of me. The kind eyes looked troubled, "We are going to have to send you to the Maternity hospital, St. Michaels. You need help delivering," he said, patting my hand. I was terrified, I tried to talk but my voice was very hoarse because the labour had been so long I was dehydrated. Because I had been in labour since the Saturday early morning and it was now Monday afternoon, the birth was what they call 'dry' All I know is, that this 'normal labour' suddenly became abnormal and a hospital delivery was called for. Then I was scared.

I was carried out to an ambulance and the midwife came with me. I had gas and air during the journey and we had to stop twice because the ambulance men thought the baby was coming. On reaching the hospital, everything was a blur.

I was very tired and feeling unwell, the consultant attending tried to prepare me for the worst. He said he was sure my baby had died and I was to prepare for a stillborn child. I couldn't cry. I had no tears, but my heart felt as though it were breaking in two. They said something about forceps and a third degree tear but I wasn't listening. Then after what seemed like an eternity, a final wrench of my body and I heard a scream.

"Is that my baby?" I croaked through a very dry throat.

"Well it's not bloody mine!" came the reply from the attending doctor.

"Is he alive?" I continued, almost holding my breath.

"What does it sound like to you?" he laughed. "I will have to put you out Cassie as I need to do some surgery from the tear, it's quite severe. We will put your baby in the nursery."

He tried to be reassuring but I didn't want 'him' put into a nursery, I wanted to see 'him'. The nurse came over and asked me what name I wanted put on the crib. "Mark," I said, "he will be called Mark."

This midwife laughed and suggested I had a rethink, as Mark was indeed a girl.

"Melissa then," I said, "we'll call her Melissa." They took her away and a nurse began to wash my face, a needle was put in my arm and I drifted off into a warm wonderful sleep.

The day after delivery I had a visitor, Mum, she acted the part of the concerned mother and played to the audience of nurses and doctors, expertly, she had had years of practice. Whenever she had an audience, she performed well. I had hoped, that perhaps my being a mum now, might bring us closer together. Hope was still a much over used emotion.

The last two days in the hospital I was given something to make me sleep. I adored my daughter, but I was so exhausted that I couldn't sleep. The consultant told me that many new mothers had this problem and while I was in his care, he wanted to help me rest. The tablets made me feel how I felt before when I was taking the sleeping pills Dr Oxley gave me. Floaty, calm and happy. After a few good nights of sleep, I felt much better.

But it wasn't to last long. I was very poorly when I took Melissa home and Edward tried his hardest to look after me. As I recovered I kept the house clean and tidy and made sure my wonderful baby was asleep in her cot before my husband came home from work. I had been given some pills, Mogadon, to take if I needed them to sleep but I wanted to be awake and aware, in case my tiny child needed me. I put them away safely.

The house showed little signs of a baby's presence when Edward arrived home for his tea. I suppose this was the wrong thing to do, but I wanted my marriage to work and so I wanted to keep my husband happy. Again, it was like having another secret, another *pretend*. As time went on and I had recovered, there was no longer a reason, an excuse, not to have sex. I tried but it was no good. Edward's attempts to make love to me, ended as it had always done, me hysterical and in tears. How stupid was I, thinking that now the evil was gone, now the *nasty* had died, my past would die with him. How naive to think that now, although the horrendous sexual abuse I suffered all my life was over, I would be able to be a normal loving woman.

To me, sex was dirty, nasty, and bad. Edward didn't understand, I shouldn't have expected him to. I had never told him about my childhood and the horrors of my early life. He knew a bit about Mum, he knew and had seen evidence that she didn't love me. But I never told him about Bill. So, no, it wasn't over, Bill was dead, but his legacy lived on. My marriage to Edward was the first casualty of the damage that had been inflicted on me during my childhood. We tried for another year but then decided to go our separate ways. He went back to live with his parents. Our marriage ended but we remained friends.

During this time I had seen my GP a few times because of the surgery after the traumatic birth. I had confided in Dr Oxley that my marriage had been in trouble. He didn't ask me why; he didn't try and get to the bottom of the problem. It wasn't his remit I suppose. "You know life can be hard Cassie, and you are not a 'coper'," he told me.

*Not a coper!!?*

I had been *coping* with horrendous sexual abuse since I was a baby, living in a home with no love.

*I had coped.*

*How dare he say I wasn't a 'coper'!*

He knew that the inability to make love to my husband was a big problem but never asked me if there was any reason why I felt how I felt. No questions, no concern, no help. No kind eyes now. He offered me something 'to make me feel better'. At first I refused, but the headaches came back as I watched my marriage fall apart and saw the pain of seeing Edward and Dottie so upset.

Once again I went back to the cold, now hostile doctor's surgery and saw Dr Oxley. This time the waiting room was crowded. There was some kind of bug going around and the last thing I wanted was to wait among sick people. I had Melissa with me and possibly looked a bit anxious. Miss Pringle came out from her side of the reception area and took me through to a room I used to come to when I was pregnant. It was the nurse's room and was even more sparsely furnished than the consulting room. Just a couch and a trolley with medical things.

I walked over to the window, cradling Melissa and waited, looking at the flowers in full bloom in the garden below. It had been a lovely summer, 1969, and everything was so colourful. "Wait there Cassie," she said, quite kindly I thought. "I will see if the doctor will see you first. We don't want baby to catch anything do we?"

I was relieved at this act of kindness, no 'we didn't want' that. After a few minutes Dr Oxley came in, and took me into his consulting room. He looked different from the last time I had seen him, perhaps that was because I had been in labour then and things were a bit distorted. He gestured to the chair opposite his desk and I sat down. I wasn't sure whether I should just tell him how I felt and so with nothing coming from this man in front of me, I spoke.

"I'm getting the headaches again," I told him. "They are really bad now and I can't concentrate as well as I need to with a baby. I'm still not sleeping and if I do manage a short sleep, I still get nightmares. Could you give me something to help? I don't want the pills you gave me before because I had problems when I stopped taking them. I just need some painkillers"

That sounded quite strong I thought to myself. I felt quite strong. I'm a mother now; I had to be strong for Melissa. He reached for his prescription pad in his usual way, sighing and looking exasperated. He began writing and without looking up, he said, "It is isn't the pills that give you a problem when you stop Cassie, it's you, as I have told you. However, I will prescribe another kind, a safe drug to make you sleep. Mogadon is new and it will also help with your headaches. I would like you to go back on one of the original pills Librium, in my opinion, you need them."

I didn't bother to say that I had had these, Mogadon, in the hospital and they had helped with my sleeping, I didn't see the point. He felt I needed more than sleeping tablets, Librium was the name of the pill I had been on before, the ones I had been on along with the Valium, so I didn't bother. I needed to feel well. He was the doctor after all. He once again, stood up, walked towards the door, handed me the piece of paper and ushered me out. So keep taking the tablets seemed to be the treatment! I stood outside, in the high ceilinged waiting room and hoped, that word again, that this time I would be fine.

After Edward and I had split up and he had gone back to live with his Mum. I still cared about him and his parents but we had both agreed that we couldn't have gone on the way we were. Edward provided for us, as best he could and I was to stay in our home until such time as it had to be sold. Although I was obviously upset at this failure, I was still happy to be Melissa's mum.

The *happy at* this time was my little girl. She was a joy to have, my blessing I called her. I loved every minute I had with her. We did everything together and I know she kept me sane. Although I was still taking the pills that had been prescribed, I didn't feel like I did before. The swimmy, not really here feeling didn't happen. Perhaps I was too happy and too busy looking after a baby and a house on my own to notice any side-effects. I was being a mum, a good mum I thought and that's what was important. So I was lulled into a false sense of safety about taking them. We played together, my little girl and I, we had picnics, went to the seaside and the zoo. She was a bright, bubbly enchanting child and everybody loved her. She had blonde hair like spun gold and the biggest beautiful blue eyes I had ever seen. I loved her with all my heart.

I found it hard to manage on the money Edward gave me, although it was a generous amount I don't think he realised how much a baby could cost to keep. I decided to look for a job, it had to be in the evenings when my little girl was asleep. She slept through, every night so my being out wasn't a problem. Christine, my friend and neighbour offered to sit in with her when needed. She was a pretty woman with black hair, cut short and in a modern style. She didn't dress as a Naval officer's wife usually dressed. I had met many such women over the years when Claire married her Officer, 'all twin sets and pearls' Dottie used to say. Christine was a bit different and wore jeans and a sweater most of the time, unless going out with her husband. She was a happy confident person and I liked and trusted her.

The only job I could get was in a pub that belonged to a friend of Edward's parents. It was here that I met a man with whom I began a relationship. I wasn't worried about sex, it wasn't on the agenda, but it happened anyway.

I began dating a man who was an important person in the local town and went to many social gatherings. His name was Larry, he was quite tall with thick dark brown hair that was always tidy and in place. He was seventeen years older than me. One evening, about six months after we first dated, we went to a dinner dance and Christine loaned me a gown. It was a pretty blue, my favourite colour and reached down to the floor. I had some white shoes and she let me use a tiny white bag that matched the shoes perfectly. My neighbour was married to a naval officer and went to many such occasions. I didn't have anything near suitable.

On the night of the ball, I was nervous so took my pills as usual and Larry picked me up outside of my bungalow. I didn't drink while working in the pub, but did have a few glasses when we were out. I didn't think about the effects of combining alcohol with the medication and there was nothing said on the bottle. The dinner dance was amazing, something I hadn't experienced before and I found myself chatting to Larry's friends and having a great time. He seemed proud to have me on his arm. He was so confidant and strong, I felt safe. I loved dancing and it had been a long time since I had had the opportunity.

When we arrived home, I asked him in for a coffee and before I knew it we had made love. I don't know how or why but we had sex and it seemed okay. No flashbacks, no fear it just happened. I was confused by this, I had loved Edward and couldn't do this with him but I had with Larry. Could it have been the alcohol? Could it have been a mixture of that and the medication? I didn't know but accepted, that as I was now in a relationship, it would possibly happen again and I needed to take precautions against pregnancy. The next morning I went straight to the surgery and was given the contraceptive Pill. No questions, just another pill but this one was necessary.

Then one morning in December 1970, a few days before Christmas, it happened. I felt sick when I got up. I suddenly went cold. My period was later than usual but I thought that might be the pills. I knew I could get pregnant from having sex once. Hadn't I become pregnant the only time I could bear to make love with Edward? Could it really have happened again? I began to panic. What would Larry say? Hope came back big time. I hoped he would be happy. I hoped he would say he will be there for me and the baby.

*Hope was away.*

*Anger was here.*

I asked him to call round to my house, I didn't hint at why and he came round that evening. We hadn't made another date and he must have thought I just wanted to see him. When he arrived at the door, I didn't know what to say. I asked him in and pointed to my little sitting room door. He walked in and stood in front of the fireplace, oblivious to what was coming. I sat down on my little green sofa and this must have alarmed him. No greeting, no kiss on the cheek to say hello. I just sat down.

The thoughts going through my mind were ones of excitement, fear and apprehension, I began to speak and was very shaky. "I'm pregnant Larry," I said softly, "I'm going to have your baby."

The way he looked at me, he might as well as slapped me. A look of horror came across his face.

*So no happy then?*

He questioned how *I* had become pregnant! How *I* let this happen! Like I had done it on my own! "How could you be so stupid!" he growled turned away and walked out into the garden.

*What did he expect to find out there?*

*An answer?*

I felt sick with fear. When he was angry, he sounded like the man I had feared all of my life. Memories of Bill, growling at me in anger. Another time when I was being blamed for something that was not my doing. Another time when I was scared and felt alone.

*"Oh for God's sake! He spat and growled at me! I suppose you expect me to clear that up!" Bill was angry. He had forced me to perform oral sex on him and I had been very sick. I tried to say it wasn't my fault but he just continued to hurt me, shouting horrid things, saying that it was all my fault.*

Yes, now I was scared. For a moment it was as though Bill were back in the room. Not only did Larry take me back to somewhere I had tried so hard not to visit, but also to someone I didn't want to think about.

*The nasty...*

*The evil…*

The father of my child came back into where I was sat, what he said next horrified me.

"You can't have it" his voice sounding rough and hard.

Did I hear that?

*It! It!*

I wasn't having an 'it', I was having a baby, a baby whom we had made, Larry and I!

I began to shake, felt unsteady and couldn't speak. Larry came towards me but didn't seem able to look at me. He said we would go and ask my GP to arrange a termination. Suddenly there was a 'we', he said 'we'. I hoped above all hope that he would accept that this baby was ours, not just mine. But the 'we' was to ask for the pregnancy to be ended.

*How could he do this?*

*I was having his baby*!?

I tried to argue, to plead with him that we were the baby's parents, his mum and dad and we would love him. But he shouted I was wrong there, he wouldn't love it, I was going to see the doctor and have 'it' done. It dawned on me then, I was just a girlfriend to him. No long term partner, not someone to have his child. To have sex with yes, but he wasn't going to settle down with me. Perhaps it was just the shock. Perhaps in time…...

With this he left.

I was mortified and walked in to the bedroom where my precious little girl was sleeping. I reached down and placed my hand on her sleeping body and my other hand on my tummy where her tiny brother or sister was growing. I will keep this baby, no matter what, I won't let anyone take him from me. It was the 1970s and I knew that only a psychiatrist could authorise an abortion, and it wouldn't happen straight away. I was hoping that Larry would change his mind and be there for me.

A few days later, having told no one about the pregnancy, I was still hoping things would work out. I was in our front garden, cutting some wallflowers that were still flowering, to place in the house. Larry arrived and told me to get ready. He had made an appointment to see a doctor. Perhaps this doctor would persuade him that having our baby would work out. But on the way to the clinic, he seemed very upbeat.

I didn't want to see this doctor, the person who could decide whether our baby could be aborted. I didn't want to go but was I afraid of Larry now. Memories of the times with Bill, when I was scared and had to keep quiet because of that fear, afraid of what he might do, came flooding back.

So the appointment made, we were on our way to the clinic. I had taken my usual tablets unaware of any danger to the baby. Dr Oxley had told me there wasn't a problem if I had taken them during pregnancy with Melissa and I hadn't been able to stop shaking. Feeling very sick and a bit spaced out, we approached the large Victorian hospital and were shown into a formal looking room and asked to sit and wait until we were called.

*There it was again.*

*We.*

The room had huge windows and as I couldn't sit still and Larry seemed to have lost his means of communication. I walked around and looked out at the gardens. It was very pretty but made me think of another time, when I was trying to fix the problems with Edward through 'Abreactive Therapy'. These memories were not good.

That fear, once more was enveloping my very being. These thoughts made me feel very sick. I began to panic, shake and I went to run to the door, when a nurse arrived and asked me to follow her. I followed. She was tall and dressed in a grey uniform and had large black spectacles that had a chain to keep them around her neck. Her hair was short and neatly shaped around her face. A pretty lady.

The room she showed me into was much smaller than the first room, where Larry was waiting and at first there was no one there. It was warm and had pretty blue wallpaper. Again, blue, my favourite colour. But it did nothing to alleviate my fear. There was an armchair and a small sofa and in the corner of the room was a desk and chair. No window in this room I thought. Nothing to distract me.

"Take a seat Mrs. Payne. It is Mrs.? "She in the smart uniform asked, bringing her glasses further down her nose and looking over them at me.

"Yes, Mrs." I answered too scared to be annoyed at this question.

"The doctor will be with you in a few minutes" she said pointing to an armchair and with that she left.

I don't know how I managed to stay on the chair. The medication usually kept me calm but not now. To say I was terrified was an understatement.

*Should I take another pill?*

*Will it help?*

I was reaching for my bag when the door opened and a middle-aged man walked in smiling. He was dressed in a smart suit as most of the doctors I had seen over the years wore, and had a set of notes, presumably mine, in one hand.

"Hello Mrs. Payne, Cassie isn't it?" he asked while holding his hand out for me to shake. I nodded and was now sitting on the very edge of the chair. I leaned forward and took the hand offered and sat back on the chair.

Then the questions, lots of questions:

*Was I sure...?*

*Did I want...?*

*Did I think...?*

At that point in my life, I wasn't sure of anything, I didn't know what I wanted and what to think? Well, I tried not to do that.

The interview, or at least that's what it felt like, went on for a long while and the thing I remember most about it, was, this doctor who could end the life of my baby, kept asking me to be sure it was right for me. He said that it didn't matter what anyone else wanted or said, I had to want to have the pregnancy terminated. No room for doubts. Suddenly, I was sure, I didn't need to think, I knew I didn't want that. I didn't want and couldn't have an abortion. And that was that!

After telling the psychiatrist of my decision and getting up from the chair, he smiled and shook my hand. 'Good luck Cassie," he said with genuine care and I left the room. I felt quite strong. I had got myself into this and I had to cope with the consequences. I would have this baby. I left the room in silence and didn't speak to Larry all the way home. I wasn't asked what had happened and I didn't volunteer anything.

On reaching home, as I got out of his car, this man who had fathered my unborn baby eventually said,

"So when are you going in to have this taken away?" His face was void of expression as he looked fleetingly at my tummy, "You can't leave it too long, you know. When it is all over we can get back to where we were."

*Get back to where we were?!*

*After I had killed our baby?!*

"I can't do it!" I cried, "I can't have a termination; it wouldn't be right."

His face contorted and he went scarlet, memories again of Bill came flooding back.

"Right for WHO?" he roared, "right for WHO, it wouldn't be right for anyone if you have a baby with no father."

*But he has a father.*

*You are his father.*

I was terrified, we had had this conversation before. There was no change of mind. Hope had let me down again.

"If you continue with this pregnancy you're on your own and don't think you can come to me for cash I won't give you a penny." With that he slammed the door of his car and drove away, leaving me shaking with fear and sobbing. I managed to find my keys in my handbag and let myself in to my house.

*My safe.*

*But it isn't safe.*

*I didn't know what to do.*

*Where is safe now?*

*And... where was hope?*

My little bungalow seemed huge. Huge and lonely. My precious daughter Melissa was with her Nan, Edward's mum, and I was glad. I didn't want her to see me like this.

We had been so happy, the two of us. Before Larry. Before pregnant. She was my blessing and I loved her to distraction. How could I let her know of my sadness now? But how could I keep it from her.

I had been here before. Sad, scared and lonely.

*Before the safe.*

*Before the happy.*

*Before.*

With my little girl and our little house, we had been 'okay'. Yes, my marriage to Edward didn't work out, but we were friends now. Of course he was hurt when I told him about Larry but he thought it was because Larry was that much older and experienced and had been able to get me to make love to him, where he, Edward couldn't. We talked about it as, much as I could talk about sex and he was okay as long as we remained friends. Life had seemed more than okay. Perhaps I had been fooling myself into believing, that after everything that had happened to me, life would be good to me now.

*Perhaps things will always go wrong.*

*Perhaps Bill and my mother were right and I deserved to have pain.*

*Perhaps...*

This time of lonely I had only myself to blame. The medication often seemed to blur my judgement but I was to blame. I took a chance, without thinking and became pregnant. I had become pregnant the first time Edward and I had made love and now it had happened again but this time I was on my own. I knew I couldn't blame anyone now, I had to be strong. I had to do this, on my own and I would.

I was scared at first but I had Melissa, on the days that were dark and scary, she would give me a hug and everything was right with the world. I never told anyone of my plight. I don't know what I was expecting to happen, all I did know was that if I didn't say the words, *perhaps*, that word again, perhaps things would turn out okay.

*Stupid stupid me!*

Although I had seen Mum in the early years following Melissa's birth, she was the last person I could tell. I didn't even try and think how she would take the news. I couldn't face it. I also hoped; my old friend hope, still hoped that once my baby's father had calmed down, he would come back to me and we would live happily ever after.

*He'll realise what he's missing.*

*He will come back, he will.*

I never learn. Of course he wasn't coming back.

During Christmas 1970 I was working in the same pub where I had been introduced to Larry, and it was an awful time for me. He came in several times and never spoke to me. Then the New Year celebrations came and I really thought this would be it. The 'it' that would make it all okay. A midnight kiss and all would be well.

There was a midnight kiss, in fact many, but Larry wasn't sharing it with me, the mother of his child. No, he danced and kissed a woman whom I didn't know and left the pub with her. Leaving me lonely and alone.

# Chapter Eleven

The New Year arrived, 1971. I had promised Mum that I would look after the house for a few days from the first of January to look after my dog. Bobby was getting old and Mum didn't want to leave him on his own. It must have been obvious that something was wrong, but as usual, she didn't ask at first. But then suddenly, she looked at me and must have noticed my sadness or anxiety. She asked where Larry was as it was a holiday. Relieved to be able to talk to her, thinking stupidly that she cared, I broke down and said that we had ended our relationship. She became angry and before I could stop myself I blurted it out.

"I'm pregnant," I cried.

There was nothing, *perhaps*, that word again, perhaps I thought this woman who was my mother, would understand. After all, wasn't this how I was conceived, outside of marriage? Perhaps I thought that this would give us a common bond and she would look at me with compassion and love.

*Why should she?*
*What was in it for her?*
*How could she do the undoable?*

No, true to form, she did none of this. Instead she screamed at me that I would have to 'get rid of it'. That 'he' was right. She went on to tell me that I was stupid and that my feelings of right or wrong about having an abortion would do me no good now. And then that word, that name, the name she had called me years and years ago.

*I arrived home late from school to see Bill leaving in his car and was so relieved he hadn't seen me and mum was waiting for me. I hadn't seen her this angry for a while. Apparently Bill and she had had a row and she said I was too blame. She grabbed me as I came in the door, "you did this" she screamed. "You have ruined my life. If you hadn't been born, none of this would happened. You have spoiled everything Get to your room you little bastard." I didn't know what the word meant but knew it wasn't anything nice. I ran upstairs scared and avoiding her blows.*

My mother was referring to my unborn baby as a bastard.

So, she was right then, and right now, I suppose, having a child out of marriage meant exactly that but in a bad way. I could never have referred to my baby as that! I wanted to shout at her the way she was shouting at me, but I didn't have the energy. I was drained, scared and so tired. With this, she left for her holiday leaving me, once again alone. Well at least I knew where I stood. Where I had always stood. No-where to her. I had hoped she would sympathise with me. How stupid was that! It didn't really come as a surprise and any thought that she would help me or support me died, as it had always done. Once again I was an embarrassment to her, in the way.

Apart from the worries around the pregnancy and what I would do, how I would cope, I was suffering panic attacks and horrendous night terrors. I knew that Dr Oxley had been told of my being pregnant, the psychiatrist I had seen said he would inform him. I had stopped all medication since finding out I was pregnant and rang his surgery to make an appointment.

I once again walked into the unfriendly consulting room where my GP was sat, as usual at his desk. Nothing had changed, it still felt gloomy, dull and today quite hostile. This time, the man with the kind eyes, looked straight at me and obviously expected me to speak. "What can I do Dr Oxley?" I asked getting very uptight. "I can't go on like this, it's affecting me every day."

I'm sure I heard him sigh, no, I know I heard him sigh, "I have told you Cassie, the only reason you are having these panicky feelings is because you can't cope without the medication. It isn't the fact that you have stopped. It is because you need the tablets, especially now, with this unwanted pregnancy, the stress is too much for you," he sounded very cross, in an 'I told you so' tone.

*Unwanted pregnancy?*

*Unwanted?*

He wasn't listening, he wasn't seeing me, he was seeing the scared, edgy Cassie who was not only drained and washed out with the worry but suffering withdrawal from the medication he had prescribed.

*It wasn't me!*

*I could cope!*

*I had been coping all of my life!*

I hadn't planned this baby but *I wanted* it now it was here, but no one else did. Not Larry the baby's father, not Mum and not my family doctor, who was now telling me, that adoption was the only way. I was tired, alone and scared and didn't know what was happening to me.

Yes, I was pregnant but that wasn't what was giving me the nightmares, the daytime anxiety and panic. I was sure it wasn't. I had been pregnant before, so I knew, didn't I? This was different; I knew it was from coming off the medication.

I spoke, softly but trying to sound strong, "But I told you that I felt like this when I came off the other tablets and you said that it wouldn't happen if I stopped the new ones. But it has."

By this time I was crying, life was bad enough through my own stupidity. I hadn't even thought about becoming pregnant when I first met Larry. I hadn't been able to sleep with Edward, my husband, a man who loved me. I hadn't been able to sleep with anyone, so I never imagined that I would have been able to sleep with a man I was just going out with. But I did and now I was paying the price. I had gone back to see the doctor for help, not to be told I would have to give my baby up for adoption. Help to work something out. But 'working something out' was ending the pregnancy and going back on the pills or planning the adoption of my second child. How was that helping! I left the surgery with the doctor's words ringing in my ears but determined that I would keep my baby and get through this on my own.

I didn't go back on the medication even though I was told it would be for the best and the next few months were the hardest in the whole of my life. Worse than the abuse, worse than the treatment by Mum. All through my pregnancy, my mind was scrambled; I had horrific dreams, would run from my bed to check that Melissa was still in her room, safe. I was getting flashbacks of Bill and the abuse and had no one and nowhere to turn. My only bit of sanity was Melissa. The time I spent with her became my *happy,* my *safe.* The only time I truly knew who I was, her Mum.

Dr Oxley had put me in touch with the Church Adoption society. Although I had told him I would keep my baby, he said it wouldn't hurt to talk to them.

He thought it was for the best.

*Whose best?*

*Not mine, not my baby's.*
*So whose?*

During the following months, I tried so hard to keep it together. I didn't fall out with Mum, if I had I wouldn't have been able to see Dad. I know Dad would have wanted to see me but he never argued with his wife. I think he learned over the years, that she was the 'boss'. Whatever she said was how it would be. Questioning would get him nowhere. There would have been no point, her word was law. I was only allowed to go to their house when Mum didn't have visitors. She didn't want to be embarrassed by her pregnant, divorced daughter. Throughout the pregnancy I had to check to see if the coast was clear before I visited.

*Here we go again.*
*More secrets.*
*More pretence.*

I felt like a criminal but went along with it for Dad's sake. I always hoped that she would come round and help me. That she would one day love me. I ignored the inner child, who had these thoughts. I ignored the warnings of one who should know, Little Cassie, the child who had hoped throughout her life; that things would turn out okay. They never had.

I went home to my *safe*; that was not so safe now. My mind seemed constantly in a daze, a fog, thinking and rationalising was so very hard. I tried to put the pregnancy out of my mind and get on with life. I stopped working at the pub and wasn't taking any medication in case it harmed the baby.

I had been assigned a social worker; this was common practice if you were to be an unmarried mother. She was a sympathetic lady but didn't beat around the bush when it came to the truth. She made me look at the reality of my life, with one daughter, a new baby and no husband. She tried to get me to be realistic about my finances, but my mind was so foggy and confused, I couldn't take it in. I wasn't ready for what she told me next, "Cassie, if you keep the baby, then both of your children will suffer."

*If I keep my baby?'*
*There is no 'if'!*

I was determined that not only would I keep my unborn child but that I would love him or her as much as I loved Melissa. Nobody would take my baby from me. "It will be an act of love, if you love your children, you will let the new baby go, you have to decide." she continued warmly but almost flippantly, trying to soften this blow. Like it was making a decision about which dress to buy! I was in no fit state to choose what to have for dinner, let alone make decisions about my baby's future. I was so scared; 'let the baby go' wasn't even an option I had considered. I wouldn't do it. But I was too weak to fight any more.

My GP was telling me I couldn't cope without the pills and sometimes I felt he was right. When I had been taking them, life became easier, although my mind was sometimes numb or swimmy, and I didn't get the nightmares or the panic attacks. I lived in a kind of daze. But when I stopped them, all the panic and bad dreams began again. Perhaps he was right; perhaps I was so inadequate that I needed this medication, just to function. Would I have been different if I hadn't been on Benzodiazepine drugs? I don't know. I was 26 years old, all of my adult life, from the age of fifteen, I had unknowingly been on some kind of antidepressant or tranquiliser. Yes, they helped block out the memories of the abuse, helped when my own *pretend* let me down, during the abuse and that had to be good. So I didn't know if I could cope without them. I hadn't been without them, ever, during my young adult life. My body seemed to have become needy of them, so had my mind become needy of them as well? It seems the longer I was taking them, the less I could cope without them. I didn't know if Cassie without the pills could cope at all. I didn't really know that Cassie anymore. The horrors of abuse had led me down this path and now, I had become a lesser person.

When I was about eight months pregnant, I had a visit from a lady from the adoption society. I thought she was a little pompous and snooty. I didn't want her in my home, this was my *safe haven*. This was the only place that I felt remotely safe, at home with my blessing, Melissa, my little girl.

"We are quite excited," she said, not looking at me. Why couldn't people in authority look me in the eye when deciding my fate? "Adopters are always looking for baby boys, so if you have a boy baby, we will have them fighting over him," she laughed. Like she had said something really funny.

*Fighting over him?*

*He isn't a trophy!*

*He or she is my baby, my child.*

No one was going to fight over him, I would fight for him. He was mine. "There are lots of people who want to give your baby a home," she said abruptly, like it was all settled, decision already made.

*I can give him a home.*

*I would love this fatherless baby.*

*Me! Me!*

I didn't voice this, not to her, I just thought it. I didn't have the strength to say it out loud. The pregnancy and the withdrawal from the Benzodiazepine drugs had taken their toll. I felt completely defeated. In my heart I always thought something would happen and I would keep my baby so thinking seriously about having him adopted wasn't happening. I didn't realise that these wheels were already in motion.

Almost to the day of the due date, I went into labour. It wasn't a very long labour, not like I had had with Melissa. I wasn't supposed to see the baby once he was born, but a mix up on the ward, left him in my arms. He was so beautiful. For just a brief moment, he looked up at me, his mum, with eyes as blue and deep as oceans. My beautiful son Jack was born. My baby, my son. The love I felt was all consuming. The reality of what the social worker had said was ringing in my ears. 'If you keep them both, they will both suffer'. She had said, loving was letting my baby son go. But how could I? The pain in my heart wasn't from giving him life; it was from the thought of letting him go.

*This couldn't be loving him, could it?*

*This pain, this heartache.*

*How could this be love?*

I tried so hard to hold on, hold on to my precious child. But I failed. The young nurse who had placed him in my arms was admonished and he was taken from me and once again, I was alone. The pain of childbirth was forgotten. This new pain had begun.

I had to see him, I had to hold him and run. I didn't know where they had taken Jack but I knew I would find him. My head was reeling and I was shaking but I had to see where he had been taken to. My legs felt like jelly and my enemy, panic was coming in waves. I climbed out of the hospital bed and made my way down the corridor, looking into every side ward, every nursery. By this time, I was cold and shivery and felt very weak. When nurses came past me, I looked the other way. No one stopped me.

After what felt like hours wandering the maternity hospital, I looked in through a window and there he was. I had found him in a nursery, in a crib, with 'unknown' on his name tag. My heart broke.

*I know you.*

*I have known you for months and months.*
*You are my son, my son Jack.*

Seeing the tag and not seeing a name, it was as though he didn't have one, that he didn't belong anywhere, like he had been found.

*He does have a name!*
*He does belong, he belongs to me!*

Since there was no one around, I didn't stop to think, I rushed in and lifted him out of the cold hospital crib and held him close. Lifted him into my empty arms, the arms that were already aching for him. He was here, held in my arms where he belonged, no one would take him from me again. But before I could do anything, the ward Sister rushed in quickly took him from me and I was escorted back to my room. The realisation and the enormity of what was happening was too much for me. I was broken. I couldn't cry. What good would tears have done? How would they help me, they had never helped before. No, I didn't cry. I shook uncontrollably and was in despair. The midwife came in and gave me an injection to make me sleep.

The following day the horrors and reality of what was happening hit me like a brick. Soon after I awoke, the adoption officer arrived cheerily telling me that she didn't have much time. "It's for the best," she kept saying. I couldn't speak; I wanted to scream *"for the best, the best for whom?"* Bit by bit my heart broke.

*Couldn't she hear it?*
*Couldn't she hear my inner soul crying out for my son?*

She must have seen that I wasn't happy to do this, and tried to warn me of the consequences if I changed my mind. "If you try and keep him and your daughter, you could lose them both." She sounded cold even callous. "You won't be able to provide for them and let's face it; you're not exactly well, are you?" Yes I did want to keep him, I wasn't changing my mind, my mind had been 'made up' for me with having no choices. I wanted to do the right thing, but I was sure this wasn't the right thing.

*I want to keep them both, they're mine, I wanted to scream.*

But before I could gather any-thing from deep inside of me, the ward sister had come to my aid and carried out the *'things'* I was supposed to do to have my baby handed over. Handed over. Like a commodity. Like a purchase.

*No, like a heartache so great that it would never stop.*

In my dreams the night of his birth, I had been trying so hard to hold on, hold on to my son. But I failed. In my dream, other arms reached out for him, they were huge, metallic loveless and strong. I desperately tried to hold on to this tiny scrap of life who had been part of me for the past nine months. But I lost my grip and he was gone.

This wasn't a dream though, this was real. Terribly, horribly devastatingly real. Before I could get up from my chair, the social worker lifted the carrycot and left the room. Jack was gone. I don't remember the rest of that day.

It was July 1971 and my life was in bits. My beloved Jack was born. Born and adopted. Gone. In a fog of pain and desperation, an inability to fight the authorities and a concern that Dr Oxley might be right, I wouldn't cope, I lost my beloved son. Taken from me, after the choice given was impossible to make. All through my life I had never had a choice. Compared to this day, those times were unimportant. To have to make this choice, was impossible. Lose Jack and keep Melissa, or keep Jack and lose them both. No help, no support, no other option. I lost Jack and my heart broke in two.

# Chapter Twelve

don't remember much of the time I was in hospital after Jack's birth. I just don't remember. It was suggested that I was depressed. Depressed! Of course I was depressed. I had just lost my son! One of the nurses asked if I would like to see someone and have some medication that would help. I said no. Losing my baby, that was the cause. Pills were not going to make that better.

There is a vague memory of my having to register him and of telling the sombre faced registrar his name. "Jack," I said in a tiny voice, "His name is Jack."

I think he said, "Jack what? What is his father's name?" I think that's what he said, looking at the form in front of him. "That doesn't matter," I said, feeling numb, "It doesn't matter because I'm no longer with the father."

I didn't want to go there, to talk about the rejection from Larry; I couldn't see that it was any of this man's business. I remember looking at the wall, a plain wall with a bookcase next to it. He, the man asking these unnecessary questions, sat at a large official looking desk and it all seemed unreal. The registrar asked me the name of my son's father.

"Larry Howard," I said. He just stared at me. I wasn't ready for the next question, I hadn't thought of this being a problem.

"Do you have the permission of his father to name him on the birth certificate?" he said, as though it was the most ordinary of questions. "Do you have his written permission?"

*Have his permission?*

Of course I don't have his permission! He won't accept my baby, our baby, so no, I didn't have his permission. I felt broken, lost.

"No" I said completely exhausted, "No, I don't have his permission."

He was looking down at the desk and continued, "Then we will have to put Father Unknown on the certificate." This hit me like a slap. That word again. Unknown. Another bit of my heart broke. I felt dead inside.

The following day I went home, home to my precious Melissa. A taxi had been arranged through the social worker as I had no means of travel. It was an horrendous journey. No one had told this poor man, the driver, why I didn't have a baby with me. I was silently crying, shaking inside and had no voice. The ward Sister took to me the door where the car was waiting. I didn't really see the driver, I knew he was there but nothing registered.

She told me to take care of myself and that she was sorry.

This poor man must have thought my child had died. He didn't seem to know what to say. He began with nervous commiseration and then rambled on about next time being okay and perhaps he would be taking me and my baby home. Wouldn't that be good? He said.

*Good!*

*Next time?*
*Shut up!*
*Shut up!*
*I don't want a next time, not like this.*

On arriving at my little bungalow, Edward was waiting at the door. "Melissa's asleep," he said looking very concerned. "She was becoming a bit tired so I put her on her bed and she fell asleep straight away, that's okay isn't it Cassie?"

Okay? Of course it wasn't okay. I wanted to hold her, never let her go but it was so hot and he had been good enough to look after her. I said nothing. He didn't know how to be with me. Since we spilt, my moods were all over the place, different medication affected these in all kinds of ways. We were still friends and he was a good man but not good at showing emotion. Shortly after my return home, he went back to his mum's.

The next day was a bit of a blur, I spent most of it cuddling my little girl and not wanting to let her go. She was my sanity, her arms around my neck usually made everything okay.

But this time it was different. Instead of feeling comforted by her hugs and kisses, I felt bereft and heartbroken. Nothing, not even her kisses at first, could console me. I looked after her, even played with her but it hurt so much. I still loved her, of course I did but I felt empty, lost and grief-stricken. I couldn't eat or sleep, the burning pain inside never left me, the only reason I kept going was my baby girl.

After about a week, I couldn't take it anymore, I tried every way I could to find out how my son was. Telephoning any of the authorities that I thought might help. But no one could. Dr Oxley visited me and was concerned at the state of my emotions and he could see that I was becoming very depressed and put me back on the tablets. "You can't go on like this Cassie," he said slightly more caringly than before. "You won't cope with your little girl, if you can't sleep and you stay so down. You need to let me help you."

*Help me!*

*Was giving me tablets helping me?*

I didn't know. I didn't want to take them, but the words of the social worker went round and round in my head, *'If you try and keep him and your daughter, you could lose them both'.* The thought of this terrified me, I couldn't lose Melissa, wasn't it bad enough that they had taken my son. I took the tablets; I needed to be able to cope. No one was going to take my daughter from me. No one. Life became a dark heavy place to be. I rang the Adoption Society and was told in no uncertain terms that I couldn't see my baby, couldn't see Jack. That it wasn't possible.

*Not possible?*

*Why is it 'not possible'?*

*He's still my baby, my son.*

I sobbed down the phone, this was one of so many calls I made but to no avail. I wasn't thinking straight, life was back in the fog that was antidepressants. I managed to look after Melissa and feed her but I wasn't eating or sleeping and my head was all over the place. The medication kept me functioning but only just.

As a last resort, grieving for my loss and with hope in abundance, that even she would understand, I rang Mum. Jack was her grandson, I was sure she would help. I say I was sure, I think I just hoped. But of course she didn't. Hope as usual, had let me down.

"You're nothing to me and neither is the bastard you've given birth to!" she screamed down the phone. She made it very clear that I was no part of her family. How short a memory. Bastard is a horrid word. Didn't she give birth to me outside of marriage?

*That's what she thinks of me.*

*I am a bastard?*

*Her bastard.*

After this call, I was drained. Suffering indescribable pain at my loss, Mother Nature dealt me another blow. My breasts became full of milk.

*Doesn't she know he's gone?*

*Couldn't she hear my cries?*

*My cries for my beloved and lost son?*

When the health visitor came, she rang the surgery and told my GP what had happened.

Dr Oxley gave me something to dry the milk; the irony of this didn't pass unnoticed. I had desperately wanted to feed Melissa myself but had no milk. Now I had an abundance.

As I cried, my little girl would wipe away my tears. I hated her seeing me like this. I wasn't sleeping, or eating and felt anxious and low all the time. In desperation I rang and asked the receptionist at the surgery what I could do to ease the pain of my broken heart. After few minutes, Miss Pringle put me through to Dr Oxley's partner, Dr Ross.

"I hear you're having a few problems Cassie," he said warmly. "I've read your notes and feel you may need a little more help."

*Help. Yes I needed help.*

I needed to have Jack back with me. That's the only help I needed. But I don't think that's what he meant.

"I can't cope Doctor," I said. "I feel so desperately unhappy. Even my little girl is worried for me. It's affecting everything I do." I meant I couldn't cope with the grief, but I think he only heard 'can't cope'. I began to cry. I suppose this man who didn't know me, only heard the distress in my voice. Perhaps he was genuinely trying to help. "I think you need to increase the Valium you're taking. Take an extra tablet now and then again this evening. If you still feel like this tomorrow, increase each dose by 5 mg. and I'm sure you'll feel much better."

So, keep taking the tablets. I didn't argue, I would have done anything to feel better. I needed to show that I could cope because I couldn't risk losing Melissa. Keep taking the tablets seemed to be the message. I did as he said and felt a little calmer.

In the days to follow, I felt a bit stronger. To all the world, the decision was made and Jack was gone, but I couldn't accept that I wouldn't see him again. I continued my onslaught of the authorities, pretending to be a social worker or nurse or anyone that I thought might be taken seriously and believed, until one day, I was in luck.

I didn't have my own phone so walked around the corner of the road where I lived and used a public phone box, making sure beforehand that I had lots of coins to make the calls. The red phone box was on a corner of a leafy road, outside of a public house. I spent many hours in this box, luckily no one else needed it. I had rung the Church Adoption Society, only to find a young clerk willing to give me the telephone number of the foster mum who was caring for my son. I said something about being a social worker working for the surgery. Whatever I said, she believed me. I tried to remain calm, act like it was a formality, something I did every day, not to alarm her. I was breathing so hard on the phone, waiting for her to get me the information I longed for, that I was afraid she must have heard. My acting talent had come into its own. She obviously believed everything I had said and not only gave me the number but also the address. I was overjoyed but didn't show it. My heart was beating so fast I was scared it might stop. "Thank you" was all I was able to say to the woman who had told me this vital piece of information. "Thank you" and put the phone down.

I knew where Jack was. I had the address of the house where my son was being cared for. 29, Roseberry Avenue. But what could I do with this wonderful bit of information? How had this helped me? I didn't know. All I did know was that I had his address and that was enough. I replaced the receiver and made my way back to my bungalow. Melissa was next door playing with the children who lived there. I needed time to process what I had been told. I didn't want to talk to anyone, I played the conversation over and over in my head, relishing the words that the woman on the phone had said.

After a few minutes, it sank in. I knew where he was living so I could go and see him. I could hardly contain myself. So desperate was I to see my baby boy, having false strength from the medication that was so obviously clouding my judgement, I made a decision. I would go and see him.

*How daft was that?*

*How really really stupid!*

*How exciting, how heart -warming, how amazingly wonderful.*

I didn't act straight away; I sat and savoured the moment, the moment that I had found out where Jack was living. The following day, Melissa and I boarded a bus that would take us to the town where I had been told the foster home was. I was shaking and panicky but managed to hold it all together. I told my little girl that we were going on an adventure. She was excited and held on to my hand, trusting that where we were going was going to be good. I hadn't realised that the road I was looking for was a long way out of town. We walked for ages, my daughter and I, until we reached a long tree lined avenue. Roseberry Avenue looked very posh, with large detached houses on either side. The house I wanted was right at the end. My heart was pounding and my hands were sweaty and clammy. I never thought beyond finding him, finding my Jack. I didn't dare think beyond this so I didn't know what I would do, what my next move would be.

On reaching Number 29, I just stood there for a while, holding onto Melissa's hand. It was a large Victorian house with tall trees at the side of the drive, surrounded by a lovely garden. Then I saw it, in front of the house. It was a very hot day. There was a canopy shielding the occupant of the large dark blue pram. Was he in there? Was there a baby in the pram? Was it Jack, my son? My heart was beating fast and I felt a little light-headed.

I wanted so much to run over and look into the pram that may have held my lost baby, but I couldn't. I was frozen to the spot. Panic began to well in my tummy. What will I do if this pram held Jack? What would I do if it didn't? Terror filled my heart and before I knew what I was doing, I began to walk quickly back down the same road. I knew I couldn't do it. I couldn't look into the pram and see my baby and then walk away. I knew I couldn't. I was so scared because I suddenly knew that if I went over and saw my baby boy, I may have grabbed him and run.

*It won't work*, I told myself, I needed to think this through. A glimpse of the sensible Cassie came through. Picking up speed, with Melissa in tow, I very quickly walked back into town to the bus stop. I needed to get home to my safe. Where I knew I wouldn't be able to rush into things and make them worse.

*Worse? How could things be worse?*

On arriving home, I was shattered, emotionally and physically. Melissa was a little confused about the day's events, or possibly to her, the day's non-events. She was just over 3 years old, she asked why we had gone to the house but nothing else. I reassured her that everything was okay, gave her tea and a bath and put her to bed. I tried to think through what I could do next. I didn't want to get things wrong; I couldn't risk anything that would look bad to the authorities. But I did know that I would go back. Jack was my son; didn't I have a right to see him? I knew I had to be strong the following day to enable me to return to Roseberry Avenue and actually look into the pram.

Dr Oxley had given me some Mogadon, a sleeping tablet. I didn't use them all the time, I tried hard not to, but I knew I wouldn't sleep. Melissa was sleeping well in her own room and so I took a tablet. I needed to be fresh and strong the following day. With this, I went to bed, optimistic and excited. Tomorrow was another day. A good day, I hoped.

The following morning I went into the local baby shop and bought some blue booties. "New family member, or are they for a friend?" the assistant asked me. I wanted to shout 'No, they are for my baby, mine' but I didn't. "Yes," I replied, "for a friend." and left the shop. Melissa and I boarded the bus that would take me to where Jack was staying. I couldn't say living; that was too final, too cold, he was staying there for now, I could cope with this.

I saw the pram straight away; it was in the same place as the day before. I told Melissa to stay where she was and re assured her that I wouldn't go out of sight. I felt quite calm, having taken an extra 'headache' pill when I got up. I knew she would be safe, I hadn't seen any traffic the day before. I began approaching the entrance to the drive and could see the pram more easily. The gravel on the drive was crackling beneath my feet. As I got closer, my heart began to race. I prayed and prayed that my baby would be there.

*Don't let me lose it.*
*Don't let panic ruin this.*

God had to be listening today; I needed him to be listening. Then I was there. My heart began to race as I peered into the pram. Lying there between the pale blue blankets, was my baby, my son, my Jack. I was looking into those beautiful blue eyes that I had last seen at the hospital, when my heart had been broken in two. He was as beautiful as I remembered. I just stood there full of love for this tiny child who I had given birth to a few weeks before. I couldn't cry, I don't know why but I couldn't. Then the fear crept in, I wasn't sure why I was scared but I knew that if I didn't go then, I might have done something that the authorities would see as desperate or stupid. Like pick him up and run with him.

*Of course I want to pick him up.*
*Cuddle him and never let him go.*
*He's mine, my baby boy and I love him.*

But I didn't. I lovingly placed the bootees in the pram and ran back to my little girl. Now I was crying. Crying like I would never stop. We had to get back. I grabbed her hand and we hurried down the road in case someone had seen me. Back to the bus that was to take us home. Take us to reality, to my *safe*.

Arriving home I was lost. Wasn't it natural that I wanted to see my baby?

*My baby, yes my baby boy.*

At that moment, I would have given anything to have a Mum I could talk to, someone to comfort me. But I didn't. I had no one. I didn't want Jack to be adopted; of course I wanted what was best for him. But how could this be best?

*I want to be best.*
*I'm his Mum, surely its best he stays with me?*

My head was hurting; throbbing like it would never stop. Everyone was saying that the only thing I could do if I loved my children, was let Jack go. The adoption officer and social worker had told me that Jack would have a lovely home. His new parents would have a lovely son *but what about me!!?* I wanted to scream to the world, *what about what I want. What about my* feelings I wanted to call out to God that I wanted to keep my beloved Jack. But I was convinced that God wasn't listening. He had never listened before, so he wouldn't listen now. Jack and the people who would adopt him, would all be happy, they would be the winners. The loss would be all mine. It couldn't happen; I couldn't bear to live with the knowledge that somewhere, out there, was my son, growing up without me. How cruel is that!

I couldn't sleep, I tried, but I just couldn't. I reached for a tablet that Dr Oxley had given me and swallowed it with some water. This didn't work so I took another one. That's when sleep came to me, blotting out the pain for a few hours.

The following morning I made up my mind that I would visit Jack again, this time I might pick him up, give him a cuddle. How good would that feel, my arms ached to hold him. I was very scared and panic wasn't far away. I wanted desperately to talk to someone, ask if this was the right thing to do. But I had no one, so I hurried round to the phone box and rang my doctor. Miss Pringle, the receptionist, said he was in clinic but she would get a message to him if I rang back in five minutes.

"I'm very scared," I began, "I've found out where my baby is and want to go and see him." I think I heard her sigh. I rang quite often so I suppose she was a bit fed up with me. But this was so important.

"You sound very uptight Cassie, Doctor doesn't have any free appointments but I'll ask for some advice." She then promised to ring me back to save me ringing them. She had the number from previous calls so I replaced the receiver and waited. After what seemed an age, anxiously waiting for his reply the phone rang.

"Cassie," said a very stern Miss Pringle, "I told Dr Oxley how panicky you sounded and he said to increase the pills."

I was mortified, "But I need to talk to him!" I cried. "I need some advice on what I should do next. I don't want to do the wrong thing." My voice was rising almost hysterically now. I didn't want to take more tablets, I wanted to talk.

"Now don't get upset," the woman on the end of the phone sighed. "He said to take two more Valium, they are a small dose, only 5mg each, and so two more will not hurt you."

*You're not hearing me, you're not listening to me. I want to talk!*

But I didn't get the chance. She said I could see the doctor the following week, if necessary, but not today. Gone. Call ended. Keep taking the tablets. The same old message. They would help. No one else will help me. I took the tablets.

Once again, with strength from the additional tranquilisers, I dressed Melissa and we took the now familiar journey to where my baby was staying. Like the times before I instructed my little girl to stay where she was and I crossed the road and approached the pram expectantly. Looking in I was horrified to find that Jack wasn't there. The pram had no baby in it! I couldn't see him let alone pick him up and cuddle him. The pain returned, the deep burning pain of loss in the pit of my stomach.

*Where is he?*
*Why isn't he here?*
*He should be here!*
*As though there was someone to hear me I cried, "What do I do now?"*

I was so panic stricken that I was talking to myself. I am sure the medication was messing with my head because I felt almost unreal. Almost as if I was looking in to my life from somewhere outside, not being part of it.

And as though someone had heard me, the door opened and a lady stood in front of me looking concerned. She had short brown hair and glasses and was wearing something green, I didn't take much more in at this point. She asked me in, but I said I couldn't because Melissa was across the road.

"I'll get your little girl," she offered, gesturing towards her warm inviting home. "I presume you have come to see Jack?" I didn't answer, I couldn't answer. How does she know? Why isn't she angry with me? I tried to walk away, I could feel the tears that had threatened all day, coming dangerously close.

"Don't go" she said warmly. I tried to speak, "I didn't mean…....." My tears prevented me from saying anything else as she put her arm around me and took me inside. Then she left to collect Melissa.

*I mustn't cry.*
*If I cry then I'll never stop.*
*I mustn't cry.*

I pulled myself together, enough to prevent the tears and walked through her hallway to a lovely room, with high ceilings and warm comfortable looking furniture. There were toys on the rug in front of the fireplace and a small coffee table with magazines on. I stood looking out through the windows at the beautiful gardens where the flowers were fluttering in the warm breeze. A different world.

On her return her, holding Melissa by the hand, I heard some laughter coming from what I think was the kitchen and two small children rushed over and invited my little girl to play with them. This lady with a warm smile, sat down and patted the sofa for me to do the same. It was then I noticed more about her. She was a smart looking lady and was dressed in a longish skirt with patterns on and a lovely green jumper, her permed brown hair had a tiny hair slide on one side to stop it from falling over her eyes. Lovely brown eyes. She said she had seen me the first time, when I had stood opposite the house. When she found the bootees the next day, she realised who I was. She knew I would go back.

"How did you know that?" I asked trying once again not to cry.

"You're Jack's mum" she said and that said it all. She stood up and invited me into the kitchen of her large Victorian house, it was warm and homely with a large oak table in the centre and cupboards around the edge. It was then I saw a crib, I tried not to look into it, but I couldn't help myself. The tiny inhabitant, my precious son Jack, was just waking up. Again the pain in the pit of my tummy stopped me in my tracks.

"He's due a feed" said his foster carer, the lady with no name. I suppose she couldn't tell me, I don't know. "I'll just get some tea then I'll feed him."

*Don't get him out!*

*I won't know how to be if you get him out!*

My heart cried.

After asking about Melissa and me, over a cup of tea, she lifted my baby out of the crib and began to give him his bottle. I could feel myself shaking, desperately trying to keep myself together. He was there, right in front of me. My beloved son. Then, before I had a chance to think, she asked me if I wanted to give him the rest of his bottle. I don't think I said yes, but I know I didn't say no. She placed this tiny being in my arms.

I wasn't ready; I didn't expect the overwhelming rush of emotion that overcame me. I was suddenly filled with a huge mixture of love and pain, in complete shock that I thought my heart would burst.

This was when I cried. Tears like I had never cried before. Melissa came rushing over to comfort me, as she had in days before. "Mummy, don't cry," said my tiny daughter, "Please don't cry, I will cuddle you". This wise lady of the house told her that my tears were tears of joy not sadness, and my little girl, feeling comforted by this, returned to play with her new friends. This kind-hearted lady who was caring for Jack, encouraged me to talk. She then said the most remarkable thing. The one thing I had so wanted to hear from the day that my son was born. "Just tell me what you want for your baby and I'll see if I can help."

Was this really happening; did she really say she wanted to help me? I was exhausted from the previous awful events since Jack's birth. The medication was wearing off at this stage and the shaky feeling was coming back. She wanted to help and I believed her. I found myself telling her everything, how my young life had been devoid of love from my mother. How I had begun to take what I thought had been pills for headaches and how now I felt unable to function without them. I told her of the affair that led to Jack being born and everything since, all the time, holding on tightly to my baby boy.

I never told her about the abuse, I couldn't tell anyone about that. After what seemed like hours, I was emotionally drained. The lady who was sitting opposite me was crying with me. Then the words, the words I had never heard from anyone before "You should have kept him," she said between her tears," I'll help you if you like."

I was stunned. Did she really say that? Did she say she would help me keep my son? It seemed unreal, a dream. But it wasn't!

"But they said I couldn't, they said I would lose both my children if I didn't have Jack adopted." My voice was shaky and weak. I daren't believe her. I couldn't have this hope. Hope let me down so many times. What was happening here?

Jack's foster carer reminded me that nothing had been signed yet, Jack was still legally mine. My son. Her next words gave me the strength to make the next decision. "If you love him Cassie, he belongs with you." Love him? Of course I love him, with all my heart and soul.

*Yes he is mine.*

*Yes I will keep him.*

But then, memories of the panic, the fog of Benzodiazepine, the strange unreal feelings that they gave me, reminded me of my reality. "But what about the tablets?" I cried. "I have tried to come off them but can't seem to manage and every time I see my doctor, he puts me back on the pills, although I'm fine now."

The foster mother, who was looking after my son, smiled, she was actually listening to me, listening to my fears. She let me believe that I could cope. She assured me that my doctor would help, once he knew what I wanted. This was new to me, someone who believed in me. I felt stronger, able to face this new wonderful future with both of my beloved children. Encouraged by her faith in me and praying that all would be well. Praying that I would be able to look after both my children and asking for God's help, hugging each other and Jack, we made plans for me to take him home the next day. She called Melissa from the playroom and took us out to the front of the house. She offered to get her husband to come home early and take us back to my bungalow but I said I needed the walk. So we left, my little girl and I, smiling and went home to prepare for a future, a future that I had never thought possible.

# Chapter Thirteen

On arriving home I was feeling hopeful for the first time in years. He was coming home. My son, my Jack. My little family would be complete. After getting all Melissa's baby things from the attic, I sat Melissa down, in our little garden where I had placed the pram and began to talk to her about what was happening. I explained, that when her daddy had looked after her, I had given birth to a baby. Because I had been ill, he was being cared for by another mummy. She was getting excited and then I told her that the baby we had seen the day before was my baby, her little brother and that we were going to bring him home.

*Why did I tell her?*

*Why didn't I wait?*

Why, oh why, hadn't I looked ahead, got the right kind of help and support. But from where? Who would help me? There was no one. Of course I didn't wait, wait for what. I wasn't thinking straight, my head was all messed up and as soon as I had a chance, a chance to have my beloved baby home with me, I snatched at it. Who can blame me? Yes, I was still taking the medication and this was clouding my mind, but I loved my son and my little girl and all I saw was a chance to be with them always. A family, my family. So of course I told her and we hugged and giggled and got ready for our big day.

I couldn't sleep that night; I didn't take a tablet because I didn't want the fog that came the morning after my taking it. So the next morning I was tired and in a daze. It was like a dream. After getting everything ready for our new arrival, Melissa and I went back to Roseberry Avenue to collect Jack. It all happened like it was the most normal, everyday thing. "Are you ready Cassie?" came the question that preceded my dream coming true.

*Ready?*

*Am I ready?*

*Of course I am ready.*

The foster carer and her husband put all of Jack's things in the back of their car. My baby's substitute mum, smiled at me and I felt safe and warm inside. It will be okay, I know it will. I thought these words but couldn't speak out loud. I felt almost drained of feeling; the last ten months had been filled with emotional turmoil, pain, fear and loss. Now, today, it would all be over and I would be at home with my two children. My two children how good that sounded. How right.

On arriving back at my little bungalow and after seeing we were okay, this caring lady said she would contact the authorities and let them know that Jack was back home with me, his Mum.

I did alright at first. I was in heaven. I bathed both children and fed them and put them to bed. Melissa in her own room and my baby boy; in his crib at the side of my bed. I was so glad I had kept all my baby things from when Melissa was a small, although some were pink, most were lemon and white so Jack could wear them. The pram was a large coach built one, dark green and cream and was still in very good condition.

The crib was wicker and I had carefully stored the linen, it still looked very fresh and bright.

I hadn't however, realised how hard looking after a toddler and a baby could be. I was suddenly exhausted and went to bed. I never slept; I just lay there gazing at this tiny being, sleeping by my side. The love I felt was huge, I would love and protect him for all of his life as I would Melissa. I didn't take a sleeping tablet and wouldn't take the Valium. I didn't need them now I told myself, I was okay. We would be fine together. I didn't realise that my body had gotten used to the drugs and it needed the medication.

The next few days were spent in a daze, a fog. I cared for my children, I know I did, but didn't care for myself. I couldn't sleep or eat and it was taking its toll on my body. One morning I took both of my children to the local shops, where I ran into a friend of Larry, Jack's father, who made an unkind reference to my son. I was suddenly very panicky. Was this how it would be now? Is this what I should expect for him?

I quickly forgot what I had gone out for and made for the safety of my home.

One evening, a few days after Jack came home, when I was putting Melissa and her baby brother to bed, it started. I began to feel terrified. I felt light-headed and had a pain inside that was all consuming. I was scared of leaving my children and even after they fell asleep, I struggled at first to leave them but had this horrendous terror that made me want to run.

'What's happening to me?' I cried out. The front door of my little home opened out onto a driveway, opposite my neighbour's front door. I rushed across and knocked frantically knocked and knocked until she answered. We had become a bit closer since I brought Jack home.

This was the worst thing I could have done. She called out to her husband for him to ring the surgery and took me back into my home, holding onto my arm to support me. I know it was for the best, her calling the doctor but it began a chain of events that destroyed a huge part of my being.

After what seemed an eternity Dr Oxley and a social worker arrived. It was like a dream, a nightmare. I had no control. I didn't feel real, like it was all happening to someone else. I wanted to wake up from this dream and make it all stop. But I was powerless to stop it.

"We don't think you are coping" said this doctor slowly, as though I needed time to digest what he was saying. "We think you made a mistake bringing the child back here."

*The child!*
*The child!*
*No my child, my Jack, my son.*

It wasn't a mistake, I knew that, but I couldn't speak. I was shattered emotionally and so physically drained that I couldn't speak. The fog that was the medication withdrawal was thick and rendered me close to useless. My doctor looked out of his depth and so the social worker took over, colluding with this medical man who hadn't listened, hadn't heard me.

"You have no means to keep him, just a small amount of money for your daughter," she said as though this was a surprise to me. "I want you to think about what you have done overnight and we will decide what's best in the morning." That word again. Best. In my heart and soul I knew what was best, but I felt beaten and broken.

*And who were the 'we'?*
*What's this we?*

They left. Dr Oxley had given me something to sleep and with the help of my neighbour, I changed into my nightdress and with Jack asleep in his crib, I went to bed.

The following morning I awoke feeling very scared. I wasn't sure what would happen but I had a feeling of foreboding. I had no one to turn to, although we had become closer, my neighbour hadn't known me that long and I had no family to speak of. I must have looked, to those who didn't know me, sick and at the end of my tether and no good for anything. I was feeling spaced out and fragile, I wouldn't take any of the medication that the GP had given me. My body was screaming out for something but I was struggling to hold on, hold on to my life that seemed out of my control.

Then they came, the well-meaning authority figures, in the guise of the social worker and my health visitor, a lady who I liked very much. But that didn't seem a comfort now. I knew today wasn't going to be good. I knew something awful was going to happen and I was powerless to stop it. Things were so different back then, no help for unmarried mums like me, just shame and struggle.

I could hardly stand up, had struggled to get dressed and that had taken all of my strength. I felt a little like a broken rag doll. We stood in my small kitchen and Melissa was playing with her friend in the garden next door. Jack was asleep in his crib, in the next room. We walked into my sitting room, what used to be my *safe* and I collapsed onto the sofa. My health visitor was looking at the floor and the social worker, in her crisp grey suit was standing in front of me. I wasn't ready for the words that came again from this woman who had already warned me. I just wasn't ready.

"You have two choices," she said, speaking as if she was reading from a menu. "You can give your son up for adoption, not to the church as they won't take him back after what you did." *That's Christian! I thought.* "He will go back into care and then given to the next couple on the list."

The next couple on the list? So this was the 'best' they talked about, this was what was 'best 'for my son? It sounded like a queuing system and Jack would be given to the couple next in the queue. I was speechless. I could feel the panic rising. Jack was precious, this couldn't be how it is. But that wasn't the worst thing said to me that awful day.

"Your other option is this…"

*It had to be better.*

*This had to be a better option; hadn't it?*

She didn't look at me embarrassed; in fact she didn't look at me once. No one did. Here they were, as before, planning the future of my children and me, without even looking at me. "If you keep both children you will deny your son a good start in life."

I wanted to scream out 'If you help me, if somebody helps me, I can do this; I can get well and keep both my children. I can give them that good start in life you are talking about.' That's what I was screaming inside, but I just couldn't voice it. My whole body was trembling. Now I needed a tablet. But I wouldn't take one, I didn't want to take anything ever again because of how they made me feel, both on them and coming off.

This formal, drab dressed woman who had come into my home to destroy me continued. "You won't have enough money to keep you all, enough for food and clothing and the Social Services will keep a keen eye on you. It will be then decided that you are not giving them adequate care."

*I couldn't quite believe what she was saying.*

*I will always care for them I love them.*

How can this be happening? She was looking out of the window of my bungalow, the home I wanted to share with Jack and Melissa; she didn't turn round but quite harshly said,

"You are not well emotionally." I knew that. "It will also go against you that you take antidepressants," she said quite abruptly. Like I took them for pleasure!

*Of course I'm not well!*

*You are trying to take my children.*

*My GP gave me the medication!*

*I nearly lost Jack and these tablets have made me ill. Of course I'm not well.*

My heart was screaming out with fear. I didn't know what to do, what to say, I was all cried out and exhausted with fear and withdrawing from the medication. "So if you insist on keeping the baby, you will possibly, no certainly, lose both children."

She hadn't stopped to take a breath, perhaps she wouldn't have been able to say this to me if she had stopped. She still wasn't looking at me; she was looking for support from my health visitor. But at first, she didn't find it.

Eventually the other woman in the room spoke. "What do you mean" looking straight at this social worker, I could see she was struggling with what she had just heard and witnessing this horrendous saga, "what will that mean for Cassie's daughter?"

*They have names.*

*My children; they have names, Melissa and Jack.*

Would it have been harder for her if she had named them? Made it more personal? "Does this mean they will both be adopted?" asked my health visitor who had known my little girl for all of her life.

I was lost, confused and feeling faint. They were discussing this as though I wasn't there. It seemed like a nightmare, I was shaking involuntarily, when I heard the social worker speak the words that shot terror through my very being.

"Because the little girl is three years old and we like to keep siblings together, I don't think they would be adopted. They would both stay in care until they are seventeen," she looked embarrassed now. She still didn't look at me, but she looked embarrassed now.

My health visitor came over and tried to put her arm around me but I moved away.

*Don't touch me.*

*I'll break if you touch me.*

Someone continued to say that I had to make a choice. I wasn't sure who said it but someone did. They went on to say that there were lots of parents out there who would love to have a baby son; they would give him a wonderful home.

I wanted to shout that no one was going to take either of my children, ever. I wanted to shout that Jack, yes that's his name, Jack has a wonderful home, he has a mum. Me! But I didn't. I couldn't move or speak. What were they asking of me. Didn't they know how my heart was breaking? Couldn't they hear it screaming out in pain?

Nobody spoke for a while, nothing happened. The air was expectant, with what, I didn't know. I daren't think. Then, very softly from somewhere deep inside of me, a tiny voice spoke. "I can't lose my little girl. She's my life." With those few words, I had sealed my fate. Given myself a life sentence. Inside I was dying slowly.

I think they continued to discuss the final details, I don't know, but I think they did. I sat there not understanding what had just happened. Not understanding what was going to happen. Powerless to do anything.

After what seemed an eternity, my health visitor became upset; the social worker had said that they would arrange everything and that Jack would be handed over, by me, two weeks from that day. The health visitor could see how cruel this was but was not able to do anything to change things. Apparently I had messed up again. I had taken my son back home to live with me and now they had to start again. Begin the adoption arrangements all over again. The social worker stated her annoyance and they discussed my baby's future, again, like I wasn't there.

This was the lowest point of my entire life. Far worse than the sexual abuse I had suffered since forever, far worse than the treatment dished out to me by an unloving mother. I was as low as I could go and felt broken, empty and emotionless. Nothing could hurt me now. I was all hurt out.

Feeling numb, I was told again, that I had to keep Jack for two weeks until they found a temporary home for him. Then they were gone.

I couldn't look at my son, my beautiful baby boy. He didn't have a clue what fate had in store for him. I felt I had betrayed him. The agony I felt was immeasurable. Then an even more agonising thought entered my head. What would I tell Melissa? How could she possibly understand that the baby brother she adored, the child I loved so very much, was leaving us? How do you tell a three year old something like that? So I told her nothing. I couldn't.

My GP came round and gave me some more medication. "You have to keep it together Cassie, if you don't, you will most certainly lose your little girl," he said. "The only way you will do that is to start taking the medication again."

*Now he sounded caring. Now he was concerned. Too late!*

What did I have to lose?!

I was about to lose a son! My Jack, I couldn't lose Melissa as well. I didn't argue with him, I should have but I didn't. I was as low as I could get and he was the 'authority'. You didn't argue with authority. I took the tablets.

Those two weeks were horrendous. I looked after both of my children. I fed and bathed Jack but I couldn't play with him. I couldn't even hold him. I tried not to look at him; I didn't want to see those beautiful eyes that I loved so much. Did he know? Did he know how I had let him down? I prayed to God that he didn't. I was numb; the pills were working in as much as I wasn't really feeling. Sometimes the pain would return, these times I took another tablet, as Dr Oxley has told me to. He was the doctor, he knew best. At this time I had sunk as low as I thought was possible.

Then the optimist in me returned a little. What if I got Larry to come round? What I thought might happen I don't know. Did I think that he would fall into my arms on seeing 'our' son? Did I think that 'happy ever after' would happen?

*Stupid stupid fool!*
*You never learn!*

I don't believe I was in a position to think at all. I was desperate. But he didn't come. He told a friend who I had asked to contact him, that he wanted nothing to do with any of us. I was shattered, completely worn out from the emotions of the past months, but especially the last few days. First unbelievable highs, getting Jack back. Then the horrible devastating lows of now.

The next few days were a blur. I eventually told Melissa that Jack was going to another home to live. It broke my heart. How could I do this to her? How could I do this to him? Choice, what was that? There had been no choice. I couldn't explain to her that if I kept him I could lose her. How could I?

She was only three years old and kept asking why her baby brother was leaving us. I had no answers for her. I didn't know what to tell her. So I told her nothing. How confused she must have been. I never thought about any damage this might do to her, losing Jack. I wasn't capable of thinking ahead. It was all I could do to get through each day. All I know is that I was given no choice and I suppose I hoped and prayed that as she grew up she would understand.

The remainder of those two awful weeks, I took the tablets and lived in the fog that they put me in. I think part of me still hoped it would never happen, that somehow something would change and I would not have to face the inevitable, I don't know. All I do know is that thinking about the loss that was to come was unbearable, so I didn't. But it did come and nothing could stop what would happen.

On that awful day, the day I lost my son for ever, I asked my neighbour Christine, to look after Melissa and to make sure she didn't see anything. I knew it was going to be the worst day of my life; I didn't want it to be her worst day as well.

I wasn't ready; I would never have been ready if it had taken a thousand years. How do you get ready for a loss like the one I was about to have?

My health visitor arrived in a car, the type that I have loathed ever since, a Volvo estate. Jack was in his pram in the garden, out of sight. Did I think that if he couldn't be seen it wouldn't happen? I don't know.

But it happened. The evil social worker, for that's how I saw her now, arrived and took no time at all telling me to get my son.

"We haven't much time," she stated, again not making eye contact with me. Not much time. I had no time at all now. It was over. I went into my garden feeling fragile, like I would break anytime. Jack's pram had a tiny elephant and a small brown bear hanging from the hood. As I reached down and lifted my precious, much-loved baby boy, out of the safety of his pram, he grabbed at the elephant and the cord broke. His little hand was tightly holding onto the fluffy pink elephant. A pain so sharp it took my breath away cut through me. I was heartbroken. It was as though he knew what was happening and was trying to hold on.

*Does he know, is he hurting? Does he want to stay?*

I was devastated. With my heart breaking in two, I carried my son to the waiting car. But then I stopped. This wasn't right. This can't be happening.

*Somebody help me please.*

*God please stop this from happening.*

*But God wasn't listening.*

My health visitor, with tears in her eyes, tried to coax me to put my baby in the carrycot that was in the back of that awful car. I couldn't do it. I wouldn't let him go. I screamed that they couldn't take him, he was mine, my precious baby. There was struggle and the social worker was pulling my baby boy out of my arms. His tiny fist, still holding the pink elephant. Someone was screaming. Someone was screaming so loud that my heart broke. I tried so hard to hold on, to hold on to the baby I loved so much. But I failed. My biggest biggest failure. The car pulled away, taking part of me with it and I fell to the ground sobbing. He was gone. I had lost Jack good. Something deep inside was broken never to be whole again. It was the end and the beginning. The end of my time with my precious son, and the beginning of my lifetime of pain and regret. A lifetime that was to be filled with his loss forever.

# Chapter Fourteen

only saw Jack once more. I had been so depressed that my GP arranged a supervised visit at his surgery.

*Supervised?*

*What did they expect to happen?*

It was a cold Thursday in October and the sun was out. My excitement was huge; I was to see my son, my little boy. He was three months old.

*It would be okay now.*

*Everything would be okay.*

My medication had been increased and I wasn't thinking straight. The pills sent me into an unreal world. In this world, everything would be okay. I thought I was thinking rationally, but I wasn't. I wasn't living in the real world, life was hazy, dreamlike and I really believed, that once I was back with Jack, my world would come right. How wrong was I!

The waiting room seemed somewhat bigger than before, the ceilings higher. I sat for a while thinking about what I would say; when they took me into see him. I was alright now, surely they would see that. Alright, being slightly doped up with medication, my judgement impaired. The surgery wasn't running but there was a nurse on duty and she had let me in. I didn't see anyone else so thought Jack hadn't arrived yet. After a few minutes the door opened.

"Cassie," called the nurse, "you can come through and see the baby now."

*The baby?*

*See the baby?*

*He has a name, his name is Jack.*

*He isn't 'the baby'; he is my baby, my son.*

But I said nothing. When I stood up I felt myself sway a little, what I must have looked like I don't know. I didn't care. Yes I was ready to see Jack; I had never been 'unready'. But what I wasn't ready for was the enormous rush of love that I felt when they placed him in my arms. I thought it might not have been there, I knew I loved him but wasn't ready to actually feel it again in this way.

"Perhaps you should sit down with him," the nurse said, "We don't want you dropping him, do we?"

*Drop him, I won't drop him.*

*I will hold on to my precious son as though his life depended on it.*

I sat down. My baby was dressed in a lovely blue romper suit and his hair had grown. He was very blonde just as Melissa was and had the same eyes, as blue as oceans. Everything will be okay now, I told myself. The nurse was sitting opposite me looking slightly uncomfortable and not looking at me. The room was quite warm and I began to feel a little light-headed. The phone rang and suddenly I found myself alone with Jack. Reality sunk in, of course nothing had changed. I was still going to lose him to adoption; they were not going to change their minds. Suddenly feeling desperate and panic stricken, I stood up and made my way into the garden, behind the surgery, looking for a back entrance. Something inside of me was telling me to run, run with my baby. But where would I run to? Who would help me? I held on to Jack with all my might, cradling him close to my heart. I was hardly breathing, hot and clammy trying to work out a way we could be free. But it was futile, it was hopeless, although I was exhausted, I didn't give up. I walked quickly to the end of the garden where it backed onto the garages, I was almost crying now. I hoped I could find a way out.

*How can I get out?*

*How can I run with my precious son and keep him?*

I was panicking and crying now. Then, when I was emotionally drained, the social worker who had apparently arrived just after the phone-call that the nurse had taken, appeared, looking furious. I must have looked possessed and she looked shocked and angry. She rushed down to where I was standing with Jack and forcibly took my son from me. Hope vanished. I knew then that this was it. I had lost him for good. The pain returned, I felt shattered and lost. He was taken from me, gone to who knows where, somewhere I couldn't reach him.

It was a new beginning for Jack, although I never thought of that at this point. All I knew was that my missing him had begun and it hurt like hell.

It's surprising how life can go on when your heart is breaking in two. The grief I felt was immeasurable. I don't remember much about the following few months, I looked after Melissa during the day, but the evenings were spent just sitting, sometimes just staring into space. I had sunk even lower into depression when the reality hit me, I didn't go back to the doctor, for some reason, maybe my health visitor called him but he came to me. Dr Oxley, in his wisdom, increased my medication. He said it was necessary and I believed him. In my mind I had made such a mess of everything, I hurt so very much, that if he said it was necessary for me to take the medication, then I had to take it. I couldn't rely on my own judgement in anything, so I did as I was told. I felt more able to cope with everyday things. I kept house, went shopping and played with my precious little girl, but I didn't cry. I daren't let myself cry. Opening these flood gates would be so dangerous. It wasn't hard, not to cry, sometimes the numb came and I felt calm. Sometimes I didn't feel anything at all. That was okay. That was fine by me. Feeling nothing was good.

That year, as winter came calling, so did the social worker. For a minute my heart leapt, the medication, messing with my head.

*They've changed their minds.*

*He's coming back.*

*Back to me, his mum.*

But of course, it wasn't that, he wasn't coming back to me, good things didn't happen to me.

She didn't waste any time on pleasantries.

"Your son's new parents would like something from you Cassie," she said in a matter of fact way.

*'New parents'?*

*He didn't need new parents.*

*I am his parent. Me Me!*

At first I couldn't believe what she was saying. Wanted something from me? They had my son, what else could they possibly want? She went on to tell me that they would like a letter that they could keep, to give Jack when he was old enough to understand. I wondered for a fleeting moment, how could he ever understand? He was mine but he was living with them. How could he ever make sense of that? I couldn't!

Of course I wanted him to know about me. But what I really wanted, was for him to actually know me. Know me as his Mum, but that was never going to happen. I had to accept that.

I couldn't speak, speech had left me, I agreed, with a nod of my head, that I would write something and this cold unemotional woman left.

I tried to write to Jack, but what could I say? Do I tell him how my heart is broken? Do I let him know that I had no choice? Whatever I said, would it make it right? No, it would never be right. So writing a letter to him, was impossible at first.

A few weeks after this unexpected request, Melissa and I were on a bus, going home after shopping. I saw Larry tending his car. The car that he bought, just after Jack's birth. After he had left me. After he had rejected me and our son. The car that represented everything that was bad in my life at that time. He had said he wouldn't help me with money to keep Jack but he had bought this big car, a Rover. My irrational self, grabbed Melissa's hand, we jumped off the bus and ran towards where he was standing. As he saw us running towards him, me possibly looking like some demented woman, Larry ran and jumped into his work's van and drove away. I don't know what I was thinking. I don't know what I was doing. But I do know that I was feeling so angry that I thought my head would burst. I know I looked at the car and knew how much he loved it. His dream car. But then nothing. I remember nothing.

Suddenly I was back home, I felt sick, drained. Melissa seemed upset and confused. The next few hours were like I was in a dream. I think I must have gone into automatic. We bathed together, Melissa and I, something she always enjoyed. I know I fed her and possibly read her a story, like it was an ordinary day. But I knew it wasn't. I knew something had happened and that the something was not good. I tried to recount the day's events but couldn't. My heart was beating very fast, the panic was setting in. I took a tablet and this calmed me a bit. I felt scared but I didn't know why. All I knew was that something bad had happened and I didn't know what that was.

About eight o'clock that evening, I had a visitor. I only answered the door because I recognised the voice of the friend that I had asked to contact Larry. Sandy was a girl I met in my evening job before Jack was born. She was engaged to a friend of Larry's. She was tall with lovely long dark hair and always looked immaculate and in the latest fashion. Usually I would have commented on her clothes, but that evening I didn't notice them. She came in and we sat on the sofa in my sitting room. I stood up and turned on the fire as it was a cold night and standing in front of it, I suddenly began to shiver.

"You were at Larry's place today, Cassie, weren't you?" she said. It wasn't a question, it didn't need an answer, we both knew that I was. "He phoned me a little while ago. Someone had scratched the word 'coward' across his windscreen," she was watching me very carefully.

I had to look away, "Someone?" I said in a tiny voice not wanting any elaboration of this fact.

"He's mortified. He loves that car," she went on. She came and stood next to me. "His neighbour saw you Cassie - she saw you damaging the car." I could feel the panic rising in the pit of my tummy; I began to shake and had to sit down.

*She saw me?*

*The neighbour saw me.*

*No, that's not right.*

*I wouldn't have done such a thing.*

I couldn't have done that. Could I?

Suddenly, there was the realisation that I could have done it given my messed up state of mind. I couldn't remember the day's events, but I knew something had happened; I had a feeling that it was something bad but I couldn't remember.

*Why can't I remember?*

It took a while for enormity of what my friend was saying, to hit me. I was scared now. If I had done what it seems I had, then I had committed a criminal act.

"He'll have to go to the police, won't he?" I said in a quiet, not really wanting to speak voice.

My friend assured me that he wouldn't.

"If he reports you, he will have to say why you might have done this and that wouldn't leave him looking very good." She put her arm around me. "No, he won't report it," she said. I was grateful for the warmth of her body next to me, another human being, someone who seemed to care. I needed to cry, I wanted to cry but I didn't. It was dawning on me why I had felt afraid since returning home earlier that day.

It was bad what had happened, what it seems I had done, but what was worse was that I didn't remember doing anything. After Larry driving off at top speed and leaving me in front of this car that he loved so much, I don't remember a thing. Yes, I was sorry, but not about the damage I may have done, but for being so far down, so out of control that I could have done anything so bad and have no memory of it. Yes I was sorry, but sorry for me and my little girl who would have witnessed my actions. So, I damaged his precious car, he damaged my heart and my very soul. Unlike the car, I could never be repaired.

Sandy left and suggested I went to bed and got some sleep as I looked completely exhausted. I took a sleeping tablet because my mind was racing and I needed to switch off for a while at least.

The next day after another fitful night, on the realisation that Melissa had witnessed such terrible behaviour by her Mum, I knew I needed help. The effects of my childhood, the horrendous abuse and the treatment by Mum, had begun this slippery slope of medication. Now, with the grief surrounding my pregnancy and the loss of my baby boy, Melissa was suffering the legacy of the person I had become. It had to stop. Once again I found myself in the surgery with the high ceiling.

"Okay Cassie, what's the problem now?" Dr Oxley was looking at his desk, not at me, but his desk. "What's wrong today?" he said in an exasperated voice.

I didn't know how to begin. My life was all going wrong, not that it had ever gone right. With the exception of my little girl, things hadn't been exactly easy for me. But I didn't know what was wrong, that's why I was there. I know I needed help, but didn't really understand how I came to be where I found myself.

"I saw Larry, my baby's father, working on his car" I said, starting at the beginning, or rather the beginning of yesterday. "Apparently, after he drove away and wouldn't speak to me, I damaged his car," my voice was trailing off at this point.

"Apparently?" said Dr Oxley, still looking at whatever held his interest on his desk. "What exactly do you mean by 'apparently? Either you did or you didn't!"

I wanted him to look at me, I don't know what I thought he might see, but I just wanted him to look and hopefully understand how desperate I was. But he didn't.

"I was seen scratching his windscreen," I said, ashamed to have to admit this. "But I don't remember. One minute I was there, in front of his car, and then I was at home, with Melissa. I don't know what happened in between." It sounded so stupid, so unbelievable. How could I have done that and not remembered. Me, the meek and mild, frightened of her own shadow Cassie.

How could I have committed such an act of violence? But I did. Someone saw me, so I did. I thought Dr Oxley would be shocked, or concerned for my well-being. But no.

"Perhaps because of the trauma of losing the baby," he began, "you could have briefly 'flipped' and lost control." Well, yes; perhaps I could of because 'the baby' was my baby. So yes I could have 'flipped' as he put it! "I will change your medication and you'll soon feel much better," he sounded so matter of fact, like this happened all the time. Nothing unusual. "I will also write to the council and try and get you moved from where all of this happened. I know your husband has agreed for you stay in your bungalow but I will see if the council can re-house you now, not wait for the sale of your marital home."

*So he accepts that something happened?*

*He acknowledges that the pain and heartache of the past year could have affected me so why doesn't he talk to me about it.*

*I want to talk!!*

I didn't push the issue, I wasn't strong enough. The past events had left me incapable of thinking straight or feeling much. His words did little to comfort me. I left the surgery, once more with the little piece of paper in my hand that I would take to the chemist.

The following day Edward and I finally put our little house on the market, this had been delayed because of my pregnancy. He had been very kind to me during all of the last year, trying to help, offering to take Melissa out, but he wouldn't or couldn't talk to me about Jack. How could I blame him? He was still hurting from our marriage not working, he said he still loved me, so how could I expect him to talk to me about the baby I had had with someone else. Putting the bungalow up for sale meant that I could try and move on. Emotionally, as well as physically and so could Edward. I knew that the memories were not in the house, but inside of me, but I had to try for the sake of my little girl.

Before I could truly put some of the past to bed, I had to try and put some of my house in order. I had to write the letter, the letter to Jack. I sat down several times and tried but just couldn't. What could I say? How could I explain something that I didn't understand myself? I didn't know why he was with another family. I really didn't understand how things got this bad. So I left it, unwritten.

Eventually, after a few endless nights, thinking about my son, I put pen to paper. I wrote a three page poem and asked the social worker to give it to my baby's new parents. I only asked for one thing. Was that so bad? They had taken my everything, so one little request couldn't be that bad. I wanted them to promise that they would tell Jack how much I loved him, give him the clothes I dressed him in when he left me, his little toy that he snatched from his pram on that horrendous day when he was taken from me. I asked if they would keep all of these things along with my poem. When Jack was old enough to understand, I asked if they would give him all of these, from me. With love.

A few days later, my social worker rang to say that the adoptive parents promised to carry out my wishes. She also said that they would keep Jack as the name of their new son. This shook me. It had never occurred to me that they might change it, so I was relieved when they kept his name, the name I had given him. It was all I had given him. It was another ending, or so I thought. Jack with his new family, and Melissa and me, going to a new house. How wrong was I. It was just the beginning. The beginning of a lifetime of pain and regret. A beginning, of my missing him every single day.

# Chapter Fifteen

A few weeks later Melissa and I moved into a council house, I had been given priority apparently, because Dr Oxley had written to the council and asked that it was speeded up, because of my 'unstable mental health'.

*Now he was helping. Now he was listening.*

*Too late, too late!*

When the housing people interviewed me, before Jack was taken for adoption, I had been told that I would only be offered a bed-sit or a one bedroom maisonette. Melissa could share with me, they said. But what they gave me was three bedroom house. It was close to where Dottie and Edward lived so that was a positive. Being given this large house, really hurt. I thought of how well Jack would have fitted in with us there. Still grieving, I became more depressed and I didn't find it easy to make friends, I was emotionally drained from the year's events and losses. Also, somehow the story had gone round the estate, that not only had I been given priority over others on the housing list, but I was given a three bedroom house for just me and my little girl.

I rang the council and asked why and explained that some of the women who lived in the area had been sniping at me, saying how unfair it was. I could actually see where they were coming from; many of them were overcrowded and would have loved a bigger house. Here was me, in one of the larger houses on the estate and I only had one little girl. The housing officer said, that when they interviewed me they thought I was on my own with my daughter but when they spoke with my GP, when he rang to hurry things up, he told them I had a son and a daughter. I was being housed on medical grounds not social and because this house had been made available they allocated this larger house.

*But I don't!*

*I don't have a son, not here, not living with me!*

*How could he say that, it wasn't true!*

I was trying so hard to move on, whatever that means; trying to get over my huge loss but then life deals me another cruel reminder of what I had lost. The council told me there was nothing they could do so I had to stay put. I kept myself to myself and just said hello to the few neighbours who spoke to me. My garden fence was low and I began talking to the young mum who lived next door. I soon discovered that her husband had known my brother Tom. So life became a bit better.

I was still taking the medication that my GP had prescribed, Mogadon at night and Valium and Librium in the day. I suppose I was getting used to the large amounts because the days were slightly clearer now, not so much fog. I knew that the tablets affected my judgement in the past but they also numbed the pain, the heartaches and grief. I wasn't getting as many flashbacks of my childhood but dreams were still haunting my sleep. The medication made life easier to bear, without Jack. Sometimes I would be overcome with sadness, something might trigger it off. A mum calling to her son, 'Jack'. That was one of the worst; it sent me into the depths of despair.

The dreams never stopped and sometimes were really bad. I was getting nightmares, about the abuse, about Uncle Bill.

*I had no reason to be afraid after such a lovely day out with the man they called my uncle, when he asked me to get into the back of the car for a cuddle. He wrapped his arms around me tightly and I felt safe and loved. But then he started to kiss my face roughly, in a way that he had never done before, and when I tried to pull away he held my head so I couldn't move it. Next his hands started to touch me all over-on my back, my bottom, then between my legs-and I knew instinctively it was wrong.*

*"No, you're hurting me!" I cried. "Please don't do this. Please stop." It was as if he didn't hear me. He was a big man, a strong man, and all my pushing him away made no difference. He was professing his love for me but at the same time he was hurting me, his big rough hands gripping my skinny little body, his fingers poking inside of my panties. I was terrified. "Please stop." I began to cry. At last he pulled away.*

I don't know why these were happening again. The nightmares had stopped for a while but now they had returned with a frenzy.

I would wake sweating and screaming. My bedroom was pink and pretty but when I awoke from a bad dream, it seemed dark and menacing. Sometimes Melissa would come in, climb onto my bed and hug me helping me come out of this awful fear. I had thought that the past was dead. Dead and buried when my abuser died. But it never dies. Never ends. I could sometimes convince myself that none of the *'nasties'* in my life, actually happened. Fooling myself was something I had become good at. It didn't mean that I had forgotten, it meant that I didn't think about them all day, every day.

For the past couple of years before Jack, having my little girl, I was able to push any thoughts of my past into the back of my mind. I so loved having her around me, spending every minute of every day with this wonderful child who had made me whole. The bad memories didn't stand a chance. But since my affair, the nightmares had come back. Larry reminded me so much of Bill, after I had told him I was pregnant, that all the fears were right there, in my every day. Life had gone so wrong, the abortion specialist, the pregnancy and withdrawal from the drugs and the subsequent loss of my son, these much bigger horrors had overcome the memories of abuse.

At this time, losing Jack was much, much worse than that. After a while, after the latest visit to see my GP, when Dr Oxley had increased the Valium and Librium, the days had become almost bearable, I found I was actually enjoying things. But in the wee small hours of the morning, the demons surfaced and the reality that was my life, haunted me unbearably.

A few months after moving house, I met an old friend from college and she invited me to a party. I didn't want to go, but she insisted. My neighbour offered to look after Melissa, so off we went. It was here that I met Robert, a carpenter. He was strong, good looking and seemed very nice. He had a good sense of humour and fun and I liked that. He was taller than me with a shock of dark brown hair and the darkest of brown eyes. He liked me enough to make a date and from that, the romance blossomed. I hadn't told him about the tablets; I didn't even think about it, my daily regime of medication, had become normal, part of who I was.

We would spend many evenings listening to music. The sitting room of my new house was large and had French doors looking out towards the garden. A bright room and I had made it our home, I had brought most of the furniture from the bungalow as Edward said he didn't want it. He had been seeing a girl for a while but it wasn't serious. The sofa was green and I had made long Brown drapes either side of the large French doors. The walls were a soft cream giving a homeliness around the room. Robert would often sit on the floor, leaning against my knees, while I sat on the sofa and we would chat or just enjoy music. One evening he looked very serious.

"I need to tell you something Cassie," he said hesitantly. He had sat on the floor in front of me as usual, with his head in my lap but he sat forward, not looking at me, and continued. He said he was concerned about how I would take what he had to say. Nothing he said would shock me, I thought, nothing after the life I had experienced. "I've had extensive surgery on my hips," he said, "This will mean that I'll have to take tablets for the rest of my life."

*And?*

*So what?*

I didn't see this as a big deal, at least it wasn't to me, but obviously was for him. I didn't understand how much this had affected him and how difficult it had been for him to tell me. Perhaps I was still too wrapped up in my own grief, not to appreciate how big an issue it was for Robert. I assured him that it made no difference to how I felt about him.

*Now's the time to tell him about me.*

*About Jack.*

"I have something to tell you" I said in a tiny voice "I think you should know before we get any closer." I was surprised at how difficult I found this. He tried to get up and sit with me, but I wouldn't let him. I made him stay on the floor with me behind him, so that he couldn't see me. This was one time when I didn't want to be looked at. I struggled to say the words. It was quite late in the evening and the pills were wearing off. I was shaky and sweaty but put this down to my fear of having to relive my story, to someone else. How do you tell someone that your precious baby had been taken from you? How do you say that without breaking down completely? And would he understand? *I didn't.* But I had to tell him. So through my tears I told of the affair, my shame and guilt. I told him about giving birth to my precious son and eventually I told him of the horror of those final days, when I lost him for good. I did try not to cry, but by the end, I was sobbing like I would never stop.

"I know," Robert said, "I know all about it." He hadn't moved. He wasn't looking at me so he didn't see the shock on my face.

*Why didn't you say something?*

*Why did you make me go through all of that?*

Shaken by what he said, I asked him why he hadn't mentioned this to me before, trying not to be angry with him. He said he knew I would tell him in my own time. I chose to believe that. I left it there.

A few months later Robert asked me to move in with him. I think I loved him, I think I did but maybe my judgement was already so impaired that I could have mistook my feelings. He said he loved me and Melissa, and I so wanted to be loved. We moved in together. It was a bit unusual back then but some friends of Robert had lived together for a few years so I thought it would be okay.

He had built the house we moved to, it was in a kind of period style with a glass porch at the front. It was beautifully decorated and with Robert's furniture and the bits I had, I turned it into a comfortable home. It was on the edge of the city and overlooked allotments so was very quiet.

Things started off okay, we were happy at first. When I say happy, I knew I could be happier. With Jack in our family. I wasn't thinking straight, I knew really that it was too late. I knew in my reality that it wouldn't happen. But in my Benzo fog, I sometimes didn't see reality. Sometimes, the truth of a situation and my dreams, became confused. Hope was alive and I dreamt that somehow, someday, we would all be together. Melissa, Jack and me. Things seemed good with Robert and so I broached the subject with him and wasn't ready for his response. He was angry, he told me that I couldn't try and get 'him' back. He seemed horrified at the prospect and said if I did try and gain custody of my son, he might call off the relationship. I was mortified.

*Call it off?*

*Why would he call it off?*

I should have ended the relationship then but I didn't. He could see I was upset and tried to make things right.

"Look Cassie, he's with his new family now, you did the right thing, the best thing for him." He tried to console me, his voice softer.

*The best thing?*

*The best thing for him but what about best for me?*

*How do we know it was best?*

*What about me?*

I wanted to shout that it wasn't fair. Couldn't he see my pain? But I didn't, I didn't say anything. Perhaps he was right and I was being selfish. Robert had said that Jack would be settled now and what about his family I didn't care about his family, I was his family, me and Melissa. We loved him.

But things were never going to change. There was nothing I could do, so I did nothing.

From then on, with the help of my pills, I pretended that all was okay. But inside I ached for my lost child.

Life went on, Robert was okay with my little girl, but not loving, and not in the way I wanted him to be. I wanted this relationship to work, it had to work, but Robert's family also never really accepted Melissa and treated her differently from his sibling's children. That hurt the most.

Melissa had made a lot of friends in the quiet road where we lived and I had become friends with their mums, so life wasn't too bad. In the October I realised that I was pregnant. Our lovemaking had always been tense and I never enjoyed it. But from past experience I knew that this was what men wanted and so we made love. I think I loved him, I wanted to love him and I believed he loved me and to keep him loving me, I let him have sex. I was having flashbacks and sometimes I would have to push him away when memories became too strong. I never told him why, after all, it was my demon, not his. Sometimes I would pretend to be asleep when he came to bed, he would try and coax me to have sex, sometime I did, and sometimes I couldn't. And then I was pregnant. I wasn't sure how he would react, the other men in my life, the fathers of my two children, hadn't been happy about my having their child. So I wasn't sure how he would be when I told him. I had come off the contraceptive Pill a few months before, when I was having pains in my chest, so he knew it could happen. But I still wasn't sure. Association is a powerful weapon and my past experience told me to tread carefully.

We were in the kitchen and I was putting away some dishes when Robert walked in from the garden. It was a cold but sunny day and I had been standing by the window watching Melissa play with the falling leaves. The room was quite small, just the units and a little kitchen table in the centre. He sat down at the table and picked up the paper that I had brought in for him.

"You know I was sick the other morning?" I asked tentatively.

"Yes" he said, not looking up at me. "We thought it might have been the fish we had, although it hadn't affected me."

He looked quite calm, not concerned that it might be anything else. "It wasn't the fish," I said, as he looked up. I was watching his expression for any tell-tale signs. "I have had a test and I'm having a baby!" I stood looking at him. I wasn't sure what his expression was telling me at first. He just sat there, staring at me.

Then he shouted, "This will show my family!" He stood up and walked around the kitchen, he seemed to be shouting to himself 'this will show them that I'm still a man'. I suppose that meant he was happy, I wasn't sure but then he surprised me, I didn't expect what came next.

"We'd better get married then," he said. It wasn't the most romantic of proposals, but I didn't stop to think, I said 'yes'.

*That would make it safe, no one could take this baby away from me if I was married.*

I did love him, I think. Later, in the evening as we sat in our sitting room at the back of the house, I asked him about his exclamation, when I told him about the pregnancy. The early autumn sun was throwing shadows into the room. It was a large through lounge and was softly decorated in blues and browns. A lovely homely room. Apparently his family had said, that he wouldn't be able to be a father because of the operation on his hips. An old wives tale about having surgery on his lower body, so just a story, a silly story and this baby was to prove it. So I could understand his elation at this news. I was more than happy, having another baby, a brother or sister for Melissa, this would make our family complete. Jack could never be replaced but a new baby would be good.

I knew I had to see our GP immediately, about stopping all the medication. The following morning I visited the surgery.

I had changed my doctor when I first moved in with Robert and went to the surgery that he used. I had only been once to have an update of my medication. The GP had my notes and from then on I just requested repeats. No questions asked.

Again, like my old doctor, the practice had a huge house as a surgery and it was only a few roads away from where we were living. I gave my name at reception and sat down. This room was smaller than Dr Oxley's waiting room and a bit old fashioned. I didn't know the receptionist's name but she was a young woman with pretty blonde hair and wore a white coat. She told me to go in when the bell rang. I sat there for a while and thought how different this visit was from most of my previous visits to doctors. This time, I was happy, pregnant safe and happy. This time all would be well.

The bell rang and I entered the room where the GP was sitting. He looked up at me and then back down to the notes in front of him.

It was a nice room with an obscure window onto the road. There were a few clinical things around, a trolley with a few instruments, a couch and a desk and chair. I noticed a photo of a child on the desk in front of me so assumed he was a family man. The doctor was sat one side of the desk and gestured to me to sit opposite him. Dr Winter was younger than my previous doctor, slim and sandy haired. I didn't notice if he had kind eyes, I didn't really look. I knew I had to be strong and tell him why I was there.

"I'm pregnant Doctor, I want to stop everything I am taking," I told the medical man sat in front of me. "I know it will be hard but I am worried about the drugs harming my baby." I was agitated, my legs were shaking and moving almost at their own will, back and forth. I was ready for a fight, ready to be told I need these drugs. I knew the effects of stopping but to my surprise and relief, this doctor agreed that it would be okay. "Yes" he said calmly, "I agree that you should stop everything, nothing will happen, you'll be fine."

*Be fine?*

*Doesn't he know about withdrawal?*

*Is it as Dr Oxley had said, all in my mind.*

*They can't all be wrong.*

Before he could change his mind, I smiled and stood up to leave. He didn't look up, just asked me to close the door on my way out. No change there then. So, hoping, that now that life was better for me, coming off the tablets wouldn't give me any problems; I stopped taking them. When I arrived home I put all my pills in a bag to go to the chemist the following day. I didn't need them anymore. I would be fine, the doctor had said so.

The pregnancy was horrendous, the withdrawal symptoms were worse than when I stopped with Melissa's pregnancy. I was sick all the time, morning sickness had nothing on me, I felt sick and sometimes was sick, all day. I was shaky and weak and was afraid to sleep because of the dreams. The nightmares were worse than they had ever been before and I was having flashbacks from childhood. The memories of the houseboat where Uncle Bill used to take me, to abuse me, came flooding back, times that I thought I had pushed so far back that I would never have to look at them again; were in my every waking hour.

*"Take your clothes off!" he ordered, and I began to cry. "Get them off!" he shouted again when I hadn't done what he said. I obeyed. Slowly I unbuttoned my school cardigan and shirt, pulled my vest over my head and then sat on the edge of the bed to take off my socks and shoes. All the time Bill was staring at me, touching himself and making groaning noises. "Lovely, you're lovely and you're all mine." I couldn't bring myself to remove my panties but Bill came over and ripped them off me and pushed me back onto the little bed, forcing my legs apart. Then the pain. Once again the abuse was horrendous.*

When things seemed too much and I couldn't manage the housework or the shopping, Robert would criticise me. He would tell me how inadequate I was, in many ways, and how pregnancy was normal. It didn't make any difference when I tried to explain about the medication.

Some days when I was really low, it was as though Mum were there, telling me how useless I was. I could see her in front of me, making scathing remarks. I knew that they were just flashbacks from my childhood, living with her and my family, but they seemed so real. I hadn't seen Mum since I had given birth to my son, Jack. I rang sometimes, when I thought she would be out, to speak with Dad, but I didn't see her. She knew that I was married because I had seen my youngest sister Anne, we had met up a few months after I moved in with Robert. I had told her we were getting married by special licence, so I know Mum knew but I didn't hear from her. No one from my family came to our wedding. It was all arranged very quickly. We married but I don't remember very much about the day. It was lost in a fog of panic and sickness.

I think I was okay, I think it went smoothly, except for Robert's displeasure at my having my long hair cut into a midi-cut, for the wedding. This style was all the rage, the top of your hair was layered and the rest left long. I thought it looked good. But when I arrived back at the house, he just stared at me. "What have you done to your hair?" it sounded more like an exclamation than a question. "I only fell for you because of your lovely long hair," he said, running his hand over my new hairstyle. I froze then shuddered. Like a ghost walking over my grave.

*What was it about my hair?*

Bill loved my hair and the memories flooded back. They were never far away these days, but Robert touching my hair brought it all back, sent me back to times I would rather have not revisited. Memories of when I was a small child and had set my hair alight, brushing it in front of the electric fire. I was terrified, and had run into the garden where Mum was talking with a neighbour. It was after this traumatic event, that Mum seemed really angry and said that Bill loved my hair and she was cross that he might be upset; that she had to remedy the accident. She cut it, really short to take out all the singed hair and had shouted and screamed at me. No thought for me and my fears, just thoughts of the man who had abused and hurt me.

So, on my wedding day many years later, Robert not liking my hair, started a panic that lasted all day. Flashbacks of childhood haunted me and I felt shaky and sick. I don't remember the service at the Registry office so I expect it all went to plan. My friend Christine and her husband were witnesses I think.

We had a meal planned that evening, just a few close friends. I was okay to begin with but a friend of my new husband asked about my new hairstyle and Robert reiterated what he had said to me earlier in the day; this remark started the panic rising and I had to leave. I rushed to the toilet and Christine followed me. I told her I was pregnant and felt unwell and she suggested she took me home. She went back into tell my new husband and we left. Robert stayed. Melissa was staying at her friend's house, a few doors down from our house.

Christine left me at the door at my insistence and I let myself in and ran upstairs. The panicky feelings took over and I crouched down at the side of my bed and screwed my eyes up to the world. The shaking became violent and the terror was overwhelming leaving me unable to move. That's where Robert found me, a few hours later. I had many days and nights like this, times of not understanding what these horrific attacks were but almost sure they had something to do with the medication. I had spoken to our GP about these attacks, at the beginning of this pregnancy, after I had stopped all the medication. I had asked him about these awful panicky episodes.

"Is it because I have stopped my pills?" I said, convinced that it was. "Is this some kind of withdrawal from them?" He just looked at me almost patronising. "Cassie, there is no withdrawal from these tablets. You have had a bad time recently, what with the baby and things."

*The baby?*

*I hate that.*

*He was Jack, my son Jack!*

"It is possible that when this pregnancy is over and you have this child, that you will need to go back on the medication. You don't cope well without it." By this time, he had stopped looking at me and looked a bit annoyed, "After the delivery I will give you some new pills that will help you and all these feelings will disappear."

How dare he! He knew nothing about me. He didn't know what had happened to me, the abuse, my treatment by Mum, he knew nothing, so I suppose he wasn't to blame. But I was angry. I was twenty-three and had been taking tranquilisers and antidepressants since I was fifteen, even though I hadn't realised that that's what they were. Nobody told me. But I did wonder how he knew I wouldn't cope? I had never been allowed to find out if I could cope without medication. Things happen in my life, bringing back the memories and fears from childhood. Then the hugeness of losing Jack, and coming off medication for the pregnancy. That had brought panic and huge anxiety. I became depressed and the tablets were always the answer, at least that's what it seemed like.

As my third pregnancy went on, I became more depressed, the flashbacks and nightmares took their toll. Not only was I having memories of the abuse but flashbacks of the awful day Jack was taken from me. Having a new baby on the way brought with it, terror that I would lose this child. I wasn't physically very well; coming off the medication had caused panic attacks so strong, that I would shake from head to foot. Sometimes, if I was alone, the walls seemed to be closing in on me and I would run from room to room. On one occasion I was in my back garden, shaking and walking round in circles, when my neighbour called out to me.

Valerie was a lady who had lived there for quite a while, she knew Robert very well. She was tall and slim and always immaculately dressed with her auburn hair cut into the latest style. Even though she had two little boys, she seemed so efficient and in control that I was left wanting in her presence. We spoke, over the garden fence but I hadn't made a friend of her.

"Are you okay Cassie?" She sounded very concerned. "Shall I come over?" I didn't want her there, but I didn't want to be alone either.

"Yes," I called back, "please come over, I feel a bit unwell." This was an understatement. I had thought it might be my stopping the tablets that had caused my panic but my GP had assured me that it wasn't. So maybe I was ill, so, yes, I did want someone with me. She appeared at the garden gate looking very worried.

"Shall I ring Robert?" she asked, obviously not sure she wanted to deal with me. "I have his number, shall I ring him?" I wasn't sure about this. Robert didn't like me contacting him at work, even though he was his own boss, but I felt so weird that I said yes. She had gone indoors to telephone him and when she returned, she looked a bit cross.

"I spoke to him and he said he would come home as soon as he could. He did say he was very busy." I could tell by the way she spoke that she wasn't convinced he would come. I reassured her that I would be okay and went indoors. My husband didn't arrive home until the evening, his usual time. I wasn't surprised; work always came first with Robert. I had calmed down by then. Felt better, so it was okay.

Apart from the withdrawal symptoms, the pregnancy brought back everything that had happened with Jack. I became irrational at times; terrified that someone would take my new baby from me. I was quite possessive about Melissa, keeping her with me, afraid she would be taken. I knew this was silly, that she was safe and so was my unborn baby, but what with the withdrawal and sickness I had all day, every day, I wasn't thinking straight. I became afraid to sleep because of the nightmares; on one of my antenatal visits my GP noticed that I looked very tired. I wasn't seeing the midwife at this visit, just Dr Winter.

"Are you having trouble sleeping Cassie?" he asked almost as soon as I had entered his room. When I said I was, he gave me a prescription for the tablets

I had previously been taking. "These will help and also make you feel a little brighter," he said, passing a prescription over his desk. "What about my baby?" I worriedly questioned, "Will it be okay to take these with my being pregnant?"

"Cassie, I wouldn't give them to you if they weren't safe, would I? Librium is not a strong drug but will make all the difference to you." Reassured, I left and returned home. I had taken them before, admittedly I hadn't been pregnant, but he said it was okay and I believed him. At this time, the panic feelings and nightmares, were regular occurrences and what with looking after Melissa and running the home, I was exhausted. I began to take the pills given me and felt a little less anxious. At least from then, I managed a few hours' sleep at night and the panic attacks stopped.

The pregnancy went on for forty-three weeks, well overdue as the pregnancy dates were taken from the test the GP did and not from my dates, which they said were unreliable. I was still struggling to cope physically, suffering sickness all the way through the pregnancy and was relieved when my GP took me into hospital to have the labour induced.

# Chapter Sixteen

The birth of my second daughter was as horrendous as the first. They had induced me because I was late and the baby was showing signs of distress. I was in a side delivery room, a stark grey place with ceilings so high they made the room seem huge. This time there was a crib, that's the first thing I noticed, this time my new born baby would stay with me. There was also, a trolley and the delivery bed. My baby was being monitored before she was born because of the foetal distress. The staff were lovely, trying to assure me that this sometimes happens. But I was scared, terrified that something would go terribly wrong and I would lose her, even though at that stage I didn't know she was a she. After a few hours, my little girl was born but rushed away to the special care unit because she was blue.

"What's happening?" I yelled. "Where's my baby?"

"It's okay Cassie," my midwife whom I knew as Jo, had stayed with me and tried to reassure me. "She's okay, just a bit blue, try and sleep and you can see her in the morning." Jo was a big lady, smartly dressed in her uniform and her blonde hair was tied back with a band. She looked a bit fierce when I first met her but

I soon began trusting her as a midwife. "But I want to see her now! I need to see her!" I was almost hysterical. I had lost one baby; I wasn't going to lose another. Trying to get out of bed, my mind all over the place, another nurse stopped me. "It's just a precaution," she said reassuringly "just to make sure she is okay. Your midwife is right, try and sleep." There was no arguing, I was very weak and slipped back under the cold hospital sheets.

The next day, my new baby girl who I had called Lucy, was brought in to see me. When I saw her, held her, I began to cry. Tears that I had held on to for years. My midwife thought I was crying because my baby was a girl. I couldn't believe what she said next, "You were wanting a boy to make up for the previous one, weren't you?" I gasped. "The one you lost," she continued.

*The 'previous one!'*

*I didn't 'lose' him. And nothing could 'make up' for that huge grief, for the massive loss of my son, my Jack.*

My tears were all mixed up, some sad, some happy and relieved. I didn't know how I felt, but I did know that no one would ever take Lucy away from me.

I stayed in hospital for a few days until Lucy was feeding well so life wasn't too bad for a while. Melissa adored her baby sister and I thought Robert loved them both the same. I didn't understand, why I couldn't feel as happy as I should. Robert had said he would adopt Melissa, I thought it was so that we could be a complete family. This made me happy, we would be safe now, happy and safe. But this brought other feelings, other concerns. What about Edward, Melissa's dad? Melissa was still seeing him but it was not an easy relationship.

This was through no fault of Edward's but he could only see her on a Sunday and he didn't really know how to be with her. Dottie, his mum and I had remained close after my marriage to Edward ended; she was like a mum to me. I wasn't sure how Robert wanting to adopt Melissa would be accepted by either of them. But I needn't have worried, assured that I would still take her over to see Dottie, her Nan, and Edward's belief that he was doing what was best for Melissa, they both agreed to Robert adopting her. I still wasn't sure, things were not really right at home but I thought adopting my first child might make things better. I was still struggling a bit with panic and although I was told I could increase my medication I fought against this.

I had really thought that Robert loved Melissa and wanted to make her as much his as Lucy was. But I soon realised that the adoption wasn't for that reason. Robert was very materialistic, very money orientated. Back in 1973 you didn't get Family Allowance for the first child, not until you had a second child. So adopting Melissa meant that we would have this money from the government. I was so angry when he told me this. Adoption was a serious thing; I knew that, it wasn't a way of getting money! He seemed slightly amused when I told him how I felt. I couldn't shake off the feelings of betrayal. My eldest daughter, who was only five years old, was being used for financial gain. He had promised he would love her and I wasn't sure he did. I wasn't sure that adoption was something that I wanted if it was for the wrong reasons.

It was at this time that I noticed that Robert and his family were treating my daughters differently. I spoke to him about this but he just shrugged it off. I was very worried about how things were going, we began to argue and I knew this wasn't good for my little girls. I began to back down. Even though I was back on medication shortly after Lucy's birth, it wasn't as much as before and again, I was feeling weak and shaky. I should have been stronger, fought against the adoption, but the submissive Cassie was back.

Our sex life suffered because I was beginning to have flashbacks of the sexual abuse I suffered in childhood. I still hadn't told Robert about any of these horrors, so he didn't understand, why should he? With my marriage failing I rang my GP. He said he didn't need to see me. His answer to my problems was to go back onto the regime of tablets; I had been on before. Valium and Librium during the day and to start taking Mogadon at night but at an increased dose. I said I wasn't happy with this and thought there must be some other way.

This was the first time I actually told the doctor how I felt about the medication, the first time I had spoken up for myself and so he sent me to see a consultant psychiatrist, at a local hospital. I didn't have to wait for the appointment Dr Winter said there had been a cancellation and so I went the following day. The hospital, St John's, used to be the local mental hospital but that didn't worry me. I knew they carried out many clinics there because of lack of space in the General. The building was a huge Gothic looking place with long corridors and tiny dark consulting rooms. I wasn't in there very long and the consultation was very brief. I was nervous and shaking and I think that was all that was seen by this psychiatrist.

The conclusion of this visit was that I had post-natal depression. Mr. Godden, a stuffy little man who didn't really ask me anything, put me onto Lentizol at night and Librium during the day. So I didn't really gain anything from trying to stand up for myself, I was back where I started before my pregnancy. I can't blame the doctors; all they could see was a frightened, anxious patient, a woman depressed and afraid of her own shadow. What they didn't realise, was, that this was how the medication affected me.

Withdrawal left me climbing the walls in terror, sick, shaky and unable to cope. Being on the medication, either rendered me totally submissive or agitated and afraid. The Cassie who stood in front of these medical men had been on 'headache pills' since she was fifteen. How could they have known the real me? How could they know if I could cope or not? I didn't. I didn't even know Cassie, the woman, as she might have been, if this dependency hadn't happened. No one knew me or what I was like if I had been drug free. So, no, I didn't blame them.

Taking the advice of the medical men, those who knew better than me, I took the tablets. My mood soon improved but life became foggy once again. I couldn't think straight and some-days could hardly function. I did feel better, well in one way, I didn't feel weepy or depressed. This time I didn't feel so submissive either, so something was better. I began to stand up for myself at times, something that seemed to shock Robert. The arguments increased and for a while, I refused to take the children to his parent's house, until he asked them to treat Melissa the same as they treated their other grandchildren, including Lucy.

He never did this, stand up for us I mean and life became very fraught, I was back to being frightened and often would just go along with what he said. If his mother told us to be at her house, that's where we would be! I didn't feel the same about Robert now, he didn't seem to understand my feelings around the way his mother was with Melissa or how he was with her. I felt betrayed, he said he would love her, but I could see that he didn't. Our sex life was worse than before. I didn't want sex but gave in sometimes to keep the peace. What with the flashbacks of the times with Bill and the abuse, I was not able to have sex easily. This was the second marriage where my childhood abuse had affected my ability to be a wife, in the proper sense of the word. I wanted this marriage to work, so much.

When I talked to Robert about not being sure about the adoption, he began to shout at me.

"You can't change your mind now, you said it was a good idea!" He was irritated because I was questioning him.

I should have said that I didn't think he loved Melissa. I should have been insistent that we waited. For what, I'm not sure. But I said nothing. The shouting scared me, brought back all kinds of horror from my young days. The adoption happened. We became a 'complete' family and the only consolation I felt, was that we were safe, or so I thought. I had to make this marriage, this family work. I had to!

But things became much harder; Robert was becoming impatient about my inability to make love and insisted that I 'get it sorted'. So again I saw my GP and my tablets were increased. *Why didn't I refuse to take them? Why did I just do as I was told?*

Would my life have been different, would my children's lives have been different? I don't know. With all the medication I was taking, I didn't have the strength to argue or question. Lucy wasn't an easy baby; she cried constantly and didn't sleep well. I would sit by her cot and put my hands through the rails and massage her legs until she dropped off to sleep. As she grew, she couldn't do the things that other babies her age could do. I compared her to others in the mum and baby clinic I went to and she was way behind. I spoke to my health visitor many times and she suggested I took Lucy to see our GP. I didn't like confrontation and with everything that was wrong at home, I was nervous and shaky. The pills, were by this time, not as effective as they had been in helping these symptoms.

So this first visit, I think all my doctor saw was a 'neurotic' mother. He didn't take me seriously and so I kept going back to him and because I went on about how I thought something was wrong, he sent her to see a paediatrician. By this time, Lucy was vomiting every time she moved and screamed for hours on end. I knew there was something very wrong. We went to see the consultant, a Dr Lewis but he didn't seem to think Lucy had a problem. I tried to be strong, tried not to just accept this, 'diagnosis' that wasn't. After about three months of fortnightly visits, at my insistence, he became a bit impatient. "Mrs. Johns," he said like a school teacher talking to one of his pupils, "There is nothing wrong with Lucy; it's you."

*How can it be me?*

*How can her vomiting and losing weight, be because of me?*

I wanted to ask him these questions, but I didn't. I was suppressed by the many pills I was taking; I didn't have the courage or the strength to question him. "Just go home and give her some Phenergan, she will be fine." Phenergan was something used to help babies sleep when they were teething. Once again, standing in front of me was a medical man who was guiding me towards the door. I was dismissed.

A few days later, I had a visit from my health visitor and told her what the consultant had said.

"He said it was me" I exclaimed, "How can it be me? My baby is losing weight and screaming with pain. I don't cause this, do I?" She looked at me with what I thought was a mixture of concern and pity. "Cassie," she said, "you worry all the time, you're depressed, so yes, this will affect Lucy." If she was trying to reassure me, she failed. Now I felt worse, guilty and a failure. "Are you taking your tablets properly and regularly?" She went on "You aren't missing them are you?"

Sometimes I would take the Lentizol and other

times I didn't. Whether I did or not, I still didn't sleep, this left me feeling wretched all day. Life was exhausting and it was only the numbness I had after taking the medication that allowed me to cope. I told her that I was taking most of them and she insisted that I take them as my GP had prescribed and then everything would be okay. I wondered how taking all these tablets, could help Lucy. I wanted to question her statement; I wanted to ask so many things of these health professionals. But I didn't. I was tired and drained, emotionally and physically. I just had to accept that they knew best. Back on the regime prescribed I went. After a while, I didn't get angry or happy, upset or excited, just levelled off, almost devoid of emotion.

*That was okay, that didn't hurt.*

Lucy didn't improve, she was still losing weight and one day she was really quite poorly. I called Dr Winter. "She looks a little blue," I said over the phone, feeling very scared, "could you come out and see her?" I tried not to bother the doctors, didn't call them out but on this day I was really worried. "I don't think that is necessary Mrs Johns," he said sounding slightly exasperated. "I'll ask the health visitor to call on you." And with that, he rang off.

When the health visitor came, she too looked a bit frustrated with me. She walked over to Lucy who was lying on her changing mat on the floor of the sitting room. This was the only place I could put her where she seemed relatively settled. "She is rather blue," said this woman who my doctor had sent, "she doesn't look well at all."

*I know that!*
*I know she isn't well!*
*Why doesn't anybody listen!*

She asked to use the phone and called an ambulance

191

before I had a chance to catch my breath. I was terrified. I knew Lucy hadn't been well, I had tried to tell them, why didn't someone do something before? She then came over to me. "It's okay Cassie," she said, patting my hand, "Lucy will be okay, she is going to the right place. It's for the best." A shiver went down my spine. 'For the best' where had I heard that before? I became very agitated, I had taken an extra pill as this woman had suggested while we waited for the ambulance, this was now kicking in and the numbness was clogging my senses.

*I don't want to feel numb. I want to feel.*
*I need to feel, to stay in control.*
Best for Lucy could mean losing Lucy.
*I have to stay on top of this.*

When the ambulance arrived I must have looked like a woman possessed. I was really scared by this time and past events were flashing in and out of my head. They were taking my little girl away from me and I was helpless. The paramedics were great; they talked to me, reassured me and made small talk that allowed me to feel slightly less scared. Then they said I could go with Lucy in the ambulance.

Once in the hospital, the paediatrician, Dr Lewis, who had seen her previously was called. He had been so sure when he last saw my baby that nothing was wrong. After examining her he admitted that she was failing to thrive.

*Why?*
*Why would she fail to thrive?*
*I fed her, cared for her, loved her.*
*Why?*

This time I asked the question. This time I found the strength.

"What would cause this doctor?" I asked trying to sound strong, in control. "Why is Lucy not thriving?"

My courage was soon to be knocked to the ground. I didn't expect what came next, out of this medical man's mouth. "It's you, Mrs Johns," he sounded almost smug. "As I told you in clinic, the only thing wrong with Lucy, is you." He might just as well smacked me in the face.

*Me?*

*I was to blame for my precious little girl being ill?*

*How?*

He just stood in front of me with his arms folded. "We will keep her here for a few days but I suggest you see your GP and let him help you with your emotional well-being." He then walked away. I felt like I had been hit, I had caused my own daughter to be ill. I couldn't take it in. At first I believed and accepted what he had said, but then I questioned it. Not to the medics, just in my head. Lucy vomited almost every-time she moved. She couldn't sleep and screamed for hours. She was in pain. I knew she was.

Why wouldn't anyone listen? Why do they only see me as neurotic? Why don't they really look at me? Look and see! Then they would listen to everything I was telling them. But no, they could only see the woman on tranquilisers, the over anxious mum.

After a few days Lucy was discharged from hospital and life got back to normal, whatever that meant. She still didn't seem to pick up and I was still worried about her inability to sit up, in a pram or in the shopping trolley. Melissa could do this at the same age but her baby sister couldn't. At the next appointment with the paediatrician, he reiterated what he had said previously.

"There is nothing wrong with Lucy, Mrs. Johns," he sounded fed up with my insistence, that she had something wrong with her. "Just take her home and stop worrying" with that, again he tried to dismiss me. I sat firm. I don't know how I found the strength but I knew my little girl had a problem. She was still screaming almost all night, not putting on weight and vomiting if I moved her or tried to sit her up.

"I have other patients" he said as he opened the door to his consulting room. "Please leave or their appointments will be late" I stood up and walked out into the waiting room. By this time my heart was racing and I was a little shaky.

*He has to do something. There is something wrong and I have to make him see that.*

Knowing that if Lucy was to get any help, I, her Mum would have to be strong. I walked over to a chair, carrying her in my arms and sat, just outside of this doctor's room. I sat and waited until the end of his clinic, and then I knocked his door.

"I thought you had gone," he said surprised. "I told you there was nothing wrong with your daughter, just believe me." He was angry now.

*That's okay, I can take angry.*

He looked at me and again must have seen a very anxious woman standing in front of him. This time, he was right. I was anxious but I knew I had reason to be.

"She can't sit up at all" I said, as calmly as I could.

*I have to make him listen, I mustn't appear neurotic; he must take me seriously.*

"If I sit her up she just folds over," I continued to this rather annoyed man in front of me, who I'm sure wanted to get home, it was Friday so he was obviously trying to start his weekend. "She just falls forward, let me show you." I was getting anxious now. I so wanted him to listen.

He reluctantly allowed me into his consulting room. His bag and keys were on his desk and I could see he was ready to leave the hospital.

"Okay," he said exasperated, "Let me see, but I think the problem is, that you worry too much." He took Lucy from me and placed her on the couch, she immediately vomited onto his hand and the sheet. "I must have moved her too fast" he said wiping his hand on a paper towel.

"No," I said, "that's what happens when she moves position." I cleaned Lucy and he proceeded to sit her up and she immediately fell forward. "I must have sat her unbalanced," said this consultant who didn't believe me. "Let's try again." He proceeded to sit Lucy up in the other direction. She folded up again. "Well, I'll admit that that's strange, but I'm sure it's nothing important," he said beginning to collect his things from the desk. "Take her home and I will see her in three months."

I couldn't believe what I was hearing. He had seen it for himself. My little girl, at eleven months, couldn't sit up unaided. I was becoming rather anxious now and I think, angry. I wasn't sure that was what I was feeling because I didn't have that feeling very often. With the medication emotions become quite levelled.

"No" I said and sat down. "I won't take her home" I sat looking, I hoped, like I meant every word. Because I did. I wanted, no needed, Lucy to get help and he wasn't listening. "I will sit here until you have my baby X-rayed."

*There, that told him!*

He looked at me in disbelief; I think he was so surprised that he couldn't speak at first. After a few minutes he said, in a tone I didn't like but didn't react to. "Mrs. Johns," he said sighing, "I will have Lucy X-rayed, just to shut you up."

I suppose I should have been upset at his rude and patronising manner, but I wasn't. I was so sure that my baby had a problem that he could have been as rude as he liked, as long as he looked further into her problems. I know it was Friday afternoon and he may have had a long week, but this was too important to me to be put off. I went off to the X-ray department afraid of what the problem might be, but so relieved that at last, something was being done.

# Chapter Seventeen

The following Monday morning, very early, I had a phone call from the hospital.

"Mrs Johns?" said an official voice at the other end of the phone, "Can you bring Lucy down to the hospital to see an orthopaedic consultant. Today?" I wasn't ready for that, 'today' sounded a bit urgent. "Oh yes, can you also bring Lucy's father with you?"

Now I was worried, why would they need to see us both? Robert had always left these things to me, too busy at work. Now he was being asked to accompany me to see this new doctor. After putting the phone down, I called out to Robert as he was going out to his van. "The hospital want us both to go to see an orthopaedic consultant, with Lucy," I continued more quietly. "Both of us, today."

I wasn't sure at first whether he was concerned or annoyed, but then realised that he was actually a bit afraid. "Why? What do they think is wrong?" his voice was a bit quieter than usual. "Was it something that showed up on the X-ray?" I didn't know. I couldn't help allay his fears because I didn't know, the voice on the phone hadn't even hinted at why they wanted to see us. So I just said we would have to go and began to get Lucy ready and arranged to take Melissa along to Christine, my neighbour, for her to go to school with her daughter. Yes, I was scared, fearful of something terrible being wrong with my precious daughter, but I had another emotion, one I was scared to admit. I felt relief. At last someone had looked further than the 'neurotic overprotective' mum that they had always seen. I had had to fight for this to happen, but it didn't matter. Now they knew what was wrong, it could be put right. So the fear over the imminent meeting at the hospital, was pushed aside, by the almighty relief that something would now be done. I couldn't tell Robert how I felt, so I said nothing.

The journey to the hospital was tense, Robert didn't say much and I could see he was concerned. At first he hadn't been happy to take time off work especially on a Monday morning. Time meant money to him but he did agree to go with me. I was glad of that, I didn't want to go on my own.

"I wonder who we'll see?" I asked, to make conversation "If it's the paediatrician I saw last time, he was a bit annoyed with me." I admitted to being slightly worried about any kind of confrontation.

"Don't get all worked up' said my husband, "Have you taken your tablets this morning? I don't want you to get all panicky while we're there" he sounded bad tempered now, not only because of work, but also because he didn't cope with my 'moods' very well.

*I can't help it. I don't want to be like this.*

He wasn't an emotional man and he was very difficult to talk to about anything serious. I kept most of how I felt to myself, so as not to upset him. We often argued, mostly about how he was with Melissa, or how his family was with her. I shouldn't have expected him to understand how I was, about the tablets, etc. I had never told him everything about my past, so how could he have understood?

"Yes, I've taken them, I'll be okay," I said slightly frustrated. This wasn't about me but our little girl; I just wanted her to be well. I have put an extra one in my purse, the ones I was given for panic, but I hope I won't need it." I hated these things now. I never left the house without them these days. Most women check that they have their purse or their lipstick, I checked to see if I had my pills! There was a song brought out, back in the 60's, by the Rolling Stones, called 'Mother's Little Helper'. Sometimes this was me, me and the pills. I thought of the words often when I had felt the panic rising, and I knew Robert would be mad with me if I let it show. It went: *"And though she's not really ill. There's a little yellow pill. She goes for the shelter of a mother's little helper and it helps her on her way"*

This was me; this was who I had become. The sad subject of a song. It was a scary thought.

On arriving at the huge Victorian Orthopaedic hospital, we found the clinic we were told to attend and were shown into a small consulting room. I was hoping that as it was a different place, the rude Dr Lewis wouldn't be there.

But he was there with a different man, someone I hadn't met before .The room we had been shown into was a bit drab, there was a huge desk and a strange ugly 'thing' on top. There were also a few other 'contraptions' on the desk, one of which I knew to be a Calliper.

So two doctors today, the original rude one, and a new man who was smiling at me and looking concerned. He was tall with dark hair and was dressed in an expensive looking suit. After gesturing to us to take seats in front of them, and himself sitting down, the new man spoke.

"Thank you for coming Mr and Mrs Johns. I am Mr Langridge, I'm an orthopaedic consultant and Dr Lewis, here you already know," he said pointing to the doctor who had dismissed me the Friday before. "Has shown me Lucy's X-rays. They have shown up some abnormalities." He was looking and talking to Robert, everything he said was directed to my husband. He wasn't looking at me, Lucy's Mum.

"What kind of abnormalities?" Robert asked calmly. "What's wrong with her?"

"She's ill; isn't she?" I said, as calmly, I thought, as Robert had been. "I knew she was ill, what is it? What's wrong?"

Dr Langridge continued to look at Robert, but Dr Lewis, still not looking at me said curtly, "Do stop worrying Mrs Johns" he sounded as though worrying was the stupidest emotion I could possibly have had at that moment. "We will explain what we are going to do for Lucy, you don't have to get upset or panic stricken." He shook his head and looked, again, at Robert.

*Not get worried?*

*I'm not panicking, I'm not getting upset, I asked a question!*

*Why does nobody look at me anymore?*

Memories of my family doctor, when I first went to him all those years before, came into mind. He never looked at me, the social worker when I had had to let my precious son Jack, go, she never looked at me either. Were they worried that they may have seen the real me, behind the haze of medication? Were they afraid that if they met my eyes, they would have had to listen?

*Look at me!*

*See me!*

This Cassie was trying hard to be strong.

Dr Langridge went on to say that Lucy had a condition called Hip Dysplasia, a congenital problem they thought. "She would have had this from birth but it went un-noticed," he said sounding slightly fraught.

I tried to speak; I turned to Robert "Do you remember when I had to put her in double nappies?" I was sounding urgent now, I knew I was. "The doctor who had delivered her said she had a hip problem, remember Robert?" he was just looking at me; his expression was one of disdain.

"Cassie, calm down" he said. I wasn't aware that I was anything else. I wasn't panicking; I was just stating a fact. "But the young doctor, he was Australian, said…" I didn't get a chance to finish what I was trying to say. Dr Lewis asked me if I wanted a glass of water.

*A glass of water!*
*Of course I didn't want a glass of water!*
*I wanted to be heard!*

They weren't interested in me; perhaps at that point, again, all they saw was an anxious mum. Perhaps Dr Lewis had already made up his mind, that I was a neurotic mother who was overprotective of her little girl. On my last visit to him, he had only had her X-rayed to 'shut me up' He never took me seriously. I am sure he thought the X-rays would be normal. He couldn't see me, through the fog of medication that was affecting me, any more than I could see through it.

"Well Lucy will have to come into hospital. We will have to put her in traction and she will go into a Denis Brown splint." Dr Langridge directed these words to my husband. He proceeded to show us contraptions that she would have to wear if the splint didn't work. The ugly 'thing' that I had first noticed on his desk was what he was referring to and it was breaking my heart, that my precious little girl was going to have endure this.

He held it up for us to see it properly, as if that would make it easier for us to accept. It had a curved top and two straight bars going down from each side. Onto these were leather straps to hold the child's legs to the bars. Once stood up, the curved piece would hold her from under her pelvis. As I said, a nasty thing. I couldn't and wouldn't envisage my baby having to cope with that!

Before the shock of their disclosures had really hit home, Lucy was taken into the children's ward of this hospital, that day as they didn't feel they could waste any time.

*What had I been saying!*

*Didn't they hear me when I said there was something wrong?*

She was put in traction and was left lying on a hospital bed with her legs strung up from an overhead hoist. She was eleven months old and I couldn't do anything to help her. She screamed continuously. I went home and collected Melissa, bathed and fed her and then asked Robert to babysit while I went back to the hospital. He was not happy about this and told me I should let the staff look after her. But as her 'Mum' I had to be with her as much as I could, I didn't want her to be afraid. I would have to share my time between my daughters.

On one occasion, when I arrived at the hospital, a nurse said. "She won't eat!" pointing to my tiny daughter with only the top of her head touching the bed and her feet in stirrups way above her head. "We will have to feed her intravenously if she won't take her food."

*Take her food?*

*I wouldn't 'take my food' if I was strung upside down from a hoist!*

But of course I didn't say this out loud. "Give me the feeder, I'll try and feed her, she took some for me yesterday." The nurse gave me the dish and left. Lucy would often take a little feed for me as she did that day. I was at the hospital every morning early. I would get up, get Melissa ready for school and take her to Christine's. Then I would make Robert's packed lunch, prepare an evening meal and leave for the hospital. I would always have to take an extra pill to be able to cope. At around five in the afternoon I would go back home, cook the meal, bathe and put Melissa to bed and go back to Lucy until around ten o'clock. I was exhausted.

This went on for about ten days and then, to my relief, Lucy came home in the splint. It wasn't easy; we had to buy a double, not a twin, a double pushchair to accommodate the width of the splint. At first Lucy screamed all the time. She couldn't see anything or anyone as she was lying down. I decided that if we propped her up and supported her, she might feel a lot better. This we did and she smiled for the first time in weeks. It was difficult to get around because I had to walk everywhere, the pushchair was too heavy and too awkward for me to take on a bus and I didn't have a car. So Melissa, Lucy and her chariot and me went everywhere on foot.

Life was tense, Robert wasn't a generous man and we argued all the time about money. The sex problem had become a huge thing for Robert but I still couldn't tell him about my past. I suppose I was lucky that he stayed faithful to me, I suppose in his own way, he did love me. I did manage to have sex once during this time because he made it so difficult otherwise. Perhaps if I had told him of the abuse, it might have made him understand, I don't know.

Carrying Lucy around the house, balanced on my left hip, was exhausting. I had begun to take Melissa to school again with Lucy in the pushchair and keep the house as Robert liked it. One morning I was very sick. I was on my own, Melissa was at her friends and Lucy was asleep. I was scared, I knew this kind of sickness; I had had this before. I was taking the contraceptive Pill but with the state my mind was in, with all the medication, I must have missed one. I knew I was pregnant. No joy this time, only fear.

# Chapter Eighteen

The day I decided to tell my husband of my pregnancy was a Friday and we were sat at the kitchen table having our evening meal. Well, Robert and Melissa were eating, I couldn't face food. Lucy was in an adapted high chair, playing with her food as babies do. I didn't mess around, just knew I had to say the words. Pregnant. Baby. His reaction couldn't have been anymore different from when I told him about being pregnant with Lucy

"You can't be!" he exclaimed as though I had done this all on my own. "I thought you were on the Pill?" I was almost afraid to confirm the fact that, yes, I was pregnant. But I had said the words so had to carry on with this news. "I must have missed one," I said. It sounded pathetic. Missed one! Like it didn't matter. Robert looked at me with a mixture of dislike and infuriation. "So what do we do now?" he shouted, "what do you suggest, as it was you who forgot to take the pill" he was really angry.

*How could this have happened?*
*How could I have let it happen?*

My mind was in a fog all the time, I was always taking pills it seemed, so I didn't realise that I had missed the one that was possibly the most important. "Well you had better see the doctor and see what he has to say," he shouted, leaving the room. I was upset, why was it that I never seemed to get it right. Having a baby should be one of the happiest times of your life but it never had been in mine. First with Melissa, Edward was shocked, not angry but not happy, just shocked. When I was pregnant with Jack, Larry was horrified and left. My pregnancy with Lucy was the only one that was met with happiness and now, well, now was a disaster and I didn't know how my marriage was going to survive.

The following day I went to see our GP. The practice had taken on a new doctor in Dr Winter's place, a Dr Weller. I found myself in the same drab consulting room I had sat in many times before. Dr Weller was a young stout woman, I knew she was married with two children, I had heard this from Christine, so I suppose thought she might be more understanding Her clothes were rather drab and looked as though they had been put on in a hurry. She seemed nice enough at first but she also appeared to be shocked, when I told her that I was pregnant.

"How can you be sure Cassie?" asked this lady doctor, who was actually looking at me. Looking at my face, my expression! I was surprised to find her looking straight at me, they didn't usually, doctors, they never seemed to look at me when they spoke. But she was. "How did this happen?" she continued sounding surprised.

*There it was again.*

*What a stupid question.*

*They know how it happened; I had sex and got pregnant.*

I was confused as to why this seemed to be such a surprise. Dr Weller looked slightly annoyed "Did you miss a pill?" she asked sitting back in her chair. "Is that how this happened Cassie? Have you forgotten to take your pill?"

Was it that unusual for someone to forget? Was I the first woman ever to forget? Because her surprise and Robert's surprise made me think that I was! "I seem to be taking tablets all the time," I said, getting quite upset now. "I must have missed one, I don't know, everything gets jumbled up and sometimes I am not sure what I have or haven't taken." I looked at the floor.

*There's nothing down here there that will help you.*

*Nothing that will help you now.*

I heard a scrape of a chair, then a hand on my arm," It's okay Cassie" this slightly stunned doctor was saying,"Let's make sure first, that you are pregnant and if you are, we can decide what to do about it." I looked up and she was half-smiling, trying to reassure me. After providing a urine sample for her to send away and have tested, I left the surgery, not sure how I felt and didn't mention the visit or the pregnancy for the next few days.

But as I already knew, a few days later it was confirmed, yes I was pregnant with my fourth baby. I didn't tell Robert straight away, I didn't want to see his anger and annoyance, I went back to see Dr Weller and she gave me the news that wasn't news to me. It was June 1974 and Lucy was almost a year old. She was still in her splint and would be for about another eight months, my marriage was not very strong and I was not at all well. The last thing we needed was a baby. But, as far as I was concerned, I was pregnant and that was that!

"You will have to decide what to do Cassie," this now compassionate GP said to me. "Talk it over with your husband and come back and see me and we will arrange a termination, if that's what you decide. We will have no trouble getting it done as you not well and are on serious medication. Go and talk it over with Robert and make a decision."

*Not again. Decide whether to have a termination again?*

*I had done this before and wouldn't have it done.*

*I couldn't do it then and couldn't do it now either. I won't do it!*

"I will stop the medication. I have done it before, I will do it this time," I could hear my voice getting louder, stronger but she wasn't listening.

"Go home Cassie, talk about it and let me know what you have decided," she said, showing me to the door. Again I was dismissed from a surgery.

On arriving home Robert asked what happened. I didn't tell him about the suggestion that I had the pregnancy terminated; I wanted to hear what he thought.

"Dr Weller is a bit concerned about my health but thinks the pregnancy is okay. I will have to stop the pills though." I had told the GP that day that I would stop everything in case it harmed my baby. I think this alarmed her more than the pregnancy itself.

Robert looked at me, folded his arms and shouted, "You can't have this baby!" Decision made. "What if there is something wrong with it, like with Lucy? What would you do then?" he said getting really angry.

I noted the 'what would *you* do then'. Yes it would be up to me, not us, just me. So I should make the decision surely?

"Go back to the surgery and ask for a termination, that's the only answer." He then turned away looking like he had made everything right with that statement. What is it with men; that makes it so easy for them to say 'have a termination'.

*It's a baby.*

*Our baby.*

I wanted to shout at him. But I didn't.

"I'll go back tomorrow and ask, what the chances are that this baby will have something wrong with it."

I tried to sound strong, firm but had to leave the room because I didn't want him to see how upset I was.

The following day I went back to the surgery. It was quite a long way away from our house and the walk made me tired. When I arrived I was told that Dr Weller was off sick but that I could see her husband another partner in the practice, instead. On entering his room, he didn't look up but gestured towards the chair. Like most consulting rooms, this one was quite austere and clinical. Dr Weller's husband was a Dr Wales; his wife had kept her maiden name to avoid any confusion. He was, like her, quite young and was slim and neatly dressed.

"I see you're pregnant again," he said, slightly infuriated "Fourth baby isn't it?" he asked, still not looking up. "Your daughter Lucy has Dysplasia?"

*Am I supposed to answer that?*

*Does he think I don't know?*

"Yes, Lucy is in a Denis Brown splint," I told him, just in case it was news to this doctor who was stating what I already knew. "And it is my fourth pregnancy. But the reason I am here, is that I am taking some antidepressants and tranquilisers and want to know if my baby will be okay?" my voice tailed off at the end of the sentence. I hated talking about the tablets, the pills that kept me going, blocked out the nightmares and flashbacks. I didn't like talking about them. "Dr Weller suggested I might have a termination but I don't want one, I just want to know if the new baby will be okay and that the problems Lucy has, won't be repeated in the baby I am carrying."

*There, I've told him that a termination is not an option.*

Now he looked up. He looked straight at me. This didn't happen very often. "I think you should seriously consider having this pregnancy ended," said this now serious looking man sitting opposite me, in his brown smart suit and slicked back fair hair. "You're on a great deal of medication and have already had a child with severe disability," he continued.

*Is he blaming me for Lucy's condition?*

*Does he think it was my fault?*

I must have looked shocked because his voice softened. "You won't be able to cope with another baby at this stage, Lucy will be in her splint for a long time yet."

I didn't know what to say, the fact that my little girl was incapacitated didn't give anyone the right to end a pregnancy. I was getting irritated now, something that I didn't do very often. The pills made sure of that. But now I was irritated.

"Is there any way I could find out if my new baby could be deformed, or affected by the medication that I have already been taking?" I think I sounded strong "I have stopped everything now; I haven't taken anything today, which is why I am a bit shaky. How can I know for sure if my unborn baby is affected?"

Dr Wales sat back in his chair. "We could arrange for a genetics expert to see you," he said, realising that I wasn't going to be easy to persuade, "I will ring someone this afternoon and get an urgent appointment. We don't want to wait any longer if you are to have the pregnancy terminated."

He began to write and I felt I was dismissed. I left the surgery when I realised my time was up! I think I was in shock. He hadn't said a straight no, to there being anything wrong, he was willing to find out! This must be good.

The appointment was made for the following afternoon at our doctor's surgery and Robert was asked to attend with me and our GP. Things at home were very tense and although I was worried about the effects of a new baby on our marriage, I didn't want a termination. On stopping the medication that I had been taking for so long, once again the withdrawal from these drugs, was affecting me. I wasn't sleeping and couldn't eat, most of the time I was shaking and sweating. But I kept praying that this expert we were going to see, would put everyone's minds at rest and I could get on with the pregnancy and look forward to this new addition to our family.

At the meeting with the genetics specialist, I felt very apprehensive. When we arrived he was already sitting in front of the desk and asked us to sit opposite him. He was a portly man, around fifty I would think and had lovely brown curly hair and a warm welcoming expression. He told us he had studied our history and said that there was no reason to think that Lucy's problems had been genetic and he could see no reason to think that the new baby would have anything wrong with it, as far as he could tell.

He was a bit unsure about the medication I had been taking as the amounts were quite high and he didn't have any comparisons to draw from. But that was okay. The meeting didn't last very long and as this expert left the room, he wished me luck and smiled. Now I could get on with the pregnancy with no worries about my baby but worried about how it would affect our marriage. Robert didn't even thank this man and after I had said how pleased I was with his news, we left the surgery and made our way home.

I was overjoyed; I prayed that my baby would be healthy and normal and that instead of our marriage deteriorating, this new baby would bring us together. What a responsibility I was putting on my fourth child.

I wasn't sure now, how Robert felt about the decision to have this baby, he wouldn't talk about it; all

I knew was that I would love my new baby as much as I loved my two girls.

It was an awful pregnancy; I was very sick and didn't seem able to sleep very much. Carrying Lucy around on my hip was difficult and the 'bump' wasn't helping. The effects of stopping the medication took its toll in a big way. I would have serious panic attacks and find myself running from room to room crying. No tears, just huge sobs. I was terrified but I didn't know what I was terrified of. Sometimes my whole body would shake and sweat and I would get cramping pains in my tummy. I told the doctor many times about this. On one of my antenatal visits, when I was at the surgery, I said it was getting worse. I was about four months pregnant at this time.

"Will this upset my baby Dr Weller?" I asked directly I entered her consulting room. "I am so worried that all of this, the panic, the shaking and sweating; the horror and pain I feel most of the time, might hurt my baby." I must have sounded almost hysterical; I hadn't even sat down before I started to speak.

"Why are you worrying so much Cassie?" she said, looking quite concerned, "Your pregnancy is going okay but you are so stressed."

*Stressed, no I'm not stressed, I'm terrified.*

"Every time I stop the pills I am taking, I get like this."

*I am stressed now.*

I needed her to help me, to re assure me that this was expected when you stop the tablets.

"What can I do? What can I do to feel better?"

Hope was back, hope that this General Practitioner in whose hands I placed my fears, would help me. "Cassie," she said slightly condescending, "it isn't the tablets that are making you like this, it's you."

*There it is again.*

*Not the tablets, just me.*

So that's supposed to make me feel better is it? If it was, it failed miserably. She went on, "I think it is safe now for you to have something to calm your nerves." She reached for the dreaded prescription pad.

*No No, I don't want pills, I just want it to stop!*

I have to be fair to her, all she saw was a young woman who appeared to be at the end of her tether. Yes, I was anxious and scared. Yes I had a lot on my plate, a five year old not settling in school, a baby girl in a splint, a marriage on the rocks and now a new pregnancy. I think I was still grieving for Jack, but wouldn't allow my mind to revisit this. But these issues weren't the problem. The problem was the withdrawal from these awful GP prescribed tablets. I knew it was that, it happened every time I stopped, I knew it was the withdrawal from the pills but I so needed to feel better. I wanted to shout 'No, I don't want more pills, I want it sorted!' but I didn't. My marriage to Robert was falling apart, this new baby, even before it was born, was causing us to drift further apart. I wanted this baby and I wanted my marriage to work. But I didn't want the pills.

But I wasn't coping very well now, with the panic and shaking, I didn't see any other way.

"If I take these I will only have this problem when I stop taking them again?" I was sounding almost hysterical, even to me. "Can you give me something that won't leave me terrified and shaky when I stop them?" I asked, desperate to avoid feeling like this ever again.

"If you go back on the Valium during the day and the Lentizol at night, you won't become dependent and you won't have problems coming off, if you ever stop," she said, confidently. "Things will be better after the baby is born and you may be more able to cope. But

I am not sure you will ever cope without medication." She was handing me the prescription, knowing that I believed her and would do as she said. I did believe her about the pills making me feel better and the 'not sure you will ever cope without medication', had to wait for another day, when I was stronger. I left the surgery and made my way to the chemist. I was back on the tablets again, but I had no choice.

# Chapter Nineteen

$\mathcal{B}$ack on medication, I was feeling calmer and actually a bit better. But then it happened. One morning, around eight o'clock, when I was about five and a half months pregnant, I felt unwell. I instinctively knew there was something wrong. I phoned my GP and told her that I felt ill and that I was suffering severe pain in my back and tummy. She said she would be round later that morning. I rang my friend Christine and she took the girls for me. I had asked Robert to stay at home, but he had work that needed finishing and left the house with me in tears and in pain.

Then I began to lose blood, I crawled upstairs to the bathroom, in agony and then after what seemed like hours of excruciating pain, I lost my fourth child. The baby I already loved was gone. Alone, in the cold bathroom, I gave birth to my baby, the child whom everyone wanted me to abort, was lifeless on our cold bathroom floor. This was a nightmare of the waking kind.

After a while I crawled down the stairs and lay on the sofa waiting for my GP to arrive. I had left everything just as it had happened, just as Dr Weller had told me to. Left my poor dead baby where it had been born. I hadn't looked, I couldn't look. I crawled in agony down to our sitting room where I laid on the couch with a towel under me. My beloved special cat, Thomas, lay on my tummy. He was special because he had been given to me by a neighbour when I had left the bungalow I shared with Edward. This giant of a cat was born on the same day as Jack, my son, whom I had lost to adoption.

Now, as always, Thomas was there, comforting me in his way, lying on my sore tummy, purring as if to try and make things better.

I don't know how long after this my GP arrived. She asked me where I had miscarried and went upstairs to see what I had passed. She said it as though it was quite normal to have 'passed' this, on the floor, on my own. When she came down to where I was, she told me to look in the nappy bin she was holding.

"No, I can't!" I cried, "I don't want to see." She turned my face round and placed the bin where I could look straight in. "It will help you Cassie," she said softly," Just take a peek and you will feel better."

How could I feel better by actually looking at my dead baby? The baby that only I had wanted so much.

*She can't expect me to look, I don't want to see.*

But this thoughtful doctor, knowing it was important, insisted, she said it would help. Help me come to terms with my loss. Reluctantly I peered into the plastic bin that usually held soiled nappies. There it was. There he was. My baby boy. My, oh so tiny, baby boy.

*How cruel was this?*

But it wasn't cruel really. Only too clearly I could see what my doctor had meant. My lost child was deformed; he had been suffering from Spina Bifida and Hydrocephalus. So I suppose now he was not going to suffer as he would have done if he had lived.

Comfort? I'm not sure. Relief for him? Yes. I tried not to cry. What good would that do now? But then suddenly, I felt another feeling. Horror and disgust. Not only had I lost my baby. Not only had this little scrap of life died but he was now being held in a nappy bin! I could feel my heart begin to beat faster, my arms and legs began shaking, and panic was beginning to set in. Even though I was back on medication, it was not as much as my body had become used to over the years. I hadn't gone back on the full amount, because of the pregnancy.

Now it showed. Nothing could stop the panic now. I tried to take the bin from her; I tried to hold on to the precious contents, my baby, my son. But Dr Weller quickly stood up and taking the bin with her went outside. When she returned, it was without the bin. I was distraught now, sobbing and shaking. I wanted to ask her what she had done with my baby. Where had she put him? But I didn't. Suddenly I felt numb. It was as though it wasn't important. She was more concerned for me and whether the afterbirth had been delivered. During the panic and my feelings of horror and pain, nature had been given a helping hand. The weight of my 'giant' companion, Thomas, had put pressure on my tummy and the placenta had come away naturally.

Because of my distress my GP thought I would be okay not to have to go into hospital. My friend Christine had come down and Robert would soon be home, she said, so I was well looked after. She gave me something to make me sleep. "If Cassie feels panicky, give her one more of these," she said handing Christine a bottle of pills. "They won't interact with her Valium and when she is up to coming in to the surgery, I will assess her medication." She left and I must have drifted off to sleep.

On waking I could hear someone crying. I looked up and was confused as Mum was there, in my home, crying, She had never been there before, never been interested in me, my home or my family, so why was she there?

*Why is she crying?*
*What does she want?*

I didn't understand. Memories of another time, Melissa's birth came flooding back. Mum acting the loving caring parent. I didn't want to think of the woman who never loved me at this time. I closed my eyes and then, the realisation of the day's events hit me. My baby was dead. I was no longer pregnant. It was over, I had lost another son. The last person I needed was my mother.

In her wisdom, coming from a loving family herself, Christine had rung my mother and now she was here, with my dad. I had begun seeing them again a few months before and they showed no interest in my baby, or rather the woman who was my mother didn't. Dad would talk about it when we were alone, but not in front of this wife he adored. I had never told Christine about my early life, she knew I hadn't always been in touch with my parents but nothing more. The relationship between her and her mum was good and strong. She placed her arm around the shoulders of the crying woman who was my mother, giving her comfort, not knowing that once again, my mother was playing the caring parent to an audience.

Playacting, something she was so good at doing. Tears came easily to her, she could convince the world that her heart was breaking, all the time, scheming and gaining the attention she craved. No thought for anyone but herself. Mum looked over at me and I had seen this look so many times before, now, this tragedy had become all about her. Just as she always wanted. She didn't care about me, my baby or my loss. Another blow but expected. Dad tried hard to give me comfort and strength saying that God had been testing me. That He, God, gave me the baby and I was given the choice of taking, what some would have said, the easy way out by having a termination, or continuing with the pregnancy. In Dad's mind, I had chosen the harder way.

*So I had passed?*
*Is this how passing feels?*

I know Dad was trying to help but nothing could help. I didn't understand how a God who loved someone, could do this to them. But I had learned a long time ago, that he didn't listen to me. This was just more proof.

They didn't stay long, my Dad and the woman who was my mother. I was very tired and the doctor had left something for me to take so that I would sleep. I took the pills and took my sadness into my dreams.

After losing my second son, I became very depressed and the medication was increased. I needed to be able to function and it seemed, every time I tried to stop the tablets, I couldn't. So back on the pills I went, usually more than I had been on before.

Robert worked for himself and speculated in property. We moved several times and Melissa and I found it hard to make friends. As soon as we did, we seemed to be moving house. Finally we ended up living in the same street as his mother. I wasn't happy about this but didn't get a choice. I wanted this marriage to work and so agreed to almost anything my husband wanted. I was only barely surviving, the medication now just seemed to dull my mind. I kept house, looked after the girls and managed. I wasn't happy but neither was I unhappy. As long as my children were okay and with me, life would be fine. I don't think I was a good wife to Robert. We didn't have much of a sexual life, the medication took its toll there. Not that the lack of sex bothered me. I would let him have sex but I felt nothing. We argued a lot but I always backed down, too tired and scared to do anything else. He was mean with money and this caused many of the spats we had. When I say argued, it was more my saying how things were and him shouting at me until I agreed with him. He always put work and his family, his mother and sisters, before me and the girls.

I had never fully recovered from the loss of my baby, not been able to share my grief. He would never talk about it or allow me to. It was as though it never happened.

*But it did happen.*

*I had lost another son.*

My grief for Jack was also still unresolved and both lay heavily on my heart. Sometimes after taking my morning pills it was as though I was living on the outside of my life. Not really there, just watching from the side-lines. The only enjoyment I had was from my children. I loved both of my girls in a way I never thought possible. I was determined to mother them as best I could. Every day I would show them how important they were to me and how much I loved them. Mothering them in a way I was never mothered. Loving them in a way I was never loved, with my time, care and protection. Sometimes I was overprotective, so afraid that someone would hurt them. I never let them spend any time alone with a man. Any man. I didn't trust men around them. I suppose that was unfair to the men in our lives, but if the man they called my uncle, the man who fathered me, could inflict such horrendous sexual abuse on me as a child, then I couldn't trust any man around my precious girls.

Sometimes, every now and again, I felt almost happy but most of the time, I felt numb. I began to be even more submissive with Robert and his family, particularly his mother, who was a very strong domineering woman. A great many of the rows we had, Robert and I, were because of the way his family, mostly his mother, treated Melissa.

There was one incident that stands out for me; that demonstrated how Robert's mother, Doris, treated Melissa differently from her other grandchildren. She had been to Disney World in Florida and had summoned us round to her house on her return. This was something she did regularly and we always went. Even before we lived so close to his parents, if Doris said come round, there was no argument we went round.

All the family were there, Robert's two sisters and his brother, all with their partners and children. We were summoned as was usual, into her sitting room and gathered around this almost matriarchal figure. There were gifts and things on the table next to her chair.

"Come here Lucy," she commanded my youngest daughter, on this day after her return from Disney. It wasn't a friendly grandmotherly way of asking, it was a demand. Her manner was always austere and commanding, reminding me a bit of Mum. "Look what I have for you dear." She was holding up a yellow T-shirt with Mickey Mouse on the front, the picture was made of leather and was very bright. All her other grandchildren were already there, holding onto little yellow shirts with various motifs on the front. They were all older and bigger than Lucy.

She was only about three at this time and Melissa was around eight. Lucy had just begun walking, having had the hip problems when she was born. She started to walk awkwardly, towards her Grandmother. Melissa got there first.

"Oh it's lovely, Nan" my eldest daughter said excitedly, reaching up to touch the T-shirt.

"Don't touch it" Doris shouted, making my little girl stand back with a start "It isn't for you, it's for my granddaughter!"

If she had slapped me it couldn't have hurt more. Her granddaughter...!

*Melissa WAS her granddaughter.*
*Hadn't her son adopted her?*
*Didn't that make it so?*

I was so angry, it was like being a child again in my family home, being treated so differently from my siblings, but this was much worse. This was my little girl receiving the same treatment from Robert's mother that I had had from my own. I wasn't going to stand for that. I wasn't sure what to do, Lucy was taking the T-shirt from her grandmother and Melissa was standing very close to me, trying, I think, not to cry.

We had talked about this, Robert and I, I had said how unfairly his mother treated Melissa and he said that was rubbish. But he must have noticed this. *Surely?* This was played out in front of his whole family. But he said nothing. No one said anything. His mother looked over at me daring me to complain. I didn't know what to do. I always took an extra pill when we visited her home, I found these visits very intimidating and the pill helped me cope. I summoned up all the strength I could.

"Come on, Lucy" I said, holding on to Melissa's little hand, and "we are going now." I looked at Robert who was becoming a little riled

"We're not going yet, we haven't been here very long," Robert said in an authoritative voice.

"It's a bit rude to just take the presents and leave," he continued.

*Rude?*
*Rude?*

*Do I care if it's rude!*
*That's nothing to how my daughter has been treated!*

"I'd like to go home now," I told him. "I think it's best if we go." I was walking towards the front door hoping he would come with me.

"What's up with you?" he snarled at me. "Whatever is the matter now?"

*Couldn't he see what the matter was?*
*Did I really have to spell it out?*

I didn't answer, I couldn't, if he didn't see why I was upset and how this had, once again, affected Melissa, then I would be wasting my time. Life was very hard at this time; physically I found everything I did an effort. The pills I suppose. So I was tired and drained all the time. When something like this happened, I had no reserves to fall back on.

"I'm going Robert; are you coming with us?" I was looking straight at him, trying to see that he should understand how we felt, that he agreed that his mother was out of order. But he didn't.

"I'm not coming," he retorted. "If you want to go then go, I'm staying here!" And with that said, he turned away from me and continued talking to members of his family. All I heard was, "I don't know what's wrong with her, she gets upset over nothing."

*Nothing! Nothing!*

Yes, I was shaking and angry but I was also feeling incensed that my little girl was being treated the same way as I had been as a child. I wasn't going to just let this happen. This was a step too far. I turned around and taking the girls by the hand, left the house and made my way down the street to our home.

# Chapter Twenty

A few weeks after this incident, we were summoned to the school that my eldest daughter attended. Although we were both asked to attend, Robert didn't come with me, nothing unusual but I had hoped he would come. It wasn't an easy meeting, my daughter's teacher Miss Reeves, whom I had known since Melissa began at the school, was a nice young woman and I felt she liked my little girl. She was tall and slim and dressed in a very modern fashion and I think this made the children warm towards her, identify perhaps.

She told me Melissa was getting in trouble at school, being disruptive and had asked my little girl if anything was wrong, as she had thought it might be how things were at home. Nothing had changed at the school and when Melissa was asked, she had said she was unhappy at home. I was distraught, I knew things were not right between her and Robert but I was more than upset that she was unhappy. I thought I was the only one to feel like that. Because I knew how it felt to be treated differently, to feel unloved and unwanted by family, I thought this might be what was causing her change in behaviour and her unhappiness. It was suggested that we seek help. "We have a child psychologist who works with children like Melissa," Miss Reeves said.

*Children like Melissa!*

"Shall I make an appointment with him for you all?"

Because I believed both Robert and I wanted this marriage to work, I agreed to the help offered. I left knowing that this teacher would be as good as her word and would make the appropriate referral. That evening just before tea, I spoke to my husband about this coming appointment. At first Robert refused to go with us.

"There is nothing wrong with me," he had shouted. "It's you and her," he said, pointing to my little girl. "She is the one who has been naughty at school and you don't help!" he continued to shout. How dare he say she was naughty, he knew how Melissa was treated or ignored by his mother and his family, how dare he blame her. "I think her behaviour is because she feels different," I said softly, almost afraid to voice my opinion. "She doesn't think you love her as you love Lucy and that your mother feels the same." I could see he was getting angry. I didn't like 'angry' but this was important, he had to come with us to help Melissa. "Let's just go along and see if they can offer some advice. The school have made us the appointment with a psychologist or psychiatrist, not sure which, and the Matron of the unit; we have to go to." It seemed reasonable to me, I would do anything to make things right, to help Melissa and our marriage.

"There is nothing wrong with me, you are the problem, you and your daughter," he shouted. There it was again, 'your daughter', the adoption had obviously meant nothing to Robert or his family. I ended the conversation and began getting tea for my family.

A few days later, we received an appointment at a family therapy unit that was annexed to a local hospital. My husband did come, not happily, but he did come with us. When we arrived we were shown into a large sitting room. It was just like a house in a way, two large sofas, a coffee table and a book shelf. There was a huge tall window with pretty green and brown curtains and the room had a dark green carpet. There was even a television. As the school had said, we had an appointment with the Matron of this unit and a psychiatrist. It was very informal and after chatting to me about my children, the Doctor, a tall, dark haired foreign man, whose name I never remembered, asked to talk to Melissa first, on her own and then Robert alone. My husband was invited into the consulting room with the doctor, Carol the matron spoke with me. She was a big lady, with blonde curly hair and twinkling blue eyes. I liked her straight away.

"How are you coping Cassie?" she asked compassionately "How are you now, after losing your baby?" I was a bit shocked. It had been around two years since that horrible day when I had lost my second son, I wasn't ready for this question. Suddenly I didn't like this woman as much. I didn't know what I was expected to say. So I said nothing. "We will help you here you know, help you come to terms with your loss."

*Come to terms?*

*I will never come to terms with it.*

*Any more than losing Jack.*

My silence didn't stop her. She was very matter of fact, saying everything will be okay; how did she know that? It won't be, it can't be. "With the right kind of medication, you can live a normal life," she patted my hand like I was a pet or something. The right medication? Wasn't I on the 'right medication?'

Before I could take in what she had said, the door opened and Robert came back into the room, looking rather pleased with himself I thought. Smiling he sat next to me and looking at Carol said, "Well that's done, things will get better now."

I was confused. How could 'things get better' after a few minutes of him talking to the doctor? Melissa had been back taken into the doctor's room and I just sat there with my mind on her trying to understand what Robert had meant but not questioning it.

Nobody told me what they had discussed, the psychiatrist and my husband but something must have been decided. When my little girl came back out, we were told that the psychiatrist had identified a problem between my eldest daughter and my husband. Robert just shrugged his shoulders like it was nothing to do with him. I didn't want to get into a row, so agreed to the help offered in the form of us attending the clinic and we went home. It wasn't mentioned again until we received the first appointment to attend the unit.

We all went for a few sessions then Robert stopped coming. I didn't ask why, he probably would have just said that he didn't have a problem; that was his usual response. The unit itself, was in lovely grounds, parkland and flower beds giving a calm safe feeling. It was separate from the hospital and made up of two informal consulting rooms, a large play area, a dining room and kitchen and three or four bedrooms. Melissa would play with Lucy and other children who were attending and I would either see the resident psychiatrist or Carol.

Sometimes, Melissa would go off into another room with a nurse and Lucy would be with me or with Carol until Melissa returned to the main room. Each visit my medication would be checked. I don't know how it happened, I must have agreed although I don't remember doing so but before very long, I was admitted to this unit as a voluntary patient. The problem, I had been told, was between Robert and Melissa but it was me who was admitted as an inpatient!! I was on a great deal of medication by now, increasing them as things had become quite tense at home. My life was being lived in a fog, nothing seemed real. I didn't question what was happening, I didn't have the strength. I felt very little, ate hardly anything and just went from day today. When it was suggested that I become an inpatient, or rather stated as a forgone conclusion, I didn't argue, didn't say very much to my husband and used all my strength and energy trying to be a good mum to my girls. Most of the time, I felt I was failing at this.

The first few days in the unit, were not too bad, Melissa was taken to school, Lucy was given toys and played with children who came in as day patients and I just sat watching and talking to the staff. The best thing was that I was sleeping at night. The matron had changed my medication and assured me that a nurse would hear the girls if they awoke during the night and so I slept. Bliss.

I saw the doctor once, he assessed my medication and I told him that I wanted to stop everything.

"I can't go on taking all these pills can I?" I said on that day, to the medic sitting opposite me. I had been taken to another part of the building, into a small cosy room where the doctor of the unit, not the foreign man but a Dr Godridge was sitting, not behind a desk but on a sofa opposite me. I had been asked to sit an easy chair, in front of him. He was very young, or at least he looked very young with very black hair and lovely brown eyes. He was smiling as I began to talk. "Sometimes I feel like I'm not really here, that I am standing outside of me and watching my life happen." It sounded daft, I knew it sounded daft but it was how I felt. "When I take them, the pills, at first in the morning, I become a little numb but then this strangeness happens and I just seem to be existing."

He smiled again and sat back in his chair. "What would you like me to do Cassie?" he asked sounding concerned, "How can we, in here, help you?"

*It's happening again.*
*He says he is going to help me.*
*Another chance?*

"I want to come off the medication, everything, I don't need any of it anymore," I said, trying not to become emotional. Emotions didn't happen very often now, I certainly didn't want them to happen now!

"Don't get upset, you don't need to get upset. I will help you, we will all help you but you must stay here, in the unit, to enable us to do that. Do you agree to stay?"

What choice did I have? "Yes," I said eagerly, "Yes, I want to be free from this medication, I want to feel things again, to enjoy my life, my family, my little girls and cope without tablets." Suddenly I felt hopeful, he was going to help. He said so and I believed him. He will help me come off these awful drugs that had changed me and turned me into a zombie. I didn't remember what I was like before. Before the medication, before the 'nothing' that enveloped me. Before just existing. But then, I remembered, thought of the horrible withdrawal I had suffered before and became scared of this prospect.

"What about the coming off?" I cried desperately, "I have horrible nightmares, flashbacks and daydreams when I try and stop. What about all of that?" I was scared now. I was so close to getting better, so close to being drug-free that I was frightened he might change his mind.

"You will be fine Cassie|" he said with conviction, "I won't let you just come off without help. There are other drugs that help with the symptoms you describe and you will be given those and then when you are okay, we will stop them."

*Just like that!*

*Stop. And nothing?*

*Yes please!*

It was happening at last, I was getting help, help to do something I had tried and failed to do many times. This time it would work. This time I would have medical help and I believed it would work. I agreed to this new treatment.

It wasn't bad to start with, my little girls had a room next to mine and I was able to rest and relax, knowing they were being cared for. But then things changed, I was kept in bed in a room on my own and only saw my children for ten minutes in the evening. I asked to see Robert but was told that he and the doctors, had agreed that I was the one with problems. That I was the one who needed help. The problem between Melissa and my husband seemed to have been forgotten and I was once again, on my own. I wasn't allowed visitors, Robert could come in once a week on a Tuesday, and then he would have a consultation with the staff. I wouldn't be allowed to be present. I could have no phone-calls, no letters. Nothing. I was terrified, I felt like a prisoner and couldn't understand what was happening. I had no strength, no energy for anything. I don't know why but I asked Matron if I could ring my mother.

*Why did I do that?*

Carol agreed and I rang. This was a bad move, the woman who was my mother, told me in no uncertain terms that I should be ashamed of myself being in a mental unit and put the phone down.

*Why did I do that?*

*What did I think she would do?*

*Come and get me, take me home, care about me?*

So here I was, no one to help me. A prisoner. I was never left on my own. There was always a nurse with me. They, the nurses didn't wear uniforms and that was a little less clinical I suppose but they never left my side. What they expected me to do I don't know.

The room was small, with a bed, a side table, a small bathroom and a window. This view to the outside world, looked out towards the main gates. I remember thinking how cruel. I could see my escape but it might as well have been miles away, I couldn't reach it. On a few occasions I did try to 'escape'. Occasionally the nurse would either think I was asleep and slip out, or be called out to help someone and I took my chance. I just wanted to see my girls. I was always found and taken back to my room and then they would be more vigilant all my waking hours.

My medication was often changed and now I felt even more like a zombie. I couldn't react, cry or feel. Nothing. I was still taking the Mogadon, about 30mg at night I think and other tablets in the day. "If you take these Cassie," Carol said one morning when I said I didn't want them, "you won't have the withdrawal you have had before, when you eventually come off them."

So they knew? They knew about the effects of this medication when it was stopped. If they knew, why hadn't all the doctors before known? But now, this time, I would be okay. She also told me that the sooner I was better, the sooner I would have the children and go home. I took the tablets.

After this, I seemed to be swallowing tablets all day, tablets to wake me, tablets to help me cry, tablets to make me sleep. Just a round of taking medication. I asked to go home over and over again and even asked Robert but he said it was 'for the best' that I remain.

*There it is again.*
*Best, keeps being said.*
*Best for me.*
*How can this be best for me?*

One day a nurse, Mary, said I was being treated for anorexia. I knew this was an eating disorder as a couple of young girls I met, were patients when I first went to the unit. They were in bed all day and a nurse would sit with them when they had their meals. Before I was kept in bed, I would often go and talk to them. They seemed okay to me, a little pale and tired but okay. But I wasn't anorexic and I knew that. I did eat, I didn't have a fear of eating as these young girls had. I refused food sometimes because I had no appetite. I was taking all of these drugs, doing nothing, seeing no one and desperately unhappy. All the nurses saw was that person. A thin, tired, unhappy patient who was now becoming terrified and anxious. I didn't want the pills, I didn't want to be in bed; I didn't want to be there! I wanted my children and to go home. But all of that was refused.

It was 1977, the year of the Silver Jubilee and I was missing everything. Melissa and Lucy were going home now at weekends, so I didn't even have my ten minutes with them. I was pleased they were out, having fun I hoped, not stuck in the unit but I missed them so much. The girls had been to parties and had dressed up in red white and blue, but I had missed it all. I had by this time been in the unit for about five and a half months when Robert came in and shocked me with a decision he had made. He was going to gain custody of the girls and move away.

"It's for the best," he said. "You said you don't like them in here, so I will have them home with me, it's best for us all." He said as he had adopted Melissa he had the right to have custody of both of the children. I was petrified!

*There it is again. Best! He keeps saying this!*
*How I hated that word! Best!*
*He can't do this.*

*I can't lose my children.*

"Help me get out of here," I cried anxiously. "We can be together, all of us, you can't manage them with your work and everything." I was desperate now. Now the feelings were there. Now they had surfaced along with the fear.

"I've been looking into a school for your daughter to board at, then it will only be Lucy except for the holidays. It's a convent school, not too far away."

I was dumbstruck.

That said it all. *My* daughter. I was shocked. He had broached this subject before when he and Melissa weren't getting on but I knew it wasn't the answer and I would never let her be sent away.

"You can't do that. I won't let you" I tried to sound strong but he seemed to have taken it for granted, that what he said was how it would be. Without a second glance at me, he left.

The following day, after refusing my sleeping tablet, Helen my personal nurse said I had to be careful. "If you refuse help Cassie, you may be put somewhere where they will forcibly sedate you."

*Did I hear that?*
*I wasn't refusing help.*
*How is this helping??*

I trusted her, Helen, she had listened to me, tried to help me cope. She was a pretty young woman with reddish hair. She used to tell me about the man she loved and share beauty tips, not that I used to take much notice but it was good to think about something else, someone else apart from my problems and my family. I trusted that she was telling me the truth and took the pill.

The following day I asked for some writing material and was brought a pad and envelopes. I wrote a letter to my solicitor asking for a meeting. I had to stop Robert from taking my children. I had known Mr. Murfitt, my solicitor, for a few years, or rather I had known his father for a long time and met the young Mr. Murfitt a few times, when my marriage to Robert had not been good. At these meetings I had told both of these men of the Law, how worried I was about myself and the children, including the problems with the medication. I trusted them and knew they would help. I gave the letter to the duty nurse who took it and casually told me that it would not be posted.

*That can't be right!*
*This isn't a prison!*
*Is it?*

"Why won't it?" I asked, "Why can't I send this letter?" I was shocked and confused. I was told it was for my own good.

*That is that 'best' word in disguise!*

I wrote another letter and the following day, and asked if a patient, whom I had met before I was made to stay in bed, could come in and keep me company. The nurses were only too pleased to have a break. This patient Linda, arrived and I knew from the past that she had no time for the 'red tape' around the unit. She was a young mum who had been into the unit to help her 'bond' with her children who had been living with their father but who now were coming back to live with her. She had never liked the way she was treated by the staff and agreed to take the letter, with no one knowing and post it.

Apparently, so I was told later, Mr. Murfitt, phoned to make an appointment and was told he couldn't see me. Quoting the law he insisted in coming in to meet with me and came a few days after my contacting him. We were shown into the library, I was a bit tired as my medication had been increased once again, 'for my own good' and explained this to this man of the law, in his dark suit. Carol, the Matron was standing next to him and looking at me. "Can we be left alone?" Mr Murfitt asked. He was a confident young man, straight from Law school and had taken over his father's firm. He was very tall and slim, always wore a dark formal clothes and wasn't someone you argued with. We were standing inside of the library and I had been asked to sit and 'stay calm' by the Matron.

The library was a large room with a few books on a shelf on one side, a play area on the opposite side and some musical instruments and a record player at the end of the room. I had previously been taken there a few times and asked to sit and think of my son, Jack. A piece of music was played and also a Mother's hour recording of an adoptive mum, reading to her son's birth mother, 'A Letter to a Birth Mother' I think is the record. I would sit there for what seemed like hours. Carol always said, "You will cry one day, I know you will and when you do, all will be better."

*Better?*
*How could crying make it all better?*
*Would it bring Jack back?*
*Would it bring back either of my sons?*
*No. Crying was a useless pastime.*

"I can't leave her," Carol said to my solicitor. "I can't leave you alone with her, that's not in her plan."
*Plan?*
*Plan? What plan?*

Mr. Murfitt must have seen my disappointment, I needed to talk to him alone. "Cassie will be fine," he said. "This has to be confidential, so please, I will let you know when I am leaving." With that he opened the door and Matron reluctantly walked through. The door was closed behind her. I told this kind man what had been happening and what Robert was intending to do and he promised to go straight back to his office and place a 'Section F' on the house. That would prevent Robert from selling it. He would also take steps to make the girls Wards of Court, a temporary arrangement that would prevent them from being taken anywhere without my say so. Then the revelation! He said, that contrary to what I had been told, to what I had been made to understand, the unit could not keep me there against my will.

*I could go?*
*Go Home?*

I went back to my room and said nothing to anyone. Although I was exhausted and scared. Although I wasn't sure how, I knew that I would now leave this awful place, with or without the blessing of the doctors and nurses who were doing what was 'best' for me. I also knew I could wait one more day. I was very tired and needed all of my strength to do what I had wanted to do for months.

The following day, the twenty-second of July 1977, I refused my medication in the morning and when the nurses change over happened, I ran along the corridor and used the pay-phone. I rang Mary, a close friend I had made since moving into the house near Robert's mother, and asked her to bring some clothes to me and asked if she could collect Melissa from school on the way. After a fraught exchange with Carol, the Matron, who was refusing to open the door for me, I told her what my solicitor had said and she reluctantly agreed. Giving me all of my medication and insisting I didn't just stop any of it, without taking medical advice, she said as though it was news to me; if I did I would suffer withdrawal.

*No really!?!*

I went to get Lucy and her things. This done, Carol reluctantly helped me pack my stuff and wished me all the best. I agreed to sign a discharge form and left my 'prison' and went home.

# Chapter Twenty Two

1977 Jubilee year, I had missed all the celebrations, street parties and everything, but none of that mattered, I had my two little girls and was back home. Where I belonged. Back with my children.

To say my husband was angry is an understatement! He didn't mention the unit, in fact he didn't speak much to me at all. Once again I tried to make this marriage work but it was futile. I had to take the regime of drugs prescribed at the unit because I needed to be capable of at least caring for my daughters. I know it couldn't have been easy for Robert, sex had always been a problem for me and the drugs I was taking had taken away any sexual feeling I might have had. This had been hard on him I know. I was living like a zombie, devoid of feelings or sense of reason. I was taking care of family and my home, as I had before but was in a constant fog, and knew I couldn't continue this way. One day after a row, the only time we had any communication, I became afraid of Robert. He hadn't hit me but pushed me and was so angry, shouting and making threats. I was scared and called the police. My judgement was impaired for sure but I was genuinely afraid. I stayed upstairs and kept the girls in my room.

As we often came upstairs, if Robert had workmates round, discussing projects, the children just thought that was why.

When the police arrived, I was listening through the part open door. "I am sorry Officer," said my now very calm and controlled husband. "My wife has been in a Psychiatric unit and is still not right," he continued. "If you want you can check with our doctor." I heard one of the police officers, offer his sympathy and they left. I was mortified, they believed him! Robert told the officers that I was mentally sick and they left! That was a turning point for me. I knew on that day that I had to take control of my life. I had to get off these evil pills and live again.

I don't know how I did it but I began to cut down. I was still taking quite a lot of the pills but I found if I stayed busy, thought of other things, I was sort of okay. Not okay really, but sort of. I began to see things more clearly and could focus a bit better. Mary helped me a great deal and offered to look after the children, so that I could take a little job. I became a Teaching Assistant in a local school and loved it. Cutting down a bit more, although I was still taking more than I thought was okay, I managed. I often took an extra one in the morning as suggested by my GP if I was nervous.

The doctor I was seeing now was a Dr Roberts, a new man in the medical practice. I had gone to see him shortly after I had begun to cut down. This surgery was at the end of our street, again a large Victorian house. When I made the appointment, I asked for the new GP, thinking that he might not agree with these drugs and help me stop taking them. Also he wouldn't know me. I hoped that he might actually listen to me and help me come off them. When I walked in, the first thing I noticed in this warm bright consulting room, was that this new doctor was actually sat looking at me and smiling. I was encouraged straight away.

"I have been in the Wessex Unit," I said, hoping he knew of it. "I am on a lot of medication and I really want to stop everything." I watched this fair haired young doctor, he was still smiling and leaning forward.

"Yes Cassie, I have read your notes," he looked down at my 'folder' on his desk, "and I agree, you are taking a lot of tablets, but you can't just stop them. "

*I know that.*

*I have tried.*

I wanted to shout but didn't. "You will have to withdraw by taking another kind of drug and when the time is right you will be able to come off these with no withdrawal."

*What no 'you will always be on something'!*

*You can't do without them' and he had read my notes!*

Well this was encouraging. I told him I had begun to cut down but he said I was to try something else. He prescribed new pills, Ativan and told me that they were safe and when I was able to do without them, there would be no problem coming off, no withdrawal horrors. I was so happy. Soon I would be taking nothing. How good was that! After thanking this young medic, I left the surgery feeling more optimistic than I had for years. I knew that I had to stay on the new tablets for a little while, until I felt able to do without them. So take them I did.

After a few months in the teaching assistant post, I was offered a chance to train as a teacher The headmistress said she had seen how good I was at explaining to the children how to do things and how well I got on with them. Apparently there was a new way into teaching and that would allow me to go to a day college and train. But Robert wouldn't hear of it, because while I was training, I would have no income. So once again, money was more important than me or my needs. Whatever my husband said was how it was or would be. He was the boss I had no say in anything. It was at this point, when I was trying to fight my way back to normality, that I realised our marriage was virtually over.

I became very ill during this time and was diagnosed with an ovarian cyst. I had been bleeding very heavily but had tried to ignore it. I thought it might be the tablets but eventually, I was so ill that Mary called a doctor. I had been too ill to move about and the GP made arrangements for me to go into the local hospital for a hysterectomy. This meant I would be out of action for six months and this didn't go down well with my husband. But there was no choice.

While I was in having this operation, all medication was stopped. I became agitated and terrified, shaking uncontrollably and feeling light-headed. The night before it was to take place I was running up and down the corridor and wanted to discharge myself but the doctor, thinking it was just pre operation nerves, gave me an injection and I fell asleep.

The operation went okay but there had been an accident in theatre and the surgeon had perforated my bladder. I became very sick and lost a lot of weight. Women older than me, who had come in the same day for the surgery, were up and about while I was still too weak to get out of bed.

I don't know if the huge amounts of medication I had taken over the years, was documented in my notes. But one morning I was to realise just how I was seen by the staff on the gynae ward and anyone who visited me. The years of medication and the trauma of the operation had taken their toll on me. I had been too weak to stand unaided, until that day. Two nurses were trying to help me walk down the centre of the ward. It was quite a big room, long, with beds on both sides and a nurse's station, behind glass, in the middle of the left hand side. With a nurse each side, holding both of my arms, I was pleased to be out of bed. As they helped me slowly walk towards the bottom of the ward, I became dizzy and so they turned me round gently and that's when I saw it. That was when I saw this horrible, gaunt and terrified white face, looking out at me from the nurse's station. The face that I saw, shocked me "Oh that poor lady," I cried. "She must be so ill, what's wrong with her?" I looked at the nurse to my right who was looking at the floor. I turned to the other nurse who looked away. Then it dawned on me. Each bed in this all female ward had a bed table with a pop up mirror in the centre. My mirror was missing and even though I had asked for a table complete with mirror, it hadn't materialised. Now I knew why. The deathly looking face that looked back at me from the nurse's station was my reflection. That gaunt, anxious sick looking woman was me.

I fell to the floor. I don't remember much more about this until I awoke in my hospital bed and the doctor was there. I was scared and agitated, still shocked at seeing how ill I looked. "Good to see you back," the consultant said. He had been so good to me since the operation, coming in everyday to see me, he apologised over and over about the damage to my bladder but I knew it had been an accident. All I was concerned about was getting home to my girls.

"I have prescribed some medication to help you calm down," he wasn't patronising, just stating facts. He was looking at my notes. "I see you suffer from your nerves," he said, "I see you have taken quite a lot of tranquilisers and sedatives over the years and they are taking their toll on your body."

*I know that!*

*I know they are and I want to stop!*

Mr Tyrrel, was the senior Gynaecologist at the hospital, he was very tall with a dark moustache and little hair, and always wore a suit. A kindly man but I had dealt with 'kindly men' before. "What is the medication?" I asked, wanting so much to hear it was something new that wasn't addictive. "I would rather not take anything". He looked at me and smiled, "You won't be able to get well and be able to go home to look after your family if you don't stop the anxiety you showed this morning."

I was shocked at his words but so weak I'm not sure I showed it. Of course I was anxious! I had just seen how the world was seeing me! How the nurses and doctors were seeing me. But most of all, I was realising the horror, that the zombie looking woman, who I had felt so much sympathy for, was me. That this was what my precious children saw when they visited.

*How horrible.*

*How scary.*

*How wrong.*

No wonder Melissa sat as far away from me as she could. Wouldn't take her coat off and didn't kiss me hello or goodbye. How scared she must have felt. Lucy being younger was fine, more interested in all the tubes and drips than in how I looked. But the reality was shocking and that is why I fainted.

*Anxious?*

*Yes I was anxious!*

I tried to say no to the medication, he wanted to put me back onto the regime I was on before I had the operation. If I refused, he offered to let me see a psychiatrist and see what he said. I had had enough of that kind of doctor, in the unit, and I was physically worn out from the surgery and the shock of the happenings of that morning. So back on the pills I went, just to be able to recover enough to go home to my family. The sister of the ward asked Robert to come in and see her before I was discharged. He did this and then came and took me home. Before he had fetched the car, the ward Sister told me she had asked him to stay home and take care of me, for a few days at least but she said she knew he didn't intend to do this. She was right. Even though I asked him to stay with me, he refused.

I had gone down from seven stone to five and a half stone and came home in a wheelchair. Without Mary I wouldn't have survived all of this. She helped me with the children, with cooking and cleaning and all of this, while holding down a job herself. I did have a home help as well and I hope that lessened the work a bit.

Before I had the operation, I had bought a puppy, a tiny mixed breed that was adorable. He was so tiny he sat in the palm of my hand when I first saw him. He was creamy coloured and had black speckly bits on his head and ears so we called him Pepper. While I was in hospital, another friend, who had this pup's sister looked after him for me. I couldn't wait to have him home. I knew this couldn't happen straight away but it was something I looked forward to.

I had made up with Mum enough to ring her and so speak to my Dad now and then and so I rang to tell her how things had gone. Mary was there when I rang and I told Mum how good she had been. "Oh I do wish I could be there to look after you" she said but I knew her playacting too well now, sounding like the caring mother, I wasn't fooled anymore. "Tell Mary I would come if I could but am not well myself." She wasn't ill, I knew that. I had given up at this point of her ever really caring, but talking to her meant I could chat to my dad again and this felt good.

Shortly after my stay in hospital, my marriage to Robert went further downhill. It was now affecting the girls and I knew we had to part. We spilt up three times but his dad was dying and so I kept taking him back. I did try, I tried to accept that this is how it was but the atmosphere was bad for the girls and I think for Robert. We had to part. He couldn't accept that our marriage was over. He said he still loved me Looking back I suppose he had never shown it, not in the way someone who loves you shows their love. He was cold and unemotional around me and my eldest daughter. When I had been in the family unit, to help mend our marriage and come off the medication, he was unkind and sometimes quite cruel. So he didn't show it but still told me he loved me. Strange kind of love and now a bit too late. Too much had happened and his feelings toward Melissa hadn't improved. I hardly recognised the man I had met all those years ago and I wondered if he recognised me. But it was no good, if he did, love me I mean, he didn't show it.

I was distraught, another failed marriage. I accepted that the trauma and grief I had suffered, both in childhood and in recent years, had affected my ability to function properly. Add this to the effects of the medication; that was increased every time I became a bit low, I don't think I was capable of functioning at any level as a human being. I wasn't making excuses for myself, I wasn't capable of doing that, I just knew that if life had been different, then I would have been different.

The pills were part of my daily life now, whenever I needed more, I just rang the surgery and they would be written up. I never had to see a doctor, I would ring and a repeat would be left, month after month. It must have been hard on Robert and on my children. My low mood and inability to feel anything, emotion, sadness or joy, must have shown. My head was completely messed up and my life was levelled out like an existence not a life. Yes I managed to look after my children. I never missed an open evening, a parent's evening, sports day and school plays. I played with them, read to them and did all the things mum's did and pretended to be okay. Pretence was back big time. So to a point, I was there for them and enjoyed being their mum but it could have been so much better. *I* could have been so much better. There wasn't a day when I didn't feel shattered. This doesn't take away the part Robert's behaviour played in the breakdown but I am sure all of this together were contributing factors.

My marriage was over and fully dependant on the drugs prescribed by medical men, I embarked on a new path to unhappiness, pain and grief. Another lack of sound judgement was about to lead once again, to my need for love, resulting in another failure.

I stayed in our home and tried to rebuild my life. I was tired all the time and never felt well. I had decided to try and come off the tablets that by now had done their damage. A few weeks after beginning to cut down, I collapsed in the local shopping centre and my GP was called.

I knew I was ill, I knew I couldn't continue this way and through the haze that was withdrawal, I asked him how.

"I have tried to stop the tablets," I cried, "I have cut down from the amount you prescribed and this is what happens, every time I try to come off them, I become so ill." He had arrived at the shop where I had been taken, after fainting in the street and was looking very put out.

"You have been taking huge amounts of Benzodiazepine drugs for years" he said as though it was news to me! "You really need to stop taking them now! Not cut down but stop. Nothing will happen, your body needs you to stop, and that is why you collapsed."

He told me, like I didn't already know, that my body was saying that it had had enough, I had to stop the tablets. This was the man who had told me I would have to take tablets, for the rest of my life. He had prescribed them for me for years without seeing me, now he was saying what I already knew. I had to stop!

*Stop?*

*Did I not tell him what this does to me?*

*How can I just stop?*

I just looked at him. This is what happens when I cut down, how will it not affect me if I just stop? He was saying stop everything and I would be okay, nothing would happen. Even though I knew this wasn't true, even though I had told him that the withdrawal was horrendous and days like this can happen, he was saying, stop everything and I will be fine. I don't know why I thought that this time it would be different, he was the doctor, he said it would be okay and so I believed him. It would be okay, he was telling me it would. He left me there and a lady working in the shop took me home in her car. When I said I would be fine, she left and I was on my own in my confused state of mind.

So for some unknown reason, the following day I did as I had been told; I stopped everything, the day tablets and the night tablets. This was the worst decision I could have made.

Mary came round after work and I explained what my GP had said and told her I had stopped all the pills. She was worried but said she would be there for me.

The first couple of days weren't too bad but the third was horrific. I hadn't slept much but dozed off a little in the early hours of the morning. Melissa and Lucy were staying with Mary to help me over the first few days. They were due back that evening. Then I awoke in a cold sweat, shaking and panicking in a way I had never done before. I couldn't stand, I couldn't talk. My legs wouldn't work and I felt so sick. I didn't feel that I had any control over my body and it seemed I was standing outside of myself watching this happen. I had had this feeling before when I tried to cut out the medication. Somehow this time it was worse. It seemed unreal.

*But this was real.*
*Help me someone!*
*Help!*

But I couldn't call out and if I did, who would hear me? Gradually the shaking eased, I am not sure how long it lasted, time didn't seem to register but eventually the girls came home. I managed to get them some tea and after they had had their bath and gone to bed, I did the same.

That was a mistake. Out of sheer exhaustion I must have drifted off to sleep. The nightmares were terrifying. The walls of my room were closing in on me, there were people trying to grab me and then he was there, the nasty of my childhood. Bill. I could hear screaming and didn't at first realise that the screams were coming from me. I got up and went downstairs, after a glass of water, I felt a little better but wouldn't go upstairs again. This continued for the next couple of days with the panic getting worse and the shaking more violent. I had bouts of vomiting and sometimes found it hard to focus.

Mary came and took the children again for a couple of days and I was so glad they couldn't witness this. My actions were inexplicable. One day I tried to bury myself in the garden. My neighbour saw me and came round and took me indoors. I had been trying to dig a hole with my bare hands, trying to hide from the terrors. On another occasion I cut my head, trying to stop the pain and fear, by banging my head against the wall. One minute I was struck helpless, unable to move and then the next I was running like some kind of wild animal from room to room, screaming. I spent the sixth night of this horrendous time, huddled in our downstairs cloakroom, desperately trying to crawl under the S bend of the toilet, wanting to die.

Finally, with me having lost a stone in weight, Mary, who had spent a great deal of this nightmarish week, when the children were in school, with me, took me back to see Dr Roberts. I looked like death. The surgery wasn't open for patients but as a nurse, my friend was able to persuade the doctor to come in especially to see me. I was shown straight into his room. The blinds were still down as surgery hadn't opened and Dr Roberts was standing just inside of the room.

"What *is* the matter?" he asked, looking a bit annoyed "What is wrong *this* time Mrs Johns?" I could hardly speak, it had taken every ounce of my strength and my courage to leave my house let alone go into his surgery. Mary told him what kind of things were happening and asked for help with these horrendous symptoms. He said he needed to speak with me on my own and she went out into the waiting room. I think I was shocked when he eventually spoke. "There are no withdrawal symptoms from Benzodiazepine drugs. Withdrawal does not make these things happen."

*What was he saying?*

*I know they were happening, they were happening to me!*

Then it dawned on me, he didn't believe a thing I was saying. He went on to tell me that I was inadequate and that it was all in my mind. He gave me two alternatives. Pull myself together, or keep taking the tablets.

*How dare he!*

*I've been to hell and back!*

*How dare he!*

Although I was angry beyond words, I felt demolished. His reaction broke me, any little strength

I had, vanished at these words. I made a decision, if what this man in whom I had put my trust said, was true, then I must be going mad. If I had imagined these things happening and it was all in my mind, then I couldn't go on. He offered me nothing, no help, no advice, nothing. Just gave me more of the pills he had prescribed and I was dismissed.

I wasn't thinking clearly, if I had been, I would have accepted that Mary had been there, watching my terror, my panic and fear, so it wasn't 'in my head' as he had said. But I wasn't thinking clearly and I couldn't take any more. I know some it is was down to me, that I hadn't been strong enough to fight back, but the cruelty, the abuse, the failures, had all affected me, I knew that. It was me who had taken the pills although they had been prescribed and said to be safe, I had taken them and so that part was down to me. I had gone to see him that day for help. What he told me stunned and destroyed me. I couldn't take anymore. I was no good to anyone like this and I couldn't go on. My head felt like it was exploding. Perhaps I should finish it all.

What happened next is a blur. Melissa and Lucy were staying with friends, someone's birthday party and they were having a sleepover. Mary had to go home and said she would try and come back that evening. I must have seemed okay because she left. Suddenly calm overcame the pounding in my head. I took the tablets that the doctor had given me and began by taking the amount he had prescribed. If the only way to stop this horror was to go back on the pills, then perhaps that was what I was doing. I'm not sure. I don't think I was going take more than I should take, but I'm not sure. I began to get a bit drowsy and lay down on the sofa in my sitting room when Mary appeared at the door. I could tell by the expression on her face that she was scared.

"What have you done Cassie?" she cried, "how many have you taken?" She ran to the hallway where she rang the ambulance service. When it arrived, the ambulance staff were friends whom she knew from her nursing job and were very understanding. They checked I was okay and gave me something to drink, I hadn't taken too many and then they left. I'm not sure about the next few hours, can't really recall what happened. I didn't feel ashamed, guilty or anything, I was numb and exhausted. Did I mean to overdose? I don't know. Mary said she thought I was reaching out for help. I don't know if that was true either. Yes help was what I needed but my doctor wasn't going to help, so back on the pills I went.

# Chapter Twenty Three

The next few months were hard and I found it difficult to think straight because of the medication. After the collapse in the shopping centre and the days that followed, I felt I had no choice but to continue taking the tablets. They became part of my routine, part of my day. Part of my life and who I was or had become. The last thing I checked every-time I left the house, was that my medication was in my bag. Not my purse, or my mirror, but my pills. They were my lifeline, my sanity.

All the time I took them, especially the little night time ones, Soneryl I think they were called, the nightmares didn't come and in the day, being on the medication had stopped the flashbacks of the abuse, so life felt better. I was resigned to this now. Just accepted that it was just the way it had to be. Eventually things became a little clearer, things settled down and I decided to look for a new job. I needed it to be during school time, although Mary would look after the girls if I had to work when they were home. She worked nights and could manage to sleep during the school day.

I managed to get a job in an accountants and enjoyed this work. The people were friendly and I suppose, with them not knowing my past, they treated me as one of them. Normal. That was good. As I felt better, I tried once more to cut down on the drugs, just a little less everyday but the same things happened as they had every time before. The panic, shaking and sweating. One day I couldn't get to work, the nightmares had been horrendous and I couldn't see straight. I knew this couldn't go on or I would lose my job. I went back to see Dr Roberts.

As I walked in to his consulting room, I could see by the expression on the health professional's face, that he was annoyed. He was in a different room, light and airy and was sat at the desk, just looking at me. "Sit down," he said brusquely. "What is the matter this time?" he almost shouted.

*What is it with medics?*
*Either annoyed or cross.*
*I am here for help!*

I was shaking too much to talk at first. Mary was not able to come with me so I had to try and tell him why I was there.

"I have tried to stop these pills but the same things are happening again. I know you said they can't but they….." He waved his hand at me to stop talking. "It has nothing to do with the pills," he said really fed up now and didn't try and hide this feeling, "it is you Mrs John, it is you who can't cope without them." He began to write on the prescription pad on the desk in front of him. No help, no talking about things, just another prescription.

*How were more pills going to help?*
*How does that help make things better?*

"I don't want more pills, I want to come off everything," I cried. "I don't want to take them, every time I try and stop, this happens!"

"Then don't try and stop," he said sounding at the end of his tether now, "I am putting you back onto Valium during the day and one Ativan and continue to take the sleepers, Soneryl at night. You need these Cassie," he said using my first name I suppose to sound more caring. "You will always need to take something, in order to cope with your life."

*Cope?*

*I coped for years without anything.*

*This' anything' has just made things worse!*

I was almost in tears now, shaking badly and feeling sick. He must have noticed how I felt about what he just said and followed it, with what I think he felt would help.

"Cassie, if you are ever in a position to stop these medications then nothing will happen. It will be easy, just stop."

*You haven't listened to me!*

*You haven't heard or believed me.*

*JUST STOP DOESN'T WORK!!!*

I thought all these things. I wanted to shout them at him but didn't have the strength or courage. He had seen me when I tried to stop. He knew! But he said it was just me. It seemed again, that I had no choice. I needed to be able to function to look after my children and hold down a job. I stood up, looked at him, took the prescription and left the surgery.

*Off to the chemist then Cassie.*

*So off I went.*

Mary had become a good friend to me, friend; sister and substitute mother. I had told her most things: how I lost Jack and my other baby boy; how Mum treated me; and how unloved I had felt as a child. But I had never told her of the abuse. I couldn't tell her because I was afraid she wouldn't believe me. My past had made me feel bad, dirty, so I couldn't tell. I had told only one person, Mum and she didn't believe me, so I didn't take the risk.

I needed to be loved, I knew that Mary fulfilled most of this need but she had her own family and I was increasingly guilty about the time she devoted to me. I missed being loved for myself, just for me as others were. Perhaps I was being selfish to want more, but I did. If only I hadn't been in such a rush, if I had waited, I wouldn't have fallen for the first man who showed me the affection I craved.

John was a junior partner in the firm I was working in and had kissed me at the firm's Christmas dance. He was handsome and well thought of and I was swept off my feet. We got engaged and married within a few months but the fairy-tale romance became a nightmare of the waking kind.

One evening, soon after our wedding I was out with Mary and her friends at a local pub. Here I found out, that all the time I was planning our wedding, John was still married. When I confronted him, he was furious. He denied it all and said that whoever told me was wrong. I explained that it had been his brother-in-law who had recognised me in the pub and scathingly accused me of ruining his sister's life. He went on to say that his sister, John's wife at that time, had suffered a breakdown because of this.

We were upstairs in our bedroom, I stood by the window that looked out over the park and John was in front of me.

"How could you do this?" I cried. "You told me you and your former wife were still friends and that you had been apart for a few years." I wasn't ready for what happened next, I didn't see it coming but I felt it. John's anger had left me falling to the floor as a result of his blow to my head. Of course he was sorry the next day, and I so badly didn't want another marriage to fail that

I forgave him when he promised it would never happen again. But it did.

Life continued and I was afraid to bring the subject up again.

The worst part of this relationship was the sexual side. I was managing to have sex, sometimes it was almost bearable but believing John loved me, I tried very hard and it was not as traumatic as it had been in the past. There were times though, when he was physically and sexually violent and I hated it. One evening, after he had promised he would never hit me again, we were dressing for a party and he ordered me to undress. He didn't ask but ordered me. Alarm bells began to ring in my head.

*Not again.*

*Please not again.*

I was almost ready to go out and I refused. He became very heated and ordered me to strip in front of him. I was feeling scared, not only because a few days before this, he had hit me but because his voice sounded like a ghost from my past. A past I never wanted to go back to.

*"Take your clothes off," he ordered, I began to cry. I had been trying to teach myself to switch off from my abuse or rather to what was happening but it wasn't working. "Get them off!" he ordered again, and I obeyed because there was nothing else I could do. Slowly I unbuttoned my school cardigan and shirt, pulled my vest over my head, then sat down on the edge of the bed to remove my socks and shoes. All the time Bill was staring at me, touching himself and making groaning noises in his throat.*

*"Lovely," he leered, "You're lovely and you're all mine." I couldn't bring myself to take off my panties, but Bill came over and ripped them off then pushed me back on the bed, forcing my legs apart. "Oh I love you. You know that don't you? I've missed our games I know you must have missed them too, haven't you?" Before I could answer, there was this sudden horrendous pain*

*again. Pain like I had never felt in my young life. I was trying to scream but nothing came out of my mouth. What had I done to deserve this?*

I was back there, in the nasty that had been Bill, back in my childhood of fear and sexual abuse.

My refusal had made John even more angry but also excited. I had seen this before in my childhood and I was scared. Suddenly he rushed at me, tore off my clothes and raped me. As if that wasn't enough, all the time he was abusing me he was hitting me and I was terrified. When it was over, he casually he got up and left the room.

I couldn't cry, again, what use would tears have been. I was that scared brutalised child again and felt as broken as I had back then. The submissive terrified Cassie was back.

These incidents happened often after this, I could usually see them coming so learned to pretend I was enjoying it, then the sex wasn't so brutal. But on some occasions, it was more than brutal, resulting in his punching me and sexually brutalising me. He was clever though, after the first time, he made sure he never marked me where it could be seen. Once again, sex became nasty and frightening. It was like revisiting my past. To enable me to cope, I was switching off to what was happening. I was exhausted at this point, I had been taking more medication to handle the situation and was shattered. Life with John became scary.

I very quickly learned to read the signs. I knew when he would behave in this way, he would come home and lock the door.

He had lied to me, betrayed me and eventually physically and sexually assaulted me. He possibly would never have stopped and I wouldn't have had the strength to stop this, if my little girls hadn't witnessed one assault. I knew it couldn't go on when I realised that this was how it would be. The children seeing him hurting me, had brought me to my senses. I was having to increase the medication to be able to function and care for my daughters. After a struggle that left me with hand marks around my neck, I threatened to call the police and also tell his boss if he didn't leave the house for good. I ended this marriage and found myself on my own again.

The positive thing that came out of this relationship was that I suddenly realised that the medication was affecting my judgement and my sense of reason. I had lurched from one mistake to another and it had to stop. There must have been signs of his behaviour, before we married but for some reason I didn't see them. I knew he was married when I started in the firm, I did ask him if he was and he insisted that he was living apart from his wife and they were in the middle of a divorce, something they both wanted. I believed him.

*Why did I believe him?*

The way my mind was at this time, I wasn't thinking straight. All the signs were there as clear as day but I hadn't heeded them. I was desperate to be loved, desperate to be wanted and to make a home for my children. John promised all of that but he had lied. All my life people had lied to me, hurt me betrayed me and now this. Why did I think he would be different?

I had to get my life together but didn't know where to start. I vowed that John would be my last mistake. Life had to change, I had to change. I had to take responsibility for what happened to me and my girls. I had to stop these tablets that I was beginning to believe, had changed something in me and allowed me to be treated the way he had treated me. All the doctors I had ever had, told me I would need the medication for the rest of my life and I believed them.

*But did I?*

*Need them I mean?*

I wasn't sure of that, I wanted to be drug free and prove them all wrong but was desperately scared I wouldn't be able to do it.

# Chapter Twenty Four

A few days after John left, I watched a TV programme that would change my life. *That's Life*, presented by Esther Rantzen was about current affairs and was, at the time, a bit controversial. I couldn't believe what I was seeing in the episode I was watching. At this point it was in the early 1980s and the theme was about dependency on GP prescribed medication. Some of the pills they mentioned were the ones I was either on now or had been on. The programme showed people who were suffering horrendous withdrawal from these pills after taking them only for five or six years! I had been taking them for twenty years or more! Many had been getting these drugs, on repeat prescription without regular check-ups from their GP. They talked of living in a daze, in a shadowy world where things seemed unreal, a foggy world.

Fog, my fog, others felt this way?

*This was me!*

*Welcome to my world!*

*I wasn't alone!*

It was like the sun had suddenly come out, like all the lights in the world were suddenly turned on! Like there was hope, a reason for all the horrors I had been through while trying to quit. I wanted to jump up and down and shout, 'Thank goodness. It's true, it's real. I do go to hell and back when I stop!'

No wonder I found it hard to come off them. Some of the patients on this programme told of all the symptoms I had whenever I tried to break free from these drugs.

*I knew this!*

*I knew withdrawal was real.*

*Why didn't anyone believe me?*

Now they would! This was the wake-up call I needed. Now I knew it was the pills. The fog I experienced, the fog that was constantly in my head, was because of these pills! The feeling that my head was full of cotton-wool was all down to the drugs I was told, back when I was fifteen, and were for my dreadful headaches. At that time, my life was so full of fear, pain and horror, the pains in my head were leaving me unable to function properly. I had gone to see my doctor for help with these headaches and that lead to where I was now, having been on this medication for more than twenty-four years. Not pain killers but antidepressants!

I was dependent on these drugs. I realised that for sure, seeing the programme on TV. They had been affecting my sense of judgement and reason. I had always tried to come off them but my GP had always told me I would need them for the rest of my life as I wasn't a 'coper'. Suffering the horrors of withdrawal when I tried to stop taking them, I was left believing, that if as the GP said, there was no such thing as withdrawal, then it was all in my head, that it must just be me and that I must just need this medication to function.

But now I knew the truth. Here was an actual programme telling the world of this horrible dependency; that left people living in the fog that is

Benzodiazepine inflicted. While sometimes they were able to cope, these drugs had left them unable to think straight and left their judgement impaired. It left some submissive and unable to stand up to whatever life threw at them. Some also said how ill they felt, all the time, every day. I couldn't believe what I was hearing and seeing. Some of the patients could have been me. The realisation that I had been right, that I didn't need to be like this was overwhelming. Was this why my life was full of disasters and inadequacies? It wasn't just me? Perhaps I wasn't solely responsible for my failed marriages, wrong decisions and bad choices. I didn't know that for sure but I did know, that I had to come off these poisonous drugs and find out who I really was.

I watched the programme with both horror and excitement. At times I must have been grinning like a Cheshire cat! So happy to know there was a reason, a reason for the symptoms I had suffered, on and off for more years than I wanted to accept. This could be the way forward for me, the way back for the Cassie I hoped was still there, beyond the medication. It had to be. At the end of the programme they asked people to take part in a survey and I sent for the pack straight away. I was both excited and optimistic. This could be it! My time to break free! For the next few days I watched for the postman impatient for this new chapter of my life with support I knew was there.

When it arrived, I tore open the big fat envelope that was hopefully to help me get my life back. The pack contained information on Benzodiazepine medication and listed all the drugs I had taken over the quarter of a century until now. There was a survey and some leaflets on how to withdraw safely. The whole pack was very informative and encouraging.

It also suggested that you inform your GP before commencing on the program. Inform my GP? That wasn't something I looked forward to. I did wonder if I could do this without having to tell him, as he might try and talk me out of it. After all hadn't he made it clear that I needed this medication to be able to function? Hadn't he told me that withdrawal from these 'safe 'drugs couldn't happen? Well now I knew different, the pills could have caused a lot of my symptoms, withdrawal did happen, this pack and Esther's programme told me that!

I suddenly felt very strong. He couldn't argue with the facts, these were now, in front of me in black and white! I read everything and was more determined than ever that I would break free and regain my life.

When I rang for an appointment I was told Dr Roberts was away but I could see the locum. I made the appointment and the next day, armed with the literature I made my way to the surgery. Feeling very nervous but determined, I walked into the consulting room.

Nothing had changed but the new face in front me was actually facing towards me. Encouraged by this, the fact that this doctor was looking at me, I began to tell him about the programme. I don't know what he saw when he looked at me. I was very thin and a bit gaunt looking. I think the medication had made my appetite almost non-existent and with the panic attacks and terror I felt at times, I seemed to have a permanent scared look on my face. I took a deep breath and began speaking. "I watched this programme yesterday, *That's Life*, and it was about tranquiliser addiction." Nothing. He didn't speak so I went on, "The drugs mentioned were all the ones I have been on for more than twenty years." I could hear my voice rising.

*Stay calm Cassie I told myself.*
*Don't let him think you are stressed.*
*Stay calm.*

"I couldn't believe it at first," I continued, "seeing all those patients feeling just how I feel." He held my gaze, I wasn't used to this so I started to look away. "This is my last chance doctor," I said, not remembering his name. "I have to come off everything!" By this time I was shaking.

He looked at me for a while and then sat back in his chair. "I am not sure you can do this Cassie, is it okay if I call you Cassie?"

*It's my name*

*Why should I mind?*

*At least you are acknowledging me, the person in front of you.*

I nodded, unable to speak. I was so scared he would just offer me more pills, not any kind of support or help. He went on, "It will be very difficult to stop. I have read your notes and you are taking large doses of medication and have done for quite some time. The withdrawal symptoms from this kind of medication can be very severe."

*I know!*

*He is telling me like I don't know.*

*I know!*

What was amazing and shocking to me, was, this doctor whose name I couldn't remember, was telling me 'how hard this will be'. I knew that, I had tried and tried! But he was telling me he knows! He is acknowledging the facts about withdrawal and the dependency!

If he knows, should the other doctors who had given me these drugs not have known?! Letting me have these drugs on repeat prescriptions for years and years and making me believe that there was no problem with them, or coming off them,! Did they all know? I'm not sure how this made me feel. Angry? Yes. Shocked? Yes but most of all betrayed. Again. My young life had been stolen from me by the horrendous sexual abuse and cruelty from the people who were my 'parents'. My young adult life had been affected by my own inability to cope with this legacy. All of that had led me to who I was now. Controlled by a dependency on Benzodiazepine drugs, unbeknown to me, that a GP had originally given me for headaches. Held hostage by the effects of this medication and having no help to break free. For years on and off, I had suffered withdrawal symptoms every time I had tried to stop these pills and each time, told there was no such thing as withdrawal. Now, this young fair haired doctor, was sat in the chair that Dr Roberts previously sat in, when he discounted with ease, my fears of withdrawal. This new doctor was telling me that coming off this medication can be very hard and the things I knew could happened, were real. Yes, I was angry now. I had been told I couldn't cope without the drugs.

As a child I had been vulnerable, scared and alone. I must have been stronger than I thought because *I survived*. As an adult up to this point, I had manage to keep house, hold down jobs and look after my daughters, all while on this harmful medication. I wondered what I would be like minus the drugs. I had to find out. If I could survive the horrors that were my childhood, I could suffer anything that coming off Benzodiazepines could throw at me.

I stood up and looked into the eyes of the man sat in front of me. "I am going to come off everything doctor," I said, sounding quite strong I thought. "I would like to have you help me but I will come off with or without your help."

I went to walk away but before I had reached the door, he spoke. "It will be very hard," he said, again, as if this was news to me, "I am not sure you will succeed but I could see you at regular appointments if you think this will help. Then if you need to go back on to them, I will be here to help you."

*Go back onto them!*
*Did he really say that?*
*Did he not hear my determination, doesn't he believe me?*

I will succeed, I will get off everything and never 'go back on them'. I said this in my head, I wasn't strong enough to voice it out loud yet. I thanked him, I think and made for the door. I left the surgery and went home. I felt scared and strong at the same time. I knew how hard this would be. I knew I would struggle but I had to do this. I had to be drug free for the first time in my adult life. I knew that and I also knew, that whatever it took, I would do it. The strong Cassie was there, behind me spurring me on. I needed to get to know who she really was and I would!

# Chapter Twenty Five

After taking Benzodiazepine drugs for all this time, I began to cut down following the advice from *That's Life*. I was taking huge doses at this time, 40 mg daily of Valium, 20 mg of Ativan twice a day and Nitrazepam at night. I decided to cut down on the Valium first.

I had sat Lucy and Melissa down after my doctor's visit and told them what was happening. I think they understood. Melissa never said very much, especially when she was worried, but Lucy wanted to know so much more. "Is it like taking a tablet for headaches?" she asked inquisitively. I wanted to shout 'Yes', exactly like that. I looked at my beautiful daughters and prayed that this would not affect them. I hoped God was listening at last.

If nothing else was a success in my eyes, my children were. They were beautiful. Melissa was now almost fourteen so not really a child. She had short blonde hair styled in a modern fashion and vivid blue eyes, and Lucy who was almost ten at this time, had dark long hair and her eyes were pools of chocolate brown. I was so lucky to have been blessed with them and loved them both to distraction. Even when life was very hard, my love and care for my girls never faltered.

I went on to explain. "I did used to get headaches Lucy, when I was younger and the doctor gave me these pills when I first saw him. When I was fifteen years old I wasn't coping very well at school and the headaches were really bad." I was watching my children very closely, I didn't want to scare them but they knew things weren't right and I hoped they understood. "I still get the headaches but because of things that happened to me as a child and later in my life, I sometimes feel scared and can't relax or sleep. Sometimes I find life hard and feel very sad." What else could I tell them, I didn't want to go into the horrors of my early life, I didn't want them to know about any of that, not now, not yet. Not ever.

Bringing children up, holding down a job and keeping the home and family together was hard and sometimes I took these pills to help me cope with the fears and anxieties that my past visited upon me. But I didn't want to burden them with all of that. There wasn't any need to go into it any more than that. I hoped they would understand. I had always been honest with my girls and wasn't about to change that now. Melissa looked at me and had tears in her eyes. "Is this sometimes when you think of Jack?" she asked in a very quiet voice. "I know that makes you sad. Do you take tablets to forget him?"

*Forget him?*

*I will never forget him.*

*Has my eldest never forgotten her little brother?*

I moved over to her side and put my arms around them both. "Yes, losing Jack is one of the things I haven't dealt with," I said honestly, "Sometimes it hurts so bad and I still can't cry." Memories came flooding back, memories of my baby boy being driven off in a car, driven far away and taken to live with someone else. Oh I wished I could cry now. Cry as Melissa was doing as I cuddled her into my arms. "Don't worry Mum," said Lucy, forever the upbeat one, "we will look after you won't we Melissa?" My eldest daughter nodded and began to dry her tears.

We sat for a while and talked about the things that might happen and they both offered to help me more around the house. I hoped with all of my heart that I could do this. The dependency that I was sure was mostly responsible for my lurching from one mistake to another had to end. With them knowing and on my side, I was determined that I would make sure it did. I saw this as my last chance.

Little notes appeared, on the fridge, in the bathroom. 'You can do it Mum' or 'We love you Mum'. Words that meant the world to me and it felt as though my children were always at my side, encouraging me to beat this evil that was the medication.

As the drugs were reduced I suffered shaking fits and cramps in my legs and arms. I began to feel very weak, couldn't eat anything because nausea was my constant companion. I tried to keep busy, tried not to think about how I felt but it was so strong, the pain and fear became all consuming. One evening, after about a week, I suddenly became terrified. I don't know what of but I couldn't get rid of the feeling of abject terror. I began running from room to room, not sure what I was running from. My skin became clammy and sticky and I felt so ill that I rang my friend Mary.

"I think I'm going to die!" I exclaimed down the phone, "I can't do this; I must take something!" That was the last thing I really wanted to do but the fear and the physical things that were happening to me, were so awful that I just wanted them to stop. I wanted to stop trying to stop!!

My friend through all of this, came straight round, I had promised not to take anything until she arrived. It was so hard. I even went and got the pills and a glass of water, I wanted at that point to go back to where I had been, taking the pills. I was okay then. That felt safer than how I felt now. I didn't feel like this when I was on something, at least not as bad as this, terrified, scared and alone. I was arguing with myself, telling me, Cassie, that I didn't want to swallow the poison that was Benzodiazepines , that I wanted to be free of them but the pain in my limbs and the terror in my heart, were saying something else.

*Take a pill!*

*Go on take a pill and all of this will stop!*

I almost gave in. Then Mary was there. Strong, capable Mary who always knew what to do, always helped me night or day. My friend.

"You can do this Cassie," she said while holding me, trying to stop my shaking. "You know you can, I know you can, we'll work through it." She held me tightly, comforting and loving me out of this horror. Eventually, the shaking subsided and I began to gain a little control of my body. Encouraged by her strength and feeling safer because she was there, the episode passed and I began to feel better. This was the first of many occasions where I would ring Mary and she would come to my aid. No questions asked, night and day. This was one of many, many panic attacks, of terrible inexplicable bouts of fear and terror.

There were times when I felt bad about ringing my friend or I knew she would be at work. In the pack from *'That's Life'* they gave a phone number, someone at the MIND organisation. There were times I rang them and was answered by one of the team. It always seemed to be the same man, probably wasn't but sounded the same. He would talk me through the panic and it would pass.

A few days into my cutting down, I was trying to hurry things up and broke some tablets into tiny pieces, and just took a very small bit of the Valium. I suddenly became violently sick and giddy. I could see black slimy things crawling out of the walls of my home. The terror became all-consuming and I was convinced these horrible things were real. They had tentacles reaching for me, trying to devour my very soul, trying to engulf my whole body. It was horrific, I was so scared that my entire body began to shake and jerk in rapid movements.

*What's happening to me?*

*Am I going mad?*

*Am I going to die?*

I sent my girls over to a friend and rang Mary. She was out.

*Out?!*

*Gone out?*

*How could she be out, I need her!*

Dependency like any other 'addiction' had made me selfish. Need had made me selfish. I needed Mary and she was out and I was angry with her. But then I suddenly came to a huge realisation. It was the medication I was angry with, not Mary. I was angry that my body needed these pills that I had become dependent on them. I wasn't taking these drugs for kicks or to get high, but I had become as dependent on them as a heroin addict is on heroin. Withdrawal made it impossible for me to do without them, I needed to be able to function as a mum, a woman and a human being. Inadvertently I had become an addict. These were not made up, they were the facts. Well these facts were not going to win! I knew at this point I couldn't and wouldn't fail. I would be drug-free in spite of what GPs had told me over the years. So Mary not being available to me, made me think about what was happening and made me take stock. I had tried to justify my feelings of selfishness so that I didn't suffer guilt. It didn't work.

I managed to get through the night I'm not sure how but the following day I asked the girls' grandmother, Robert's mum, to have them for a couple of days. She was pleased because some of her other grandchildren were staying and they could all be together. We had made our peace, Robert's mum and I, after his dad had died. She was much nicer to me and to my daughters. Maybe losing her husband made her need her family more than before. Maybe feeling so sad and depressed she understood me more, I don't know but I was glad. I was happy that she could have them and that they would be able to see their cousins. It would take my daughters' minds off me for a while.

That evening the panic came back. I knew Mary was at work and as it rose, I began violently shaking once again. I ran from room to room sobbing and shaking. I was so scared, scared to be on my own but not wanting to have anyone near me. Sheer terror ran through my body and my mind was all over the place. My next move is inexplicable. I rang my mother. I hadn't told her about the withdrawal as she had become great friends with John, my ex-husband whom I had divorced on the grounds of cruelty. I never understood this, he had hurt me and she had befriended him. Why I had been surprised I am not sure. She had remained friends with my abuser when I was a child, after I had told her what he had done, so I shouldn't have been shocked. She had always ridiculed my taking tranquilisers and antidepressants, so now, when I was attempting to be rid of this dependency, perhaps I hoped, that little word again, I hoped she would at least support me. Wrong again Cassie!

"So why are you ringing *me*?" she began unkindly. "What do you expect me to do? You started on that road years ago, so what do you expect me to do now?" I thought I could hear her laughing.

*Started on that road?*

*Whose fault is that?*

*How could she be so cruel?*

But in the cold light of day, I knew she could, be that cruel I mean. She had always seemed to enjoy my pain. She had let Bill hurt me, she now had made a friend of John who had hurt me. Why did I think she wouldn't enjoy how I was now, at this point in my life?

*So why, oh why, did I ring her!*

*That little word hope, had let me down again!*

*When would I learn?*

I replaced the receiver, still shaking and sobbing but suddenly more determined. I would do this without her. I had survived my early years with their horrors without her, I would survive and triumph over this. Perhaps it was the extra push I needed to make sure I succeeded in becoming free, from this awful medication that had controlled my life. Perhaps, unknowingly, she had done me a favour.

Just after this phone-call, Mary rang to see how I was. I wanted to scream 'I need you please come round' but instead, I assured her I was coping on my own. I had taken up a great deal of her time and was beginning to realise how hard this must be on her and her family. As I said, dependency and addiction are selfish, I was beginning to see that now, so I reassured her and put the phone down. Eventually, with my newfound strength and determination after speaking with Mum, the terror passed and with it, the nausea and shaking.

The physical problems that were part of the withdrawal, included constipation and indigestion. I took herbal remedies for both but to no avail. I couldn't sleep because of how these made me feel along with the shaking and nausea. Then things got even worse.

I had cut down on the Valium and Nitrazepam, the latter being to help me sleep and as it didn't, I decided to cut them down.

But it was the newest of the pills that I was having the biggest problem with. Ativan, the one I was told wouldn't have the same effect as the others, when I stopped taking them. That was the hardest. As I reduced the dose I was taking, I had complete muscle seizures. My body would go absolutely rigid, my jaw would feel as though it were locking. I was terrified. These symptoms went on for a long while and just when I thought it couldn't get any worse, a new horror hit me. This was one of the worst physical symptoms, a sticky yellow stuff began secreting from my body. My clothes became damp and smelly. A smell I will never forget. I became very hot and shaky and then it would start. It was the most horrible feeling, as though my body were not my own.

I would wash for what seemed like hours after this sticky yucky stuff covered my body. I never felt clean. This brought back all the fear and terror that I felt as a little girl, when I had been sexually abused by the man they called my uncle. When I used to rush to the safety of the bathroom after his assault and scrub my little body until it hurt.

*Then I felt the yucky whitish stuff all over my fingers, making me want to retch. It was horrible and sticky and I supposed it must be 'wee'. Why would he do this to me? I was scared to death and he just didn't care. He pulled a hankie from his pocket and cleaned himself up, then he threw it on my lap. "Wipe your hands off and we'll go home," he said in a cold voice. I wiped my hands and longed to be in the relative safety of home. He dropped me off outside of my house and I ran upstairs to the bathroom and let the water run over my trembling hands. I couldn't make sense of it. I scrubbed and scrubbed my body, trying to rid myself of what had happened.*

273

The only difference now, was that I wasn't that little girl, but a grown woman. But it felt the same and so all the memories and feelings of childhood came flooding back. Flashbacks of the abuse, horrors that the pills have relieved me of. Now, this horrid smelly secretion had brought them back big time. Association was a powerful thing.

In between these times, I was having severe panic attacks and would run from room to room, sobbing and screaming until I was exhausted and would fall asleep on the floor where I fell. Sometimes this would be during the day when Melissa and Lucy were at school. Sometimes they would be there, and would try and comfort me, giving me a little strength to try harder and not give in and take the pills. If I managed to get off to sleep, many times this wouldn't last. But I would awake, terrified and not know why. The walls of the bedroom felt as though they were closing in on me and I was suffocating. I couldn't breathe properly, I didn't think I could go on; I just wanted it to end.

I came so close, so many times, close to going back, taking the horrid drug that sent me to this God awful place. I tried, oh how I tried, to do this on my own but sometimes I needed some help. I rang Mary many times and she would rush round and sit with me. At this time, she would try and hug me but I couldn't handle touch. Her hugs used to help, before the *'nasties'* of my past had revisited in my head.

"Come here Cassie" she would say beckoning to me to go to her and cuddle into her warm body. "Just a hug, you will feel better with me holding you," she said leaning forward. I leaned away. Feel better with being held? No. I didn't want to feel the touch of another person ever again. I couldn't say this to her but I felt it.

"I can't Mary" I said, "I can't let you near me. I'm sorry, I just can't". She was wonderful, she would make me tea, get clean clothes and watch me try and wash away everything that was happening to me. Just as I had as a small child. That was okay. I was okay with that, just watching. She was my friend and understood. She was a nurse so nothing shocked her. Just having her there seemed to calm me a bit.

This sequence of events went on for weeks and weeks, I couldn't eat properly and lost a lot of weight. Melissa would bring raspberries or chocolate to try and tempt me to eat. They were wonderful, my children, amazing. Melissa had taken over the housekeeping, she was fifteen now and doing a childcare course at school. She was very good at the practical things but on my bad days, she wouldn't come into my room.

"Are you okay Mum?" she would call from the door of my bedroom, "I'm off to school now. Lucy will be in soon." We would blow each other a kiss and she would be gone. It was hard for her, she was overwhelmed by what was happening and, I am sure, confused at all the events in our lives. Guilt was huge for me at this time.

Then there was Lucy, my ten year old. She would breeze into my room, leap onto the bed and tell me I looked awful. Diplomacy wasn't a trait she owned. "Are you going to get up today Mum?" she would ask with no subtlety. "You are doing so well, no tablets now or at least only a small amount. I know you can do this." With that she would give me a hug and a kiss. Holding my children was still good, for that I was grateful. They were the only human contact I could bear.

I tried very hard to find some normality. I had by this time, stopped the night time pills and only used a little of the Valium, sometimes last thing at night. This seemed to calm me more than the Nitrazepam. But I didn't seem able to stop the Ativan yet. I was down to a tiny little piece of this blue pill that had now become my new *nasty*. Leaving the house was hard. I would check and then double check that I had a tiny little piece of tablet in my purse. All through the dependency I had made sure I always had my pills, before anything else, I had to make sure my safety net was in place. Extra tablets in the back of my purse. Now, during this horrid time, I had to make sure the little bit of blue tablet was safely tucked away in my purse, in case I needed it. Then I could leave the house. Then I would be *safe*.

The notes were still coming, all over the house 'Almost there Mum' or 'We love you Mum', even ones saying that they believed in me that I didn't need the horrid pills. Everyday these little messages to encourage me to keep going. They really were little stars during this awful time.

Christmas 1983 was one of the worst Christmas's of my life. I had been awake all night. The girls, at my request, were going to their dad's house for a few hours. Not unexpectedly, Robert chose not to take part in their lives. I did try and keep him involved but he had 'moved on' and didn't really want anything much to do with them. But as things had been quite bad, I had asked if he could have them at his house for a little while. He had remarried and was reluctant but agreed.

On this 'joyous' holiday, suddenly, out of nowhere, one of the worst panic attacks I had ever had, began. The terror was rising, the hallucinations were horrible and scary. I could see bodies all over the floor, some covered in blood. Flashbacks of the abuse, memories from which I couldn't escape were rushing through my mind. I began banging my head against the wall of my bedroom trying to knock all the thoughts that were haunting me, out of my mind. I prayed and prayed that someone would come, someone would help me. If I had been offered any pills at that time, I would have bitten off the hand that offered them to me. I just wanted it to stop. I wanted to die, death had to be better than this.

I rang Mary, I suppose it was unforgivable to ring on Christmas Day, she had her own family, but as I said, withdrawal makes you selfish. I rang Mary. There was no hesitation. "I will come round as soon as the girls come back from their dad's place," she said kindly, "we will spend Christmas together, here." At first I was relieved, but as soon as I put the phone down, the shaking got worse, the sickness began and I was terrified out of my life. The horrors had stripped me of any common sense or sense of reality. I looked down, my hand had felt sticky and then I saw blood. I was back there, back to my childhood, looking at my own blood.

*I locked the bathroom door and finally my strength left me and I collapsed onto the floor, my whole body shaking. I ran some water in the bath and started to take my clothes off. It still hurt very badly between my legs and when I pulled my panties down I was horrified to see blood on them. What on earth had happened to me? All I wanted to do was cleanse my body of this horrible experience as soon as possible. What had I ever done to deserve this? Why was I being punished?*

There was no washing this pain away, any more than there had been when I was a little girl. This realisation and the memory made the terror stronger, coming in unbearable waves.

I ran out of my house and began to run down the road and round the corner towards the house where Mary lived. Several people passed me giving me strange looks. I didn't care: I must have looked demented. My head was bleeding from the head banging but I didn't think about that, I ran as fast as I could until a neighbour who had just taken a present to a friend, saw me and stopped me. I pulled away as she touched my arm.

"Are you okay Cassie?" she asked with concern. "Are you sure you should be out like this?" she continued, looking down at my feet. I think it was the puzzled concerned look that stopped me in my tracks. Why was she staring like that?

I was exhausted. I looked down to follow her gaze and saw the reason for her concern. I was still in my slippers. But that was not the worst of it, I was still wearing my dressing gown, I hadn't washed or combed my hair. I must have looked dreadful and totally out of it.

*Are you okay?*
*No I'm not okay.*

I felt shattered and hurting in every part of my body. I looked at her with I suppose, a look of desperation. She put her arm around me and I didn't care. I didn't care what happened next, she could hold me or do anything; I didn't have the energy to care. She took me back to my house which wasn't locked and I crumpled to the floor sobbing. Then she did what any kind neighbour would do, she called my doctor. I couldn't hear the conversation but gathered she wasn't best pleased with the outcome of the call. He told her it would pass, I would be fine, not to worry. He said, if things got worse, tell her to take a tablet, that will calm her down and he ended the call. She was beginning to ask me where I kept my pills, when Mary rang and my neighbour told her what had happened, including the advice for me to take a tablet.

"Please don't give her anything, I mean anything," my friend said, "I will send my husband around to collect Cassie and I will collect Melissa and Lucy from Robert's house, they will spend the rest of the holiday with us." She asked my neighbour if she would stay until Bob had arrived.

But I wearily took myself upstairs, reassuring my neighbour that I would be fine and she left. I had a wash, put on some clothes and when Bob came and collected me we spent the rest of the Christmas, cared for in the safety of Mary's family. I was physically exhausted, the panic had subsided to a point that I had learned to cope with, and the rest of the day was not too bad. At least Melissa and Lucy had Mary's children to be with taking their minds of their Mum.

# Chapter Twenty Six

Over the next few months, the withdrawal took its toll. The nightmares continued, sometimes worse than others. I would awake and find someone screaming.

*Who is that?*

*What's happening?*

Then I would suddenly realise that those awful cries of terror were coming from me. I became afraid to go to bed, sometimes sitting downstairs all night. I wouldn't answer the phone or the door and if Mary hadn't continually called round, I wouldn't have seen anyone apart from my girls. She had a key, ever since the incident when she called the ambulance, when she came round now, she let herself in. I had friends but they had stopped calling, a while ago at my request. I didn't want anyone to see me like this. I was in no fit state to see anyone.

While on the evil pills I was able to function, able to live a sort of normal life. I had these friends and often went to coffee mornings and things at school or the local church. I would model clothes for a local shop, being a size eight or ten, Annie the owner couldn't get anyone else to wear them. Even at that small size they were often much too big for me and I would have to pin them to make them look good. I managed to have a kind of social life and thought that no one knew there was anything wrong. But people were always asking if I was okay, so I suppose I must have looked ill given the amount of medication I was on. I never told them. I never told them about my 'problem' because until very recently, I hadn't thought I had a problem.

Months into the withdrawal, the girls were round a friend's house who had been given a pony for her birthday. On this day, the panic had not been as bad for a few weeks, but for some reason I began to shake and felt really cold and clammy. Then the pain started and it was like no other pain I'd ever had, stomach cramps that left me curled up in an agonised ball on the floor of the kitchen. I wanted to scream but couldn't, wanted to run but couldn't do that either. The terror was horrific, I could hardly breathe and as it reached its crescendo, I passed out.

When I awoke, my hands were hurting and as I looked down I could see that they were bleeding. The nails, that I had managed to keep long, had broken into my palms, I must have been clenching them and that was where the blood was coming from. Some of the broken pieces of nail were still in my skin and some just lying in the blood on my hands. I didn't feel this happening, hadn't felt that pain, only when I awoke from the faint did they hurt. Again I was exhausted and just sat there until I felt a little stronger, then went upstairs to wash the blood away. I was shocked that this could happen and I didn't feel it, but glad that I had been on my own.

Eventually, months later and still only taking a minute amount of medication I was beginning to see things more clearly. Not only that, I could taste and smell, things that I had not been able to do while 'drugged up'. I still couldn't cry, but one day when I was playing with my little dog, Pepper, I laughed out loud at his antics. I was on the floor of the sitting room, in front of the fire. Melissa and Lucy were near the window making some little figures with Fimo or something. I looked up and both my girls were staring at me. I was worried.

*What happened?*
*What did I do?*
*Why were they staring in such a way?*

"What's wrong?" I asked tentatively as they continued to stare.

"You laughed Mum," Lucy said. "You laughed." They both stood still and continued to stare, waiting for my reaction to her words. Lucy looked a bit worried. And then the tears came, not many but at least I cried. Not because I was sad, but because it must have been unusual, my laughing to have had the reaction it did from my daughters. That was why I was crying, shocked at the realisation of how hard this must be on them. Seeing tears they rushed over and hugged me.

"It's okay Mum," said Melissa, "It's good to cry." They both continued to hold me and we were all crying and laughing at the same time.

For many years I hadn't often felt emotions. I hadn't been able to taste food, smell flowers or perfume, become angry or even sad. All the things that normal people do. But as I improved, still taking a small amount of medication, my daughters saw the real me, the Mum I wanted to be and a normal mum, whatever that meant. Not only did I laugh and shed a few tears, again, not many, but I sometimes shouted when things were too loud for my voice to be heard. The girls were mortified.

I hadn't shouted, I never had that much energy. I said I was sorry and we talked about it; they said all of their friend's mum's shouted, it was just a surprise to hear me shout. Nothing touched me so much that I felt the need or had the voice to shout while drugged on the pills. It was like living on straight flat line, no 'ups' and no 'downs'. The fog that was the medication was so dense, nothing could come through. Perhaps Melissa and Lucy were shocked at this 'strong' Mum but if they were, they never showed it, they only had praise, encouragement and love for me.

After a year of drastically reducing my medication, as and when I felt ready, I knew I needed something to focus on. My weight had improved, I was still very thin but food was more important to me these days and so I ate regularly. I was sleeping a bit better I still had flashbacks but they were not as vivid as they had been in the early days. When I slept, the dreams came and sometimes I would awake in a cold sweat, sobbing or crying out. I would get up and go downstairs and sit in my living room and cuddle Pepper and try and remember how far I had come. Then I would creep upstairs and back to bed.

My self-confidence was still at rock bottom and going out on my own was still hard. Mary was wonderful, visiting every day and encouraging me all the time. If I did go out, I still checked that I had my pills. By now I was taking half a little blue Ativan tablet. I would put one half in my purse and then an extra half in my handbag pocket. If I was out later than I meant to be, I would always have my next dose with me. The other bit was my safety tablet, the one I 'might' need.

I decided that as the girls were in school, I would look for a part-time job. My concentration wavered as the days went on and I had serious mood swings but

I still thought I could cope part time. I saw an advert for a 'Girl Friday/Personal Assistant' with a design company. On the morning I had been asked to attend for interview, I took an extra piece of tablet. I really wanted to get through this interview but immediately on taking it, I felt upset. I didn't want to start again. I was doing so well but felt I needed that extra boost. I knew this was wrong or silly and told myself off severely.

*So, every time things are scary, you take a pill!*
*How is that helping?*

My own chatterbox came into play and I vowed not to let that happen again.

I had begun taking more pride in my appearance. My hair was looking much better than it had for years, I gave it a booster rinse with some red dye and I had grown it long again. I put on a long thick skirt, a pretty pink jumper that Mary had given me for Christmas, and a pair of high boots. I then made sure my pills were in my bag and I made my way to the bus stop for my new start. Yes, I was nervous, scared but I knew it was the right time. With a little makeup and a lot of determination I went to the interview.

On arriving at my destination I walked into the small foyer where the company were based and was met by two young men. Nothing smart or formidable about them, they were both casually dressed and that put me at my ease. I went upstairs to their offices and sat in a large low chair in front of the huge desk at which they both sat. That was a bit daunting as I felt so much smaller than them. It was quite a nice room but very untidy. No one spoke and I could feel the fear beginning. I couldn't let this happen, I had to break the silence.

"What exactly does the job entail?" I asked in a quiet voice. "What would you need me to do?"

The first one to speak was a bearded young man who had introduced himself as Christopher. "Well we have been a company now for about five years, just me and Peter," he said gesturing towards the man sat smiling at his side. "We have been to see an accountant who asked for our books, account books and we don't have any."

I continued looking at him waiting for him to go on and to answer my question. Nothing. They both sat there looking at me. I began to get fidgety, I knew panic wasn't far away. I had to say something just to stop this from happening. The panic I mean.

"And you want me to do what???" I said in a bit of a haughty voice, trying to be strong but not quite getting it right.

The second young man hadn't spoken at this point but he leaned forward smiling at me. "Well, we would like you to make up books for the company," he said and sat back in his chair as though that had made everything clear! I wasn't an accountant, or an accounts clerk. Girl Friday the advert said not magician!!

"I can't magic books out of the air," I said trying to smile and so soften my nervous voice. "I have never done any kind of financial job in my life before."

Now it was my time to sit and look at them. Christopher stood up and walked the length of the room, he reached behind a kind of screen and dragged out a huge tea chest. Bringing it over to where we all sat, he placed it before me.

"Look" he said and was pulling out bits of paper. "We have kept everything, every single thing we bought, we kept the receipts for. Even bus tickets and train tickets." He looked so proud. I just stared. I gazed into this large crate and sure enough, all the little pieces of paper were indeed receipts. I didn't know what to say. What was there to say? I wanted to leave the room, say goodbye and go home but their faces were so full of hope, I didn't at that stage have the heart to upset them.

"I really don't think I am who you need. You need someone with financial experience and that's not me." I was going to say an outright 'no' but couldn't. They seemed so optimistic but they only saw this woman sat in front of them doing her *pretend*, if they knew the truth, if they could see through my facade and see how close to panic I was, they wouldn't let me anywhere near their bits of paper or even their office! So, I decided to come clean. Tell them about the dependency, what did I have to lose? Then I could go home and forget all about the tea chest and look for another job.

I went to speak but Peter stood up and came round to the front of the huge desk, perching himself on the edge he said "Would you like to think about it......" looking down at his notebook, "Cassie, is it okay if I call you Cassie?" His voice was warm and calming, a bit like warm, velvety chocolate and I didn't quite know what to say.

"There is something I think you should know," I began, looking straight into the brown eyes of this young director. "I have been taking tranquilisers, prescribed by my doctor for more than twenty-four years and have been trying to come off them for the past year or so." I stopped to take a breath. What I expected them to say I don't know but it didn't matter because they said nothing. "I am at the end now of a hard struggle and sometimes have serious mood swings, panic attacks and agitation." Should I continue? I looked at Peter and felt I needed to explain why I was telling them this darkest secret. "If I took your job, which I am not saying I will, there will be times when I am unwell, times when I might not get to work and times when my mood may be too much for you."

*Why was I telling them this?*
*Did I think it would let me off the hook?*
*That they would say, the job wasn't going to be offered to me?*

I don't know but I had started so I had to finish. "My life has been affected by these pills in a bad way, I have two little girls to look after, a mortgage and everything else, I need to work and want to work but I won't give up my struggle to come off this medication!"

There, I had told them. The first people outside of my immediate family and friends, I had told. Peter stood up and it seemed right I should stand up. I was shaking, but he smiled at me and said to take the night to think about things. He didn't appear shocked or anything, he just smiled that warm smile. I knew they had other people to see so I didn't think they would offer me the job now anyway. I managed to smile back and said goodbye to them both and made my way out of the building.

When I arrived home and was about to ring Mary and tell her how it went, I was shocked to have a phone-call from Christopher, they wanted me to take the job. I hesitated and said I couldn't but again, he insisted that I slept on it and went in to see them the following day. By now I was shaking and feeling a bit unwell. I thought about taking an extra bit of Ativan, the little blue piece I kept for emergencies, as I was beginning to feel panicky.

I had to keep busy, take my mind off medication so I decided to make some cakes for the girls when they arrived home from school. That is something else I had begun to do recently, cook. No shop bought cakes now, just my own. Baking did indeed take my mind off the job and the panic and I decided to go back to the design company the next morning and refuse the job.

The following day, after dressing myself in my 'strong' colours, black and red, I made my way to the bus stop. If I felt especially nervous, these colours gave me confidence, so black and red it was. I had taken my little bit of Ativan as usual, made sure my emergency one was in my purse, and started the journey to the office.

Christopher met me and said that Peter might not be able to make it. I felt a little disappointed, but wasn't sure why. I didn't know these young men, but I was sad that I wouldn't hear that lovely, chocolaty voice that day. The tea chest was still there, next to the low chair in which I had sat yesterday and it was still full of every little piece of paper proof, of anything and everything these men had ever bought since the start of their company.

"We really liked you Cassie," Christopher said as I sat down, this time in the chair the other side of the desk, as he had sat in the low chair. "We think you are just what we are looking for."

I was a bit shaken by this. I so wanted a job but not this job. I thought of the things I could do with a bit more money, then I looked into the tea chest at the offending bits of printed paper and tried to see sense.

"I don't think I am up to this Christopher, as I said, I am having quite a difficult time..." he stopped me. "Peter and I admired your honesty, we would love to be part of your recovery. We can all help each other."

I couldn't quite believe what I was hearing. They wanted to help me? They don't know me. But these two young designers wanted me as part of their team and more importantly, they wanted to help me give the tablets a kick up the butt! Before I could answer, the door opened and in walked the owner of the velvety voice.

"Ah, so you couldn't keep away," he smilingly said, "You will come here and work with us, won't you Cassie?" he looked like a little boy, a child and my heart strings were pulled. I don't quite know how it happened but I said 'yes' and after a coffee or two, I was on the staff with these two wacky and likeable young men.

# Chapter Twenty Seven

It was now about fourteen months since I had begun this journey into a drug free life. I was still in the throes of cutting down the tablets into the smallest pieces possible. I still had terrific mood swings but my concentration was continuing to improve. I put the latter down to being busy at my new job and finding it all consuming, when I was there and it rendered me tired enough to sleep at night. The girls were happy to have a mum who seemed to be enjoying her life again. A mum who joined in with them after school and had lots to talk about now and was happy just to be there.

It seemed these days that the house was full of children, friends of Lucy would pop in all the time and Melissa's friends would come round and we would talk make up and clothes. Lovely times. I still had panic, not serious panic but it would raise its ugly head now and again to remind me of where I had been.

My mood swings were still severe and some days I couldn't talk to anyone outside of my family. Work was going well but Peter and Christopher were never sure to speak to me or not on some days when I must have looked different. I realised this must be hard on them but didn't quite know what I could do to make it easier.

They were both very supportive of my changing moods and made a useful suggestion.

"We think you should wear colour coded badges," Christopher said, looking at me and hoping I wouldn't jump down his throat or make my way to the door, I'm sure. "Actually it was Peter's idea. You could wear 'yellow' on a good day, 'blue' on a not so good day and 'red or black' on a bad day." At first I thought they were joking but when I realised that they weren't, I said I would give it a try and in a Blue Peter kind of moment, the man with the velvety voice said, "And here's one I made earlier." He then produced a yellow badge. I smiled and took it along with the other colours he had in his hand. If I wore yellow or blue things went well, if I wore red or black they kept clear and didn't speak to me, unless I spoke first. Clever.

I had begun to see the funny side of things again, my sense of humour and fun was returning. I had always used humour as a kind of defence, it was good now to laugh at things that didn't touch me before, but most of all I could laugh at myself. With the support of these two young men, I began to get the hang of the business. Somehow, and I really don't know how, the books were done and with the accountant within a few weeks. I was very glad to see the back of them and taught myself how to keep accounts books from then on.

I couldn't have asked for more support in this struggle, I had my daughters at home, Mary my best friend and these wonderfully eccentric young men at my new place of work. Life was getting better every day. I still had panic attacks but was able to fight them because I could now recognise when they were coming. I think, that because I didn't have to hide how I felt now, because everyone in my life knew about the medication, that I was able to handle the panic better.

The worst part of this struggle, apart from the horrendous withdrawal that I had suffered for more than eighteen months, was the letting go of the very last, tiny piece of Ativan. This took months and months. I made sure I had a tiny blue bit in my purse, but on a really good day, I wouldn't take it. Sometimes this was a struggle but I would keep busy, look at the notes that were all around the house telling me I could do this. If I was at work, I would put the appropriate badge on and would shake my head when I first came in. Peter would make me a cup of tea and come and sit with me. We would talk about the future of the company, how far it had come in the past year and talk about our love of our dogs. I had little Pepper and he had a setter, a daft but lovable dog called Rudy. He would often be left in the office with me, if the boys were both out. I think he was supposed to look after me, the dog I mean. No chance. One day I was working at my desk, which was at the front of the upstairs office when I heard Rudy running around and whimpering. I ran out to the stair well above the lower office, to where the sound was coming and saw him cowering in the corner of the top landing. I couldn't see what was wrong so I sat with him, cradling his head on my lap, trying to stop him trembling. Peter came back and found us there.

"I don't know what happened," I said, "He was okay and then suddenly ran out here and this is how I found him."

Peter smiled. "Was there a fly?" he asked. "Did a fly come in through the window?"

*Was this a trick question?*

*A fly?*

I couldn't see one at first but then, I looked up and there it was. A bluebottle on the ceiling. I pointed up and Peter laughed, "You big softie Rudy, it's only an insect." He made a brush to towards the fly, reached up and opened the ceiling window and it flew out. Straight away this big lump of a dog became himself again and walked off into the office as though nothing had happened. So, I think I was looking after him, not the other way around.

Life became better every day. I loved my job and we were getting along with each other so well, me and 'the boys', we became a happy little family. Christopher was funny and a bit of a lad and Peter, well he was Peter. Someone who became very important in my life and someone who played a huge part in me finding the real me, the real Cassie. He enabled me to see that love was actually a thing to be treasured and not feared. Real love that is.

While I was on the medication and before the withdrawal, my house had always been filled with the sound of children, boys and girls who were friends with Melissa and Lucy. It was always a fun time and I loved it all. Some of the girls would talk to me, about things they perhaps couldn't talk to their parents about. This could have been because I was always too willing to listen or it could have been that I was a captive audience. I don't know. But I had begun to miss these times.

For the past year and a bit I had been trying hard to hide what was happening to me, from anyone outside of my family. I often had to ask the girls not to bring anyone home when things were really tough, I never liked doing this but I couldn't let them see me in either panic or fear. After a few weeks, the children stopped coming home with Melissa and Lucy. Now, it was different. Sometimes when I was feeling okay, their friends would be at home with us and normality reigned. Whatever that was supposed to be. All I know is that these times were precious. They would be quiet around me but at least they were there.

One day, a few months later, just before I had let go of the last little piece of blue peril that was my security, I arrived home from work to the sound of children's laughter. I was earlier than usual and my girls didn't see me arrive back. On opening the door, I could see the children playing with some things on the floor and Melissa and her best friend were listening to music. A wonderful sight. Melissa looked up and asked her friends to keep the noise down. I waved my hand and shook my head. "It's okay, make as much noise as you want, it is okay' I said smiling. Suddenly I realised that I was back. Life was good and I was back from being dependent on medication and back from the horrors that were withdrawal. I didn't need the tablets any more, I didn't need the quiet. Cassie was back and it felt good.

It had been the longest eighteen months of my life and had sent me to hell and back many times. Arriving home to a house full of *happy* was wonderful and I had missed it so much.

It was November 1984 and I was close to my thirty-ninth birthday when I awoke one day and reached for my purse. I took out the last tiny bit of Benzodiazepine and walked to the bathroom. Many times throughout my life, the bathroom had been my sanctity, my bolt hole and now it was where I disposed of the last bit of *evil* that I would ever have. It was in my bathroom that I told 'yesterday' goodbye. I dropped this tiny blue reminder of my past, down the loo and flushed the chain. What an amazing feeling that was. I suddenly felt I was living again. I had taken back control of my life, any mistakes I made from that day, wouldn't be made in the fog that had been part of my life for around twenty-five years. I had been to hell and back and survived. All the struggles in the world, all the withdrawal had been worth it. Life would begin today and I intended to live it to the full.

During the time I first began to withdraw from the drugs, I was told to expect panic attacks and nightmares for some time and not to expect everything to be wonderful from the last tablet taken. That it would take time, I still had moments of panic and association is powerful thing. When the feelings rose in my tummy I instantly thought 'a panic attack'. But sometimes it wasn't and when it was I would keep busy, and usually do something physical, like ironing, until the feelings disappeared. It wasn't going to be wonderful from the throwing away of the last tiny piece of evil, I was prepared for this. With that in mind, although I celebrated quietly on my own at home, I planned, that one year after I had last taken any of these tablets I would have a party. Then I would know I was free and life would indeed begin at 40.

And it did!

# A Note From The Author

In 1985, I had my party and I was living a drug free life with Melissa and Lucy, still in the home I had shared with John. I had taken over the mortgage and was still working at the design company. During the time working with Christopher and Peter, life was better than it had been for many years. After the company disbanded, I continued to work with Peter. Our relationship blossomed. I fell in love. The velvety voice had won me over and we embarked on the most wonderful magical love affair. This strong man who had helped me through some tough times with his 'little badges' and comforting voice had become someone who showed me that sex wasn't dirty but beautiful between two people in love. But it wasn't to last, I wanted so much more and with many tears from both of us, I ended the relationship. Peter and I are still friends, distant in a geographical way but close as friends can be. He supports everything I do and shows interest in my work as I do his.

Melissa married young and has three children, Lucy concentrated on a career after going to University. She still lives close by.

I met Daniel my husband in 1985 and we fell in love, this time, it was a love that was romantic, grown up and right. He is the most caring loving funny man I know. He took me on 'warts and all'; with post dependency and all that threw at me and accepted my two children, dog and cats. We married and moved to Wales with his work and are now very happy living on a smallholding with our many ponies, ducks, dogs and cats. I am truly a lucky lady.

Both my parents are now dead, I see Tom and Rosie, sadly Ellen died earlier this year 2014.

I always tried to find Jack. Every year I wrote to Social Services asking after him. In the early years I sent cards. In 1993, after a Social Worker helped me find my son, we met. It was the happiest and saddest days of my adult life. I had missed so much. I was terrified he wouldn't like me but needn't have been. We met a few times after this and he met his sisters. Memories I treasure. Sadly, we only contact each other now, over Social media. He feels disloyal to the family that brought him up. I understand this but would love to have more. I will always respect his wishes and hope one day he will be back in my life.

Claire is still my best friend and we speak on the phone often, she lives a long way from me but distance makes no limitations on friendship

After Gwen died, Steve's mum, I met up with Bill's 4 sons and am now part of their family. Something I missed, most of my life, believing they never wanted to know me. I now know that wasn't true and couldn't be happier. They accept me as their sister. How good is that!

I never had therapy as such for the abuse, I worked through the worst by writing my first book I DID TELL I DID. This was painful, revisiting the horrors of my childhood but necessary and somewhat cathartic.

After moving with Daniel, I trained as Psychotherapist and gained a Masters in Counselling which involved useful personal therapy. I now have my own practice where I work with a diverse group of clients including some who have suffered abuse.

Since telling my story in my first book, I have had many readers asking for help, asking how to be free from a sexually abusive relationship or family. I wrote I DID TELL to hopefully inspire others who have suffered the way I had. The many letters, messages and emails I have, show me, that in some small way, perhaps I have. If so revisiting the trauma of my childhood horrors was well worth the pain. For this I am truly grateful. Many of my readers asked about the effects of the medication and that is the reason for NOBODY TOLD ME.I hope this book will help others who unknowingly or unwittingly became slaves to this medication.

You can break free, I did and look at me now!

Cassie

Also by Cassie Harte, the
Number-One bestseller

I did tell,
I did

The True Story of a Little Girl Betrayed By
Those Who Should Have Loved Her

CASSIE HARTE

# THE FACE BEHIND THE SCREEN

(A preview of the upcoming book from Cassie Harte)


*"hello, I don't want to bother you, but if you could please advise me?*
*I read a bit about you and your life. I am 20 and something similar is happening, I am so scared to run away or tell someone, but I want it to end so very badly. Could you suggest anything please?"* it was signed simply *'Jade'*

As soon as I read the email I knew I would help the sender.

Since writing my life story and my book, I DID TELL I DID being published a few years ago, I had helped many readers of all ages; to either come forward and tell someone what was happening or had happened to them or go to the police. In some cases they just needed to off load to someone who had suffered in the same way they had. I think victims of sexual abuse know that other sufferers will understand. Helping others was after all the reason I DID TELL was written in the first place. I was happy to be able to be there for anyone who needed me.

It was a gloomy day the 31st May 2012 when this email arrived on my desk. I had walked up to my study with a heavy heart and switched on my computer. It's a lovely room with double aspect so is quite bright. The walls are a warm creamy colour, the curtains are striped, cream, orange and charcoal, very 1930's like the house we had moved into 2 years before. The floor is oak with a large comfortable rug in the centre. A peaceful space to work. In the corner of the room is a sofa and in front of the window, is a raised dog bed for my little chums, Ellie Mae and Cody, my Shih-tzus. They sit there happily for hours while I work.

The scenes from my windows are beautiful, looking out over fields, trees and the stream, towards where the mountains meet the sky, from the large window and out to the paddocks and our duck filled lakes from the small window. Breath-takingly beautiful.

But the day before this email arrived, the beauty had been tarnished. The month of May had ended with great sadness, my wonderful horse, Evening Star, whom I had known since her birth, 23 years ago and who had lived with us for 21 of those years, had left us for that Rainbow Bridge people talk about. I hope that's true, Rainbow Bridge I mean. The loss was huge, the grief too heavy. On the 30th May the sunshine had gone out of my life and I needed to grieve.

The evening I lost this beautiful friend and companion, I had written on a social networking site, my feelings of great sadness and loss. I had many readers and friends who said they looked forward to my uplifting daily blog about my animals and my life 'on the farm'. I felt I needed to let them know why I wouldn't be writing for a while. Allow myself time to work through my sadness and grief.

So it wasn't an ordinary day when this email arrived, ordinary days had stopped yesterday, ordinary, happy days.

2012 was supposed to be a happy year. Britain was staging the Olympics, the Queen was celebrating her Diamond Jubilee, we were all optimistic that things in life were getting better. But on that not an ordinary day, I wasn't feeling that way, I was fragile and vulnerable and sad.

I had no reason not to answer this email, no reason to suspect the horror that was to unfold after I had replied. My own grief and sadness would have to wait, someone needed me and I would reply.

I sat down and began typing.

*"Hi Jade. Please tell someone, someone you trust to believe and help you. What is happening is wrong.*
*If you need support please write back and I will see if I can do anything. But please tell someone.*
*A Doctor, a priest, your Mum, your Dad anyone whom you trust. If you can't do this, then ask a friend to go with you to the police. They will make it stop.*
*Please keep in touch and let me know you are okay.*
*Love and hugs*
*Cassie"*

It was late, I didn't expect a reply, at least not as quickly as Jade answered me.

*"It's my Dad that's hurting me. Though he isn't my real Dad, I don't know who he is, he married my Mum, then adopted me when I was young. I can't tell my Mum as she died in a car accident when I was 9, the age my Dad started this.*
*He says I should be lucky, and grateful to him because he has looked after me for the past 10 years. I know I should be thankful to him, so telling someone would be like me not being grateful (if you get me?) Then there is the thought of*

*'why would anyone believe me, he's looked after me, and been kind to let me live with him, he wouldn't hurt me, I'm a trouble maker'*

*I have no-one.*

I knew that feeling only too well, having no one. My heart went out to this poor girl.

*'Hi Jade*

*You do have someone now, you have me. Whereabouts are you? Not your actual address, just whereabouts, are you in the UK? Please write back and let me help you if I can. You are not alone now, you have me. This is the first step to this ending if you can be strong enough. The hardest thing is to tell someone and now you have. Yes, he was good to you in but he adopted you so any man would have looked after his daughter, whether adopted or not. He isn't looking after you by hurting you. You have no reason to feel grateful to someone who has abused you and your mum's trust by doing this to you.*

*Please write back to me and let me see what we can do together.*

*Take care*

*Hugs*

*Cassie x*

I sat there for a moment, how could she feel grateful to someone who was doing anything but looking after her! I know how abusers can lay the blame on their victims, how the child, in this case, can feel guilty for all kinds of reasons. But whatever was happening she needed help and that is what she would get. I waited for her reply and began to get myself ready for bed. I wasn't sleeping much but went through the usual routine, letting the dogs out for their last short run around the garden and then was going to put the computer to bed when I saw another email. Part of me wanted to leave it until the morning but I could sense the urgency in this girl's messages, checked that it was from her and sat down to read her reply.

*'Hello, I can't believe you want to help me. I've gone years thinking this is my problem, no one will care, I'm a bit overwhelmed.*

*I am in the UK, Midlands. I would love for you to help me please, and I can try my best, though I don't think I am strong enough at all, I mean I let him hurt me. It's my fault.*

*Thank you for the 'email hugs' it's much better than hugging a pillow. Nobody has hugged me since my mum died, so I'm going to return the hugs.*

*I'm so scared.*

*Thank you, and you take care*

*Jade x*

My heart went out to her, no hugs for all those years. They say that there are no better hugs than those from your Mum, I wouldn't know that but Jade did and then her mum died and they stopped. I warmed to her straight away, she seemed so scared and needing help. There was a part of me that was angry, angry that her step father had been able to hurt her and then place the blame on her, leaving her feeling that she had 'let him'. But anger helped no one and I had to help this girl and that's what I intended to do.

I wrote a quick goodnight asking her to think of someone she could talk to, ask to help her. And then reluctantly went to bed.

Printed in Great Britain
by Amazon.co.uk, Ltd.,
Marston Gate.